FROM THE PUBLISHER

Dear Industry Professional:

If the recent changes involving the increased competitive expansion of our industry have taught us anything, it is that business owners, who understand what **profit** means to their operations, have remained successful. Owners who have maintained a focus on financial management through planned examination have remained flexible and competitive in the marketplace.

When you examine their approach to management, you will see that the profits these successful business owners realize are not simply hoped for, they are planned. And, that's what **Managing Your Kitchen and Bathroom Firm's Finances For Profit** is all about. Don Quigley has assembled financial management information that will prove to be essential to operating your business at a profit. He will show you why paying attention to the way you price your products and services can greatly impact your profitability. Step by step, he will show you how to track expenses and what happens when you fail to realize your true costs.

Collecting and tracking the right kind of information in a timely fashion provides you with the knowledge of when to hire new employees, lease equipment, purchase inventory, plan your advertising, and even when to take vacations. All by simply creating a financial plan.

Financial management can seem like a daunting task for most of us. For many, our strength is our technical design and construction expertise. Since not knowing this information is undoubtedly the cause of more frustrations and failures than anything else I can think of, I asked Don to present this material in an easy-to-understand format. Each of the worksheet calculations will show you how simple it is to read, evaluate and apply your own financial information.

This book, correlating profit to the element of water and our ability to control either, can become a vital tool that you can use to educate employees and subcontractors in your organization. Share this information and this book with them. Together, you will find new ways to manage your business' finances for success that others only hope for. It's your choice—let the faucet drip, and watch business drain away, or turn it on full force and realize a surge in your profits!

Nick Geragi, CKD, CBD, NCIDQ
Publisher, NKBA Books
Director of Education and Product Development

NKBA'S ELEMENTS OF SUCCESS

Earth, fire, water and air are the elements necessary to sustain life. In similar fashion, a business needs a solid Start-up, successful Management, Profit and good Business information to thrive. NKBA recognizes these basic business needs and offers this new three-book series which focuses on the elements of success essential to your kitchen and bathroom firm.

Managing Your Kitchen and Bathroom Firm's Finances for Profit   by Don Quigley
The Element of Water

Just as you can't survive without water, your business can't survive without profit. Profit should flow through your business, buoying up the equipment, the people and the services you provide. The key is to plan, and to work with your financial records to keep the profit reservoir full. If you don't, profit will slow to a trickle, and your business will eventually fail. Use this guide to help keep profits flowing in your business.

The Complete Business Management Guide for Kitchen and Bath Professionals ... Starting and Staying in Business   by Hank Darlington
The Element of Fire

Fire provides the warmth that keeps us alive, the energy that moves us and powers machines, and a source of light when things get dark. So does innovative management propel a business forward and ensure that it continues on its path. Good management can lead a company through good and bad times. While poor management, like an untended fire, destroys. Learn to manage every area of your company to keep projects moving, employees energetic and your business HOT!

The Kitchen and Bath Dealer Operating and Performance Survey   by NKBA
The Element of Air

Our intake of air is essential to life. For a company, the intake and use of business information is essential for survival. This publication will provide important financial and management comparisons for kitchen/bath businesses. You'll be able to assess your own business practices and make modifications accordingly to stabilize your business atmosphere. A must-have for every business. Available to NKBA members only.

BOOK STORE

- **Publisher:** Nick Geragi, CKD, CBD, NCIDQ

- **Director of Communications:** Donna M. Luzzo

- **Director of Marketing:** Nora DePalma

- **Executive Director:** Paul A. Kohmescher, CAE

The National Kitchen & Bath Association (NKBA) is the leading international organization exclusively serving the kitchen and bathroom industry. NKBA is dedicated to researching and providing information on all facets of kitchens and bathrooms, and will continue to pursue timely subjects that affect the industry and those working in it.

Copyright © 1997, by the National Kitchen & Bath Association. All rights reserved. No part of this publication may be reproduced, stored in a retrieval system or transmitted in any form or by any means, electronic, mechanical, photocopy, recording or otherwise, without the express prior written permission of the copyright owner.

ISBN 1-887127-10-0

Information about this book and other NKBA publications, membership and educational seminars may be obtained from the National Kitchen & Bath Association, 687 Willow Grove Street, Hackettstown, NJ 07840; phone 800-THE-NKBA; fax 908-852-1695; e-mail educate@nkba.org.

This book is intended for professional use by kitchen and bathroom business professionals. The procedures and advice herein have been shown to be appropriate for the applications described, however, no warranty (expressed or implied) is intended or given. Moreover, the user of this book is cautioned to be familiar with business management and accounting principles.

OTHER CONTRIBUTORS

- **Editor:** Janice Costa, Senior Editor
  Kitchen and Bath Design News

- **Technical Reviewers:** Stephen Vlachos, CKD, CBD
  Leslie Vlachos, M.Ed
  Atlantic Kitchen Center, Inc.

- **Content Editors:** Paul Kohmescher, Executive Director
  Nick Geragi, CKD, CBD, NCIDQ, Director of Education
    and Product Development
  National Kitchen & Bath Association

- **Electronic Publisher and Designer:** Janice Von Brook
  Janice Lamb, Office Services

ELEMENTS OF SUCCESS FOR THE KITCHEN & BATHROOM PROFESSIONAL

managing
Your Kitchen and Bathroom Firm's
finances
for profit

PUBLISHED BY THE NATIONAL KITCHEN & BATH ASSOCIATION

By Don Quigley

CONTENTS

INTRODUCTION i

1. PROFIT AND THE KITCHEN AND BATHROOM PROFESSIONAL 1

2. MAPPING THE DIRECTION FOR PROFIT IN YOUR BUSINESS 17

3. UNDERSTANDING FINANCIAL REPORTS 33

4. THE INTEGRITY OF PROFIT 51

5. PRICING FOR PROFIT 83

6. FINE TUNING FOR PROFIT 115

7. YOUR REAL PROFIT CENTER—THE CUSTOMER 139

8. IT'S WHAT YOU DON'T KNOW THAT CAN HURT YOU! 149

9. FINANCIAL RATIOS—HOW OTHERS WILL JUDGE YOU 157

10. BY THE NUMBERS 185

CONCLUSION - CREATING WEALTH 193

RESOURCES 195
   GLOSSARY 195
   BIBLIOGRAPHY 202
   RECOMMENDED SOFTWARE 204
   INDEX 205

INTRODUCTION

We'll never know the worth of water till the well goes dry. - Scottish Proverb

There is a good chance that when you decided to open your own kitchen and bathroom business, you worked from some type of plan or outline to ensure that you covered all your bases. Whether your plan was self-designed or obtained from outside sources, you used it to be sure that you were starting off on the right foot to protect your valuable investment. While a business is certainly an investment of money, it is also an investment of all the time, work, skills and effort you put into your venture and the livelihoods of those that work for and with you.

Having worked with hundreds of small-business owners, I have found that there is a common formula for disaster built into the game plan of many businesses—too few people really understand the overall function of profit.

Most small-business owners establish their own businesses because they have developed a particular interest, either through their education, job training or a hobby. We can generally recognize limitations with regard to our own and our employee's technical skills; however, it's often not as clear when it comes to viewing our related business skills. Most of us did not enter into business because we were particularly adept at management, but, rather, we thought we would be able to acquire these skills through trial and error. It's certainly true that we often learn through our errors. But, even when we learn something from our mistakes, we tend to continue to employ our known and familiar methods of doing things until someone else points out a different and better method.

Unfortunately, it's easy to become so busy operating our business that we become prime candidates for adopting an old saying, "*If it ain't broke, don't fix it.*" So our methods never really get updated.

Many small-business owners would rather give bookkeeping responsibilities to a bookkeeper or accountant than to do it themselves. The problem with this strategy is that this is your business, not your bookkeeper's or your accountant's. How can you be competitive or profitable with that approach? You are the one who works with your customers and prepares estimates, not your bookkeeper. What assurances do you have that you are covering all your costs, if, in fact, you've never sat down and thought about how to apply your overhead to each job? By delegating these responsibilities to others, you create a real opportunity for problems that occur when something is left out of the equation. Out of sight, out of mind is an adage that comes to mind here.

Do you know the function that your bookkeeper was trained to perform? Most bookkeepers will tell you that their job is to prepare a financial record or history of what you have done in the past, so that you can use it for managing your business in the future. However, it is not their job to make sure you are charging enough to cover all your expenses and earn a profit. That is a function of management.

More than a few people today are convinced that they are ahead of the game merely because they have a computer and their own accounting software. Therefore, they now have this important function in-house where it belongs. Right? Don't be so sure. If you are not financially managing the business, who is? Previously, if you had your accountant prepare and review the financial reports each month, you at least knew that someone was aware of what was happening and why. It is important to realize that accounting software is simply a tool to highlight information. It is only as accurate as the person who entered the information, or those who provided it initially. It cannot make judgments, and it cannot be sure you understand the significance of the information it is providing. You might say that is exactly why this book was written—to help you understand that significance.

The kitchen and bathroom industry is no more immune to business failures and discontinuances than any other business. If we focus on why businesses fail, we find two of the most common areas in which failures occur relate to economics and finances. Each time you underprice or undercharge for your work, you are hurting not only yourself, but the entire kitchen and bathroom industry as well.

When you offer a proposal on a job and realize you are not getting the markup you need, what usually happens? You either have to approach your clients, who may or may not let you off the hook, or you may elect to take shortcuts in an effort to minimize the loss. What effect will that have on the outcome of your work? Will you maintain the same enthusiasm and dedication as before? Will the difference be obvious in the quality and appearance of the finished product?

What is your philosophy with respect to customer service? You may be asking yourself why we are discussing customer service in a book written to explore financial management. The simple fact is you won't have any finances to manage if you don't have any customers. Your customers are going to render their decisions regarding your ability to provide outstanding customer service, either by doing repeat business with you or by recommending you to others. What preparations have you made to ensure that everyone within your organization understands and delivers such outstanding customer service? I see the role of the kitchen and bathroom professional as being as significant in these areas as I do their ability to design a functional space plan.

While you may already be using sound business management practices, there is a good chance you've forgotten much of what you once knew. Your business may have changed its original focus from just a few years ago. Being in business is an evolutionary process, one which requires constant trial and correction. Often without realizing it, we make adjustments or modifications that are not accomplished as a result of planning or design, but rather because they appear to be relevant to the circumstances or occasion.

Originally, I assembled the information in this book for the benefit of people whom I defined as "non-financial," and who own and operate their own businesses. Since that time I have come to realize that it is more like a set of instructions, the kind most of us don't bother to read because we believe we understand how it should all come together. At some point, we usually abandon our position and break down and read the instructions.

Have you ever found yourself:

- Assembling a child's toy without reading the instructions first?
- Driving an unfamiliar vehicle without reading the owner's manual, and, as a result, are unable to locate the jack to change a flat?
- Paying an overdraft charge because you didn't bother to reconcile your checkbook balance?
- Driving around aimlessly in a strange town because you followed your sense of direction instead of a map and can't find your destination?

Human nature being what it is, we often trust our instincts instead of relying on our intellect, resources and available choices.

Until we are aware and convinced that there is a better way to accomplish what we have set out to do, there is every likelihood that we will continue to repeat those same mistakes over and over again. As a result, it is often repetition which has the greatest influence on our management style.

Hopefully, some of that sense of frustration in these situations is something you can identify with, and you are now open to learning how to avoid a repeat of such mistakes in your business, where the stakes are much higher. You can create an atmosphere within your business that routinely explores your direction and the resources available to you and your staff.

My intent is to put you on an equal footing with other successful businesses, at least with respect to the tools available to you. Your true competitive spirit and advantage lie within your ability to manage your business through designing and planning for profit, not on mistakes, errors or wishes. I have tried to present this material in a clear and relevant manner. At the end of each chapter, you will find summary sheets of terms, ratios and formulas for quick and easy reference.

I don't have the only solution to operating your business more profitably, but it is a solution I know you can apply to your kitchen and bathroom business with predictable results. I may not be able to solve all your problems, but at least I will have made you think about them, which will give you an awareness of potential pitfalls and dangers that can constrain you or even put you out of business.

Much of what you need to understand about your business and its operation can be reduced to numbers. Once you understand what these numbers represent and how to use them to restructure and redirect your business, you will indeed find your business more rewarding and challenging. Knowing where you are going and how you will get there requires an even greater focus and a new set of tools.

Remember, we cannot do anything about our problems if we are not aware of them in the first place.

Chapter 1

PROFIT AND THE KITCHEN
AND BATHROOM PROFESSIONAL

Drop a pebble in the water: just a splash, and it is gone;
But there's half-a-hundred ripples circling on and on and on,
Spreading, spreading from the center, flowing on out to the sea.
And there is no way of telling where the end is going to be. - James W. Foley

One question I frequently encounter as I talk with small-business owners pertains to their views of who they are and what their business is all about. Reaching a common ground in this area will provide an excellent opportunity for success in helping you to see your businesses in a new light.

To be more aware of your responsibility to your customers, your industry and yourself, you need to explore two very different approaches to meeting your customers' needs—the **cust**om*er service provider* and the strict *retailer*.

THE KITCHEN AND BATHROOM PROFESSIONAL'S IDENTITY CRISIS

Perhaps you have opened up or expanded your business to the point where you're offering numerous retail products. You may feel you are facing an identity crisis of sorts. Are you truly a **cust**om*er service provider* who offers ancillary products to enhance the services you provide, or are you now a *retailer* who can't afford to offer service because of the influx of big retail and discount operations that in recent years have become your retail competitors? This is not so much an industry challenge as a singular one, but one which nonetheless presents a significant question for you. I would suggest that if you find yourself competing on a retail basis, you seriously consider reevaluating where your market really lies, and, within that market, how you have identified your own niche. Nobody can answer that but you.

If you perceive yourself, for instance, as a retailer of kitchen and bathroom cabinets, fixtures and accessories, then you are probably in competition with the big lumber yards and discount centers. Accordingly, you must decide how much it will cost you and how effective you can be as a direct competitor. If, however, you have identified yourself as a firm which offers experience, training and education to a specific portion of the market, a segment of the market that prefers personalized service, you have more choices. You have the distinct advantage of creating your own set of rules, which will distinguish you further from those you probably can't compete with on a level playing surface anyway.

Allow me to offer you an example of this. I recently spoke with a swimming pool contractor who had relocated to Albuquerque, New Mexico, from California. When I inquired about his business on the West Coast, he informed me that he worked around the Beverly Hills region of Los Angeles, and that his clientele consisted of many people affiliated with the entertainment industry. When I asked about the economy in recent years and how it had affected his business, he said that business was not very good, which was why he had relocated. I asked what he knew about his biggest and most successful competitor, which he readily identified. What was it, I asked, that made this other business so successful?

He informed me that this competitor subcontracted out all his work, but employed four designers almost full time, creating graphic renderings of the clients' finished products. They could clearly see and participate in the design of what was going to be the centerpiece for many of their social and business gatherings.

Furthermore, this competitor charged anywhere from two to four times what the other pool contractors were charging, and had referrals coming in every day. What made this swimming pool contractor such a successful competitor in a crowded marketplace? He had allowed himself to define who he was, rather than leaving that important function up to either the customer or the competition. Bearing the mark of a true professional, he:

1. identified a need,
2. provided a solution that no one else had thought of, and
3. packaged his business as a professional **customer service provider.**

He did this in such a way that he didn't even compete with the other swimming pool contractors. Successful businesses seek to establish themselves as the leading benchmark for performance, service and quality. If you tag yourself or allow others to identify you as a retailer, you will no doubt wind up playing by their rules, or creating a set of rules that bear no resemblance to your role as a kitchen and bathroom professional.

For instance, as a retailer, you and your competitors purchase products for resale from the manufacturer or wholesaler at one price, and then attempt to turn a profit by increasing the volume of sales. Your customers can go to virtually any of your competitors and order exactly the same thing. Price, inventory and the ability to deliver the project may very well be the determining factors in whether or not you close the sale. Therefore, your marketing strategies are influenced by your pricing.

If, however, you see yourself as a ***customer service provider***, as well as a retailer of kitchen and bathroom products and services, it becomes obvious that you do not sell exactly the same thing as the competition. Your customers don't seek out your services because they want their kitchen or bathroom to be exactly like someone else's. Rather, they want you to create a statement about who they are and what their homes mean to them.

No two jobs are alike, and, even though the estimates may be the same in their monetary value, they have, in all likelihood, been conceived using different approaches. Your ability to sell the value of the way you complete the work should be your strong point.

You are responsible for shaping your customer's perception of who you are and what it is you do. Don't leave that decision up to your customers or your competitors. You need to think of yourself as a ***customer service provider***, not just a retailer.

WHAT PROFIT IS

Profit is the residual value or surplus from a sale or investment transaction that remains after satisfying any claims for goods and/or services rendered, relative to that transaction, and after deducting the seller's expenses.

That statement tells us there are some very significant considerations with respect to properly identifying your true costs or expenses. To the extent that you do not deduct all your legitimate costs and expenses, you are overstating your profitability. By properly using accepted accounting methods and procedures for the purpose of maintaining objectivity and consistency, you can ensure your own accuracy.

For management purposes, you must be timely. In order for this information to be used in an effective manner, its timeliness is vitally important. If the information is prepared after the fact, its value is greatly diminished. Conversely, if your system routinely provides this information while it is still relatively new, it can be employed in conjunction with your responsibilities as an effective manager. Ultimately, you can use this information to make important business decisions based on your profit or loss.

DO YOU NEED TO PUSH FORWARD OR TRIM BACK?

If you have been accurate with your costs and expenses, you can use this information to adjust your overall business plan, either with regard to your overall budget or individual performance records. In addition, this information will be valuable to others who may be required to make judgments concerning the merits of your requests for loans, investments, bonds, insurance or a whole host of other financial matters. Profitability, in terms of bottom line dollars, is the language that professionals, who may need to make judgments about your business, understand, and will use to base their decisions.

WHAT PROFIT IS NOT

Profit is not necessarily what you take out of the business. The draw you take, or the paycheck you make out to yourself each payday, should not be considered your profit. In fact, depending on the longevity and maturity of your business, the money you take out could actually lead to the early demise of your business.

If you have a well-prepared business plan and a budget in place, which includes both an owner's compensation package and operating expenses, then you should have a good overall view of where your business is headed. If, however, you are not working with an established business plan that includes a carefully drawn up budget, how can you justify taking any money out of the business? Regardless of your personal financial demands, taking money out of your business without first having analyzed your cash-flow needs can be risky. If your business is not mature enough to sustain the drain of these funds, you could end up losing the business.

Profit is not simply a reflection of how busy you are. It's easy to be busy if your products or services are not priced to make a profit. Too many people believe that if you start a small business and underprice the competition, you can be successful. It may be possible, but it is a big risk, and one that can put you out of business quickly.

How can you expect to make a profit competing against the giants of our industry, if your only strategy is to lower prices? The statistics are overwhelmingly against your success if you employ this strategy for any sustained period of time. Simple economics indicates that you can't do this, and there is ample evidence, based on bankruptcy court proceedings, to support this. In fact, one of the leading causes of business failures is insufficient and inadequate profits.

WHY IS PROFIT NECESSARY TO THE CONTINUED GROWTH AND DEVELOPMENT OF A BUSINESS?

All too often, small-business owners understate expenses, and, thus, inadvertently overstate profitability. In the process, they make their jobs more difficult. If you are using the profits to pay the bills, you are understating your expenses. As a small-business owner, your goal has to be to produce enough to cover all your costs and expenses, as well as to leave enough to compensate you for your investment of time, money and effort. Whatever you do, you can be assured of a constant barrage of new competitors for your customers' dollars. In order to ensure your own continued growth and prosperity, you must be certain you are also making enough profit to assist with the development of that growth on a sustained basis.

Many small-business people have learned the hard way that rapid growth is just as dangerous as not enough growth. Over-expansion that is not accompanied by a return on the investment, but rather which leads to inadequate cash flow, will also cause the early demise of a business.

Your reputation and the visibility of your business in the marketplace must be perceived by your customers in a positive light in order for it to be profitable. You must also make sufficient profits to cover the cost of advertising, promotion and training of your personnel in the area of customer service, so that you will be seen as a leader in your industry.

There are different levels of growth and expansion throughout the normal development of any business, with ever-increasing demands for funds. For example, assuming that your business can start up and develop as you wish, the larger it becomes, the more prone it becomes to government regulation. You now find yourself in the position of having to comply with a myriad of paperwork requirements that have nothing to do with the production of profit. Yet, whatever profits you produce must now be used to ensure compliance with these same regulations and requirements, for failing to do so will result in your business being assessed substantial fines and penalties. As you can see, there is an ongoing need for profits to assist with the development and growth of any business.

CAN I EXERCISE ANY CONTROL OVER HOW MUCH PROFIT MY KITCHEN AND BATHROOM BUSINESS EARNS?

Not only can you exercise control over your profitability, but, you must do this in order to be successful. When you entered into your business, you probably wanted to apply your creative abilities and make a profit at the same time. You didn't need to operate your own business to do that. For the creative aspect, you could have worked for someone else, and, as far as making a profit goes, you could have invested your money in a variety of other options.

You would have studied those options first, and quite possibly sought some counsel on how to proceed, examining where you could expect to find the greatest return with the least amount of risk. You probably would have established some objectives and then developed goals based on those same objectives, in order to measure your progress towards achieving them.

Since your business is another form of investment, it would be wise to approach it with those same concerns and questions. This is what I believe separates the profitable businesses from those that just barely get by from week to week and ultimately wind up closing their doors.

The owners and managers of successful businesses have a shared sense of direction as to where they are headed. They have a goal. They are not merely taking whatever is available, but, rather, they are looking to create opportunities for themselves. As someone once commented, "The best way to insure a successful future is to create it."

Many who are unsuccessful in the kitchen and bathroom industry will fail, never knowing exactly why. Maybe they had a great idea. But, even with a great idea, you must be willing to develop a plan and test your idea before putting it into action. If you can turn your idea into some type of projection of future earnings, you may be able to predict whether or not it can provide a reasonable return on your investment. I find it amazing that the first thing a lending officer or investor wants to see is this information, and, yet, it is too often the last thing many small-business people learn about their own business.

HOW PROFITABLE COULD YOUR BUSINESS BE?

You, as a business owner or manager, must be accurate in your assessment of the potential costs and expenses, so that you can make a realistic determination with respect to the profitability of your business idea. By focusing on what you believe needs to be done in order to operate profitably, you can identify areas you could reasonably expect to impact your business. Now you are in a position to make management decisions or adjustments concerning these areas. By giving yourself the opportunity to anticipate potential problems, you can develop strategies to overcome them. Instead of reacting to potential problems in a defensive manner, it is possible to take a proactive stance, and develop strategies to exploit opportunities that you may not have seen initially.

Successful business owners recognize that yesterday's success won't guarantee tomorrow's profits. In order to be competitive, you must continuously search for new opportunities. Managing your business well is another function that distinguishes the successful companies from the unsuccessful ones.

Managing for profit means maximizing the available resources, so as not to waste those which are limited, and managing them in such a way as to allow the people who work for you to call upon their creative talents, with the best possible tools at hand, in order to obtain the greatest results. This brings up another very vital function you must be willing to acknowledge and address.

THE IMPORTANCE OF COMMUNICATION IN YOUR EFFORTS TO REALIZE A PROFIT

To realize a profit, the people working for and with you need to understand the process. Regardless of whether these ideas are new to you, or merely things you may have forgotten over time, you will enjoy far greater profits if you learn this information and communicate it to your employees, subcontractors, suppliers and even your customers.

The biggest challenge facing most of us is that of learning to communicate properly and in a timely fashion. What I'm offering you here is simply a tool you can use to identify how and to whom you should communicate your objectives and goals. I believe profit is the product of effective communication, and yet communication is one of the most underrated and least appreciated aspects of any business.

Our assumption that everyone around us is hearing and truly understanding what we say may be at the root of some of these problems. But, of equal importance, is what we communicate by omission; that is, what our failure to communicate says to those around us.

WHAT SHOULD BE COMMUNICATED AND TO WHOM?

In their book, entitled *The Service Edge, 101 Companies that Profit from Customer Care*, authors Ron Zemke and Dick Schaaf refer to a business' *moment of truth*. This occurs anytime your customer has the occasion to render a judgment about the quality of service your organization provides. Think about that for just a moment. How often and under what circumstances might that happen in your business, and what have you done to shape your customers' expectations and perceptions of the value of the service you provide? You might also want to consider what is happening every time you pursue a project, even with a potential client.

Before, during and after a sale, you or members of your staff are continually restructuring a new set of relationships. How many opportunities, in the course of all this restructuring, are you creating for the customer to make a judgment about the value of the service you and your associates will render? If you think about the scope of any work-related undertaking, you soon realize that there are numerous opportunities for assumptions that can correspond to mistakes.

If the interaction with you or your associates is to be perceived as a positive experience by the client, every aspect of the development process should be well thought out, planned and executed. You are the one who is putting your name on the line, perhaps both figuratively and literally. While a client or potential client has the ability to render the judgment, you and your associates should recognize this opportunity to mold the prospective client's perception of the value of the service you are offering. If you take the time, you can identify all the players in a typical project and think about the issues and concerns affecting each.

In the following table, I have identified the roles performed by one or several individuals involved in a project, as well as many issues needing to be addressed. No doubt there may be others. However, you can begin by looking at each of these issues and identifying concerns affecting them.

ISSUES THAT INFLUENCE CLIENT PERCEPTIONS

ISSUES	TO BE ADDRESSED FROM THEIR PERSPECTIVE						
	Salesperson	Designer	Installer	Sub-contractors	Owner	Client	Concerns
Time	x	x	x	x	x	x	Start, finish and availability of materials
Changes	x	x	x	x	x	x	Procedure and responsibility for changes
Prices	x			x	x	x	Increases due to material costs and changes
Project finances	x				x	x	Availability of funds and scheduled draw downs
Damages	x		x	x	x	x	Responsibility detailed up front instead of finger pointing later on
Job-site cleanliness and safety			x	x	x	x	Before, during and after
Liability insurance and bonds		x		x	x	x	Who is responsible and what policies are in force
Subcontractor relations			x	x	x	x	Mutual agreement that client's needs come first
Client privacy and security	x	x	x	x	x	x	Establish limits and enforce them for client's peace of mind
Checklists explained and used	x	x	x	x	x	x	Ensure thorough and professional completion of work without problems for client
30-day follow-up and request for referrals	x				x	x	Distinguish yourself to make yourself worth more
Guarantees implied or written	x			x	x	x	Complete understanding and agreement at beginning of job

TIME

You usually consider the issue of time from the business point of view, but, how seriously do you view it from the customer's perspective? The salesperson has a responsibility to educate the customer regarding the amount of time required to design and build the project, and the impact any changes will have if they are made at a later date, both with respect to completion and costs.

At this time, the salesperson can also help everyone involved by getting the customer to disclose any agenda not previously made known regarding personal time constraints or concerns. Encourage customers to disclose whether or not they are planning any major events around the completion of this project. Even a single unforeseen delay could have serious consequences, and it would be better to understand those up front. Take an informal survey of everyone involved in the project, including tradespeople, and try to hear both what they are saying, and what they are not saying. How close do these responses come to your customer's expectation of the outstanding service they anticipate from your business?

CHANGES

How clearly has the salesperson indicated to the customer that, while it is certainly the right of the customer to make changes, it must be understood that, after the contract is signed, those changes cannot be undertaken without additional expense? What policies and procedures are currently in effect to facilitate customer-initiated changes, and how well are they working?

PRICES

Nobody likes surprises involving money, unless it involves getting an unexpected windfall! If you are trying to maintain your company's edge as a leader in your market, you are no doubt locking yourself in with a written contract. By failing to handle this up front, you risk accusations about a lack of integrity and questionable business practices that can hurt your business' reputation. Don't let it get to that point. Instead, define for yourself what your position is and make sure everyone else is aware of it.

PROJECT FINANCES

Although it is not your job to be a banker, you will want to make it easy for the customer to buy from you. What arrangements have been made to offer third-party financing for potential customers? Failure to have the financing in place and available as needed frequently causes delays, which can cost you money. Do your salespeople understand the definition of a sale, and that it is not consummated until you have been paid in full by the customer? Is there a cooperative effort to educate your customers in this area? These are questions that must be addressed.

DAMAGES

You would be remiss to believe that damages are not going to occur. The way to lessen these is to encourage your team to deal with these issues head on, rather than forcing people to cover up or minimize the situation because they fear losing their jobs. Note that I have used the word "damages" as opposed to mistakes, errors, misunderstandings, ignorance or accidents. Those words require finger pointing, and I believe that what you really want to promote is an attitude that fosters responsibility and cooperation in attempting to correct the situation once it has occurred.

JOB-SITE CLEANLINESS AND SAFETY

Everyone has a different idea of what job-site cleanliness and safety should mean, which is why there must be a consensus reached by all those involved. Job sites that are not maintained are not safe. This can be an even bigger issue than we realize with many homeowners. Establish high standards and enforce them! Customers don't appreciate having the trash from their project sitting in their neighbor's front yard. Your name is very likely printed on your vehicles, and your image can be easily tarnished by a job site littered with debris. Safety is also a major issue, with government regulations, insurance premiums, lost work hours and lawsuits all economic incentives for insisting on a safe working environment.

Government regulations now require evidence that you are actively promoting job safety and training through regularly scheduled programs. You might try establishing a routine time for weekly safety meetings of about 10 to 20 minutes in duration. Appoint a safety officer who is responsible for ensuring that each employee actively participates and maintains records. For more information on this, in the United States, check the Occupational Safety and Health Administration (OSHA) requirements under the Code of Federal Regulations Title 29 Part 1926, revised as of July 1993.

Encourage each employee to participate by leading a discussion or researching a topic, such as information contained in Material Safety Data Sheets, which contain chemical make-up and recommended first aid for anyone exposed to a chemical. Remember, small companies are not exempt. No matter where you may be located, by adhering to these safety practices, you may find that your firm can help improve its own safety record and qualify for reduced insurance premiums. Contact your insurance agent and request information on what incentives your insurance carrier offers small employers, and whether or not they provide any resources for your efforts.

LIABILITY INSURANCE AND BONDS

Liability is a question of who is responsible, in the event of an accident, not necessarily who was there, or who was at fault. A common approach today is to sue everyone and allow the courts to decide who pays how much.

You must realize that you are responsible for what you, your employees, your subcontractors and their employees do, which are *acts of commission*. You are also responsible for what you, your employees, your subcontractor and their employees fail to do, which are *acts of omission*. Insurance is designed to spread the risk around, and should be purchased for your own protection. Make sure that your subcontractors can produce a certificate of insurance for worker's compensation, as well as for any other insurance your contracts call for, before they step foot on your client's property. Without such proof of coverage, you have no means of ascertaining whether or not their employees have any protection. Without it, in some jurisdictions, you may find that, if one of their employees is hurt in a job related accident, you and your client may be liable.

Bonds, on the other hand, are for the protection of third parties, and not for your benefit. It is a good idea to call on an insurance professional and have that person do an insurance analysis or review. There is usually no fee for such a service, and it can give you some peace of mind with respect to where your business might be vulnerable or at risk.

SUBCONTRACTOR RELATIONS

Failing to exercise some planning and coordination in subcontractor relations can only lead to trouble, if there isn't some common ground for settling disputes. Such controversies can lead to a very unpleasant experience for the customer, and can undermine the success of that relationship, to say nothing of your relationship with the subcontractor.

Decide for yourself what your policy is with regard to this issue, and then find subcontractors who will cooperate in delivering quality work and service that enhances your image as a true **custom**er *service provider*. The customer should always come first, therefore, resolve to settle differences away from the job site, and not delay or inconvenience the customer. You can usually call on local trade associations, the Better Business Bureau, or the local Chamber of Commerce, for assistance in resolving such conflicts through mediation or arbitration.

CLIENT PRIVACY AND SECURITY

Your clients' homes are their castles. A home is important in that it is often viewed as a bastion of safety and security, and, as such, most owners do not appreciate having strangers roaming about. If you want to get an edge on the competition, take every opportunity to reassure your customers that their privacy and security is an issue of very real concern to you and your team. Make absolutely certain all involved have an appreciation and thorough understanding of how they are expected to conduct themselves in the client's home.

CHECKLISTS EXPLAINED AND USED

It has long been recognized that taking a uniform approach to remodeling or construction projects provides a decided advantage. As people within the organization become increasingly familiar with the idea, the chance for errors, mistakes or oversights is greatly diminished. On the other hand, if the designer conceptualizes and designs the project using one approach, and the lead installer and subcontractors use a different method, there is every reason to believe that time and money are being wasted. One simple way to reinforce the uniform approach is to utilize tools that support the concept at every level. Checklists are something every small business can afford to use and probably can't afford not to use. Surveys relating to employee satisfaction and productivity repeatedly show that people want to actively participate in the way their work is organized and performed. Bring everyone into the process of detailing the approach you intend to adopt for your business. Without employee involvement, you can end up sabotaging your idea without even realizing it.

(Obtain copies of NKBA's Installation and Business Management Forms #4005 and #4020.)

30-DAY FOLLOW-UP AND REQUEST FOR REFERRALS

If you or your employees think the sale is complete the day you receive the final payment, you are surrendering an important opportunity to cement your relationship with the customer and enhance your reputation as a true ***customer** service provider*.

If you have done an outstanding job, as the clients expected you to, go back and share the bragging rights with them. Let them know how smart they were to recognize they were dealing with the very best kitchen and bathroom designers in town on this project. Customers value that kind of reassurance, and, if something was amiss, you now have a second chance to make it right. You can distinguish yourself and your business by once again reassuring your customers that you really do care about them and their project.

Ask to take pictures of the project, ask if you can use them as a reference and ask if you might compose a letter which includes their comments and bring it by to have them sign it. Include these letters in your portfolio.

What were the reactions of family members, relatives, friends and neighbors upon seeing the completed work? Could your customer possibly refer you to others who may be thinking about remodeling their own kitchen or bathroom? Your client may be very satisfied with the outcome of the job, but, if you don't ask for these comments or referrals, you may never get them. Ask! And, it's a good idea to share the good news as well as the bad with the rest of your team. It does wonders for morale.

GUARANTEES, IMPLIED OR WRITTEN

Have you ever asked yourself why you really use a written contract? If you think it is only because you don't want to get ripped off, you are probably kidding yourself, and, at the same time, missing an opportunity to distinguish your business from the competition. Someone once remarked, "A written contract is designed to keep honest people honest." We can certainly add that a written contract also helps to avoid confusion, eliminate legal questions and prevent a whole host of other problems as well. But, are you using it to your maximum advantage?

A written contract can and should be used as a tool to educate and reassure your customer that you are going to do and say what you said you would. Use this document to detail that information in a positive light. For instance, hold a pre-construction meeting with your subcontractors and salespeople, and establish the ground rules so responsibilities are understood by everyone beforehand.

At this point, you may be asking yourself what any of this has to do with financial management. The answer is: everything! Every one of these issues and concerns must be addressed on a consistent basis if you ever hope to realize a profit. These are the issues and concerns that have the potential to impact your business profits either in a positive or a negative manner.

CHAPTER 1

Reference Information—Terms

CHAPTER 1
SUMMARY OF TERMS

TERM	DEFINITION
acts of commission	Acts of responsibility attributed to contractor, employees, subcontractors and subcontractor's employees, such as mistakes committed and directly attributed to you as the prime contractor on a kitchen or bathroom remodeling job; a good reason to carry liability insurance.
acts of omission	Omissions attributed to contractor, employees, subcontractors and subcontractor's employees. These are omissions directly attributed to you as the prime contractor on a kitchen or bathroom remodeling job. Another good reason to carry liability insurance.
bonds	A financial commitment that certain work will be completed if the contractor defaults. It protects third parties only; contractor remains responsible to bonding company. Examples are surety bonds such as lien bonds, payment bonds and performance bonds.
certificate of insurance	Instrument issued to subcontractors which they then supply to prime contractor as proof they have obtained worker's compensation insurance coverage for their employees. Kitchen and bathroom dealers should require these from subcontractors who work on their client's properties.
Material Safety Data Sheets (MSDS)	Forms available through your suppliers for each item you use in your business, containing its chemical makeup and recommended first aid in the event your employees inhale, ingest or are exposed to it.
Occupational Safety and Health Administration (OSHA)	Agency which governs the standards for a safe workplace.
profit	Residual value or surplus from a sale or investment transaction that remains after satisfying any claims for goods and/or services rendered, relative to that transaction, and after deducting the seller's expenses. An example is Net Profit as determined on the Income and Expense Statement.
projections	Also known as pro formas. A company's financial performance as anticipated in reports assembled for future periods. Some examples are: projected annual budgets (Income and Expense, and Cash Flow Statements) and adjusted ownership at the end of the future accounting period (Balance Sheet).
third-party-financing	Project costs provided through a source of funding other than directly by the customer or contractor, such as local banks, finance companies, mortgage companies.

Chapter 2

MAPPING THE DIRECTION FOR PROFIT IN YOUR BUSINESS

A river seems a magic thing. A magic, moving, living part of the very earth itself—for it is from the soil, both from its depth and from its surface, that a river has its beginning. - Laura Gilpin

Let's begin by identifying those areas of your business which are more than likely the sources of profit and loss: *sales, productivity, customer service, business management* and *financial management*.

SALES

Far too often there is a tendency on the part of the small-business owner to equate *sales* with profitability. It is a legitimate concern, and an important indicator of the health of the business. But, beyond that, what do you truly understand about this important function within your own organization?

- Who's function and responsibility are sales?
- What real costs does your business have to meet in order to make those sales profitable?
- Is your business suffering because you are attempting to spread yourself too thin, assuming more responsibilities than you can reasonably handle, and not doing any of them well?
- Are you primarily a sales professional and/or a kitchen and bathroom designer?
- When was the last time you had any sales training or refresher courses?
- Because of your involvement in all other aspects of the business, are you able to maintain your proficiency in the area of design and product knowledge?

- Are your customers being attended to in a professional manner by your present approach to the selling process?
- Do you enjoy what you are doing now?
- What have you been successful at in the past?
- Would you be happier and more productive if you could go back to selling and design duties while assigning the business duties to a business manager?
- If you employ professional salespeople, what do you really understand about their job?
- Are they supported with the training they need and is there a cooperative effort between them and the rest of your staff? This alone is a very important issue and one I find many owners and managers tend to overlook or neglect.
- Are your salespeople truly being supported in their efforts to sell, or does the organization expect them to do the things others don't wish to do, such as deliveries and pickups?
- How effective is your marketing plan?
- What sort of advertising do you do, and how effective has that been?
- Would you be better off working with an advertising professional?
- Do you and the people in your organization solicit referrals?
- Have you correctly identified your target market?

PRODUCTIVITY

Profitability and *productivity* are tied together. To get the most out of the systems and people you have in place, you need to carefully weigh just how efficient the business is.

- Are you currently using the most up-to-date methods and technologies?
- How experienced are your personnel and subcontractors, and do they maintain their certification in their respective fields?
- Are proper inventories being maintained and adjusted as they are depleted, or have backorders and delays become the order of the day?
- How familiar are your personnel with the various product lines you sell?
- Are the members of your management team as proficient as they should be?
- Are you providing them with meaningful feedback as to how effective they are and where and how you can support them in the further development of their professional skills?
- Could you ask similar questions concerning your subcontractors?
- How well do they meet the criteria you have established for the success of your business?

CUSTOMER SERVICE

It is still the little things that count, if your organization is to distinguish itself in the area of *customer service*. Communication is vital and goes both ways. If you are not hearing what you need to hear, establish some new guidelines or procedures with the assistance of your customers and internal team members (employees, contractors and suppliers). Problems can only be addressed when they are brought into the light and analyzed. They then become opportunities from which to learn and profit.

BUSINESS MANAGEMENT

Business management is an area that is essential to the success of each and every person in the company. The size, complexity and scope of the responsibilities of your organization will influence how you respond, but, while much of this is necessary, it is not always vital to production or to the sales process, and, accordingly, you may choose to neglect many of them. However, your attention to detail with regard to business management can provide you with a competitive edge. It entails such things as dealing with your suppliers, providing training and support for employees, scheduling, purchasing, hiring, motivating, firing, negotiating, planning, advertising, promoting and processing. It's about insurance, security, leases, health issues and safety in the workplace.

- How well do you and your staff function in each of these areas?
- Do you rely on assuming you really know?
- Have you actually delegated some of these responsibilities to different personnel, or are you solely responsible?
- Could you and should you consider using outside resources in some of these areas?
- Would you be better off hiring a business manager, so you could free up more of your own time to do what you do best—designing or selling?
- How much attention have you paid to your personnel?
- Are they really as committed to their jobs as you would like them to be?
- What investments have you made in them during the last 90 days, 6 months or year?

FINANCIAL MANAGEMENT

- Are you fully aware of how you make a profit in your own business?
- You don't have to prepare a set of financial reports yourself, but, do you understand how to read them?
- Do you have a prepared budget, and, if so, do you use it on a month-to-month basis as a real management tool?
- Do you know how to find your break-even point each month?
- Do you really understand payroll burden?
- How much are you spending in advertising and how did you budget in that amount?
- Do you have a chronic cash-flow problem and what have you done to relieve some of that pressure?
- How often do you consult with your accountant or bookkeeper?
- When did you last raise your prices?
- Do you take advantage of early-payment discounts when paying your suppliers and vendors?

If you own your kitchen and bathroom business, you and you alone are responsible for its *financial management*. You need to understand the information listed above, and how it relates to your business. You may delegate it to others as part of their duties; however, the ultimate responsibility to assimilate all of this and to put it to work for your own benefit is undeniably yours. A business plan would be an excellent starting point, but only if you use it routinely to monitor your forward progress.

Employing this information may require you to change some old entrenched policies or ideas, which can be difficult at times. People frequently resist change, even when they know it is in their own best interest. If you expect to succeed, however, you must be willing to embrace change. I feel very strongly about the need to computerize your business. We are heading for the 21st century, and those who fail to employ the available tools put themselves at a severe disadvantage. Am I suggesting you should run right out and purchase a computer tomorrow? No, of course not. But, I do feel it should be an investment you will commit yourself to making within the coming year. Today, with computerized accounting packages available, you can have immediate access to information that just a few short years ago might have taken a good month or more to put together.

This means that you can exercise management decisions because you have accurate, reliable information on which to base your decisions. You are no longer at the mercy of your bookkeeper or accountant to supply you with this information a month or 6 weeks later, which by then may have lost much of its significance as a management tool.

There is, of course, a disadvantage to using your own computerized accounting software. I find many people believe that having this important function in-house gives them a decided advantage. However, if they have it in-house simply because they are trying to avoid paying an accountant, they will be doing it for the wrong reason. In the past, when this software was not readily available, a business owner went to an accountant with about as much enthusiasm as one might show when visiting the dentist. The accountant could be counted on to ask some probing questions based on the information culled from the financial reports. But, with software taking the place of the accountant, who is asking those same thought-provoking questions?

PROFESSIONAL ADVISORS

I would like to focus here on the role of your *professional advisors*, in this case, your accountant. I firmly believe you should employ the services of a professional who can assist you in preparing your tax returns and ensure that you comply with them in an orderly and timely fashion. Select someone who is familiar with the kitchen and bathroom or remodeling industry. Ask for references and then follow up, asking these people how effective the accountant has been, not only in preparing their returns, but also in guiding them and educating them. Go into your first meeting with your prospective advisor well prepared. You should have some goal or objective in mind. Ask what this person will be able to do to help you realize your goal. Ask what background this person has in the industry. Keep in mind that part of your advisor's job is to offer you advice.

Not long ago, the U.S. Government conducted a study of small-business owners, concluding that the majority of them found it difficult to relate to even their closest advisors. They felt that other people didn't understand or appreciate their plight. If you have found that your advisor's information has not been on the mark, who is really to blame? Have you been holding back some important thread of information, simply because you didn't want to appear unaware or uninformed? Remember, your advisor can actually help to enhance your business knowledge, making you a more effective manager.

HOW MANY BUSINESSES ARE MANAGED

The conduct and pace of business has changed dramatically during the past 3 to 5 years, and will continue to change in the future. You will see in the following table that a conservative estimate says that as many as 65 percent of all businesses simply go along, day to day, without a business plan or strategy in place.

Unless somebody can convince them otherwise, they will continue to travel in circles, never making much headway. You can be sure that the top 10 percent or even the top 25 percent got there by having a good idea of where they were going and how they were going to get there. With a little planning and preparation, you can build not just an income, but a future.

10%	The top 10 percent of all successful small-business owners is not necessarily the largest, but the most profitably organized and managed. They have goals, plans and strategies to achieve those goals. Everyone in their organization is involved and shares a common purpose. Owners and managers encourage their employees to motivate themselves and use their creative talents.
25%	This group is distinguished by the fact that they, too, are aiming for a higher level of achievement. They are more than likely working toward the top 10 percent, but, numerically not everyone can be there. Employees no doubt are made to feel they are partners in a cause and feel empowered to represent the firm in its best light at every "moment of truth." There is usually a commitment to look at every aspect of the business in an effort to understand how they can improve it and be more effective.
65%	This group of businesses tends to be characterized by its lack of direction toward any appreciable goal. Their primary objective is usually short term, such as the concern of finding work for tomorrow, and is frequently an example of the "tail wagging the dog." What the owners frequently miss is the opportunity to encourage their employees to function as a team. Oddly enough, many of them believe they must be in control, while for the most part, their employees feel that nobody is responsible, and they certainly don't feel empowered. Every business must begin somewhere, and the bottom line here is the starting point. Those businesses that are headed for the top 35 percent won't remain here very long. They have a destination and a schedule, and, if they fall short, they will simply pick themselves up and try again. Unfortunately, for many of those without a destination or a schedule, they won't remain here very long either. They will simply fall by the wayside. The organization has no sense of direction and no goal. These businesses are usually characterized by turmoil, and their owners feel they are constantly putting out fires.

BUILDING A BUDGET YOU CAN USE

Although the following approach to preparing a budget might be less than traditional, I am proceeding on the assumption that you have never done this before, and want to understand the process. If you have worked within an organization for any length of time, you probably have some knowledge of budgeting, at least to the extent of using a budget as a tool to restrict expenses or determine hiring and firing policies. Unfortunately, what we know about budgets has too often been learned in negative situations. There is, however, a positive side to a budget. It is a very informative and necessary management tool.

This section has been prepared for people who would like a step-by-step procedure for developing a budget they can understand and work with. You don't need a sophisticated piece of software to use this format, but you can prepare a template using a spreadsheet program. This will work equally well as a stand-alone worksheet without the benefit of a computer. If you will follow along with me, using the three-page **BUDGET BUILDER** template at the end of this chapter, we will look at this example of how to prepare a budget and the significance of the information employed in putting it together.

SECTION A - REVENUES

Here, I am referring directly to those *revenues* produced from the sale of the primary product or service the business is engaged in. This information can and very likely should be broken out by categories or departments. This will facilitate drawing profiles and extrapolating information later on. There are revenues produced within a business that are produced, not as a result of the primary function of that business, but which must nevertheless be reported. The revenues produced from the sale of an asset would be such an example, and we will discuss that later.

A word of caution with respect to estimating your sales. There is a tendency to decide that you want to make a profit of so many dollars or a specific percentage of your sales. Force yourself to justify the numbers before you adopt them.

- What evidence do you have that would indicate these figures are realistic or readily achievable?
- Are prior period numbers available?
- Have you actually done any market research that would suggest your product or service ent of the existing market to make your numbers

d map culled from your decision-making processes.
forward will bear the brunt of how reasonable your initial

SECTION B - COST OF SALES

There is a common misunderstanding with regard to the distinction between *cost of sales* and what are frequently referred to as expenses. Expenses are those items you would find it necessary to purchase or use within your kitchen and bathroom business, assuming you had no sales whatsoever. They generally consist of costs associated with the actual operation of the business. *Cost of sales*, on the other hand, are those costs which can be attributed either directly or indirectly to the production or delivery of the actual goods or services the business produces. Each type of business will have some categories of such costs which are typical to that particular industry.

Direct And Indirect Costs

What is the difference between *direct* and *indirect costs of sales*? Depending on the nature and complexity of a project, management might desire a more comprehensive and detailed accounting as to how it is actually spending money over the course of various projects. A *direct cost of sales* can easily be attributed to a particular phase or component of the construction or production process. The cabinets you install in a kitchen remodeling job would be an example of such a direct cost. An *indirect cost of sales* is one that can be easily connected to the overall project, and yet may be more difficult to associate with a particular phase or component of the construction or production process. Shop drawings, reports and schedules would be examples of such indirect costs. Labor, materials, subcontracts and equipment (rentals) are examples of typical *costs of sales* categories that would apply to the kitchen and bathroom industry.

Labor

Labor is that labor provided by tradespeople employed on the job site, or in support of the project by the business itself. This includes the costs of all payroll, benefits, bonuses and payroll burden assumed by the business in its role as the employer. It does not include those same costs when they are incurred by subcontractors, who assume the liability for their own employees. Such costs would probably be included in their overall bid to perform the work. As a rule, this does not include the cost of your administrative personnel, those who most commonly work in the store, place of business or office. The expense of employing these people will typically be recognized as legitimate operating expenses, and we will discuss the treatment of that expense in *Section E*.

Materials

Materials refers to those materials, such as cabinets, appliances, bathroom fixtures, dry wall and lumber, used directly in the project by your personnel.

Subcontracts

Subcontracts usually cover specialized work that the business itself may not be licensed for, or work that requires additional expertise. Direct costs in this category might include such things as the subcontracts awarded to the various trades employed on the job site, e.g., plumbing and mechanical contracts, electrical contract, masonry contract. Some examples of subcontracts considered indirect costs might include temporary sanitary facilities on the job site, maintenance of those sanitary facilities, temporary lighting.

Equipment

Equipment (rentals) refers to that equipment you will use during the actual construction for which you must recoup your expense. Equipment that you might lease, rent or purchase for a particular job would fall into the direct costs category.

Overhead Costs

Project *overhead costs* that might be associated with the finished product could include the salaries of the project manager, and perhaps the wages of delivery drivers employed by the business to work on this or several projects at the same time. In addition, taxes, duties, professional fees, project finance costs, schedules, reports, shop drawings, utilities, sanitary facilities, premiums and fees for bonds, permits and insurance, barricades, signs, move-on and move-off costs and site clean-up are all examples of overhead costs.

Contingency Costs

Contingency costs are a very real cost of doing business. They are often totally beyond the control of the contractor or business owner, yet they pop up unexpectedly and with a price tag that you will rarely be able to get the customer to pay for. Some businesses are more likely to incur such expenses than others, and your own job-costing records may be the best indicator of that. The kitchen and bathroom industry is especially prone to such costs, as you are continually faced with new and unexpected challenges every time you open up a wall or attempt to tie into existing utility lines. Sometimes these challenges involve the clients themselves.

For instance, you send a crew out at 8:00 a.m. to begin remodeling Mrs. Jones' kitchen. At 8:30 a.m., you receive a phone call from your installer telling you that Mrs. Jones needs to see you immediately, and won't permit them to begin work until she does. You drop what you are doing to respond, only to learn that she has changed her mind about the color of paint for the bathroom. Could you have reasonably foreseen this delay? Didn't it cost you money to have your employee standing around unproductively while you attempted to resolve it? But, do you really think you can convince Mrs. Jones to pay for that? Not likely!

Remember, a contract with a contingency fee may not always be possible, but, a contract without a contingency fee may not always be profitable. I would suggest you treat it as a true cost of sale on a percentage basis, so that it will be proportionate to the fee you are charging. It will be calculated as part of the pricing process I recommend later in the book.

SECTION C - GROSS MARGIN

Gross margin, also referred to as *gross profit*, is not really a profit at all, and many people who are not familiar with accounting terminology misuse it. *Gross margin* is simply the amount that remains after subtracting *cost of sales* from *revenues*. It is that amount from which, after subtracting your *operating expenses*, should leave you a *margin of profit*. So, although it is not actually profit, it is where we hope to retrieve our profit. You want to break out your *gross margin* by categories or departments, so that you can use such information to determine your real profit centers and to assist you with management decisions.

SECTION D - OPERATING EXPENSES

Operating expenses are frequently referred to as *overhead*, *general operating* and *administrative expenses* or *fixed expenses*, and refer to the costs associated with operating your business or office and staffing it with permanent help. It is the one single area that I believe so many small-business owners do not appreciate as they should. Designers, contractors and anyone else who must prepare estimates and formulate pricing must take a close look at what goes into this section. It is an area that is widely subject to misinterpretation, and the failure to understand it often leads to serious losses. This is where you can begin to customize your business by maintaining and exercising management processes and decisions.

Keeping your expenses to a minimum is certainly the most cost-effective way to do business, but you can't really do that unless you are aware of where and when you can take advantage of volume discounts and early payment discounts. Your cash-flow management is critical to the success of your business, but, again, you must stay on top of this information. Within this section, you must include every cost you incur on a daily basis to keep your doors open and your operation running smoothly. The sooner you can build a profile of your business, the more quickly you will be able to gain an edge over your competitors. The numbers calculated here will be an important aspect of your business' financial profile. They will help you project the peaks and valleys in your business, and plan accordingly. You will note that I have attempted to label some of these expenses with respect to the *variable* type versus the *fixed* type. You may want to do the same within your own business, as variable expenses can often go unnoticed over long periods of time, and, as a result, you will miss opportunities to rein in some of these expenses.

SECTION E - PAYROLL AND PAYROLL BURDEN

Payroll and payroll burden are areas where you must exercise due diligence if you want to manage for profit. In the service industries, some of your most notable expenses can be found within this area. This is especially true when your business depends on labor-intensive applications and highly skilled and compensated personnel. You need to audit accurately and frequently to see what you are really paying your personnel. Calculate across-the-board salaries, hourly wages, all costs of benefits you have obligated yourself to, and worker's compensation premiums for both federal, state or local taxes. Learn what it is costing you each hour of the day. Don't rely on assumptions, get the facts.

SECTION F - OWNER'S COMPENSATION

Owner's compensation can be somewhat perplexing, which is why I have broken it out as a separate entity. Your accountant will assist you in determining how your earnings should be reported for tax purposes, either as income or profits, but, for our purposes, I would suggest that a realistic allowance should be made for you, the owner. Remember that profit is a surplus over and above the cost of doing business. However, a legitimate cost of doing business is employing the owner. This is especially true if the business is your primary source of income. Lenders and investors will not be fooled if you try to explain that you don't need an income to live on. It may, in fact, send the wrong message, that you are trying to hide something.

SECTION G - BALANCE SHEET

The function of the *balance sheet* is to show what assets have been invested in the business, and what portions are owned by whom, including your creditors. Any and all payments that must be paid to creditors and lenders on a regular basis should be included in your budget. Making these payments in a timely fashion will help ensure that a *statement of cash flow* will mesh with the finished budget.

SECTION H - PROFIT FROM OPERATIONS

Profit from operations is simply the first in a list of what may properly be referred to as profit. It is intended to be a reflection of profitability, or what has truly been earned as a surplus in relation to the operation of your business. For accuracy's sake, it should not include references to other sources external to the operation of your business or the sale of any assets.

SECTION I - OTHER INCOME AND EXPENSES

Under the heading of *Other Income and Expenses*, you should indicate all other forms of income you can realistically expect to see flow into the business in the coming year, such as: income from dividends, bonds or other types of securities, interest income, rental income, and sales of any assets.

You also want to project any interest expense you will incur as a result of debt (interest-bearing liabilities), that you have obligated the business to during that period. Check amortization schedules to determine what those payments actually are.

This budget is not set in stone, and will require fine tuning as you move through the period for which it was prepared. However, it is primarily a communication tool, and it can only communicate what it addresses.

I could not possibly consider every item that you may want to include in your version, so add to it as you see fit, and learn to use it as the primary management tool in building, developing and capitalizing on your own profitability.

MANAGING YOUR KITCHEN AND BATHROOM FIRM'S FINANCES FOR PROFIT

BUDGET BUILDER

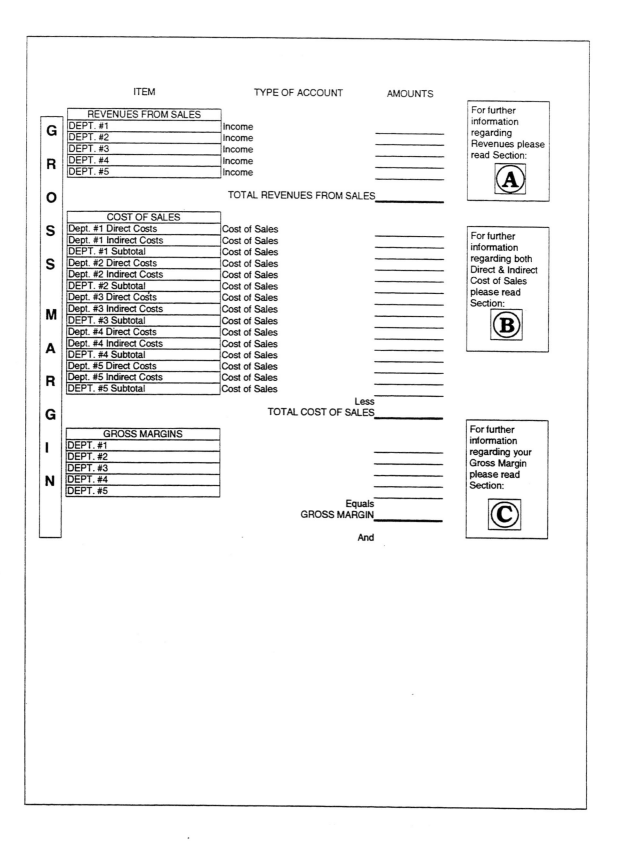

MAPPING THE DIRECTION FOR PROFIT IN YOUR BUSINESS

BUDGET BUILDER

GROSS MARGIN _____

O V E R H E A D   &   P A Y R O L L   E X P

OPERATING EXPENSES	
Advertising	Variable Expense
Automobile	Variable Expense
Bank Service Charges	Variable Expense
Computer Repairs	Variable Expense
Contributions	Variable Expense
Credit Card Expense	Variable Expense
Depreciation	Expense
Dues & Subscriptions	Expense
Equipment Repairs	Variable Expense
Insurance	Expense
Miscellaneous Expense	Variable Expense
Office Supplies	Variable Expense
Postage	Variable Expense
Professional Fees	Variable Expense
Property Taxes	Expense
Rent	Expense
Repairs	Variable Expense
Shipping	Variable Expense
Telephone	Variable Expense
Travel & Entertainment	Variable Expense
	Expense
	Expense
	Expense
	Expense
	Expense
	Expense

Less
OPERATING EXPENSES _____

For further information regarding your Overhead please read Section: **D**

PAYROLL	
Gross Earnings	Variable Expense
Fed Withholding	Variable Expense
Social Security (FICA) @ 6.2%	Variable Expense
MCare (Medicare) @ 1.45%	Variable Expense
S.U.T.A.	Variable Expense
	Expense
	Expense

COMPANY BURDEN	
Social Security (FICA) @ 6.2%	Variable Expense
MCare (Medicare) @ 1.45%	Variable Expense
F.U.T.A. @ .008% of first $7,000	Variable Expense
S.U.T.A.	Variable Expense
Worker's Comp Insurance	Variable Expense
Benefit	Variable Expense
Benefit	Variable Expense
Benefit	Variable Expense

Less
LESS PAYROLL & BURDEN _____

For further information regarding your Payroll & Payroll Burden please read Section: **E**

OWNER'S COMPENSATION	
	Variable Expense
	Variable Expense
	Variable Expense
Benefit	Variable Expense
Benefit	Variable Expense
Benefit	Variable Expense

Less
LESS OWNER'S COMPENSATION _____

For further information regarding the Owner's Compensation please read Section: **F**

BUDGET BUILDER

BALANCE SHEET

BALANCE SHEET ITEMS
ASSET ACCOUNTS
Notes Receivable

LIABILITY ACCOUNTS
Current Portion of L-T-D
Mortgages Payable
Notes Payable

Plus or Minus
BALANCE SHEET ITEMS _____

For further information regarding these Balance Sheet Items please read Section:

G

Equals
PROFIT FROM OPERATIONS _____

For further information regarding Profit From Operations please read Section:

H

PROFIT

OTHER INCOME & EXPENSE

Other Income
+ Proceeeds From Sale Of Asset
+ Rental Income
+ Other Income
+ Interest Income
  Other Expense
- Interest Expense
- Interest Expense
- Finance Charges

Plus or Minus
OTHER INCOME & EXPENSE _____

For further information regarding Other Income & Expenses please read Section:

I

Equals
NET PROFIT BEFORE TAXES _____

CHAPTER 2

Reference Information—Terms

CHAPTER 2
SUMMARY OF TERMS

TERMS	DEFINITIONS
business plan	A detailed strategy designed to communicate to you, your investors, employees and others, your mission and plans to execute these strategies.
contingency costs	Job-related costs outside your control, but which are, in fact, real costs of doing business, such as delays caused by customers, subcontractors and mandatory inspections.
cost of sales	Costs associated directly or indirectly with a project or sale. Labor, materials, subcontracts and equipment rental are examples.
customer service	The totality of the experience you offer to distinguish yourself from the competition when it comes to fulfilling your customer's wants. Look at your bottom line, and, if it is not healthy and growing, you have room for improvement.
financial reports	Reports prepared for and used by management and others to evaluate the company's financial performance. Most commonly these refer to the Balance Sheet, the Statement of Income and Expense and the Statement of Cash Flow.
gross profit (margin)	Revenue income remaining after deducting cost of sales. Not a true profit, since overhead has not been deducted yet. Revenues - Costs of Sales = Gross Profit Margin.
marketing plan	A detailed strategy designed to identify and reach your market niche, maximizing the results of your efforts by properly utilizing the resources available to you. For instance, a kitchen and bathroom dealer's overall marketing strategy as it relates to advertising, customer service, employee training and management support.
other income and expense	Revenues or expenses produced other than through the sale of the business' primary product or service. This could be revenue from the sale of an asset or expense realized because of a liability.
overhead costs	Those expenses you must absorb each day just to keep your doors open, such as rent, utilities, salaries of office staff and advertising expense.
payroll burden	Additional costs to management, beyond hourly pay or salary for which management is responsible, i.e., worker's compensation insurance, unemployment taxes, matching Medicare and social security payments.
profit from operations	As distinguished from Gross Profit Margin or Net Profit, this profit is recognized as earned from the primary operation of the business. On the Income and Expense Statement, this is frequently referred to as Net from Operations.
referrals	Leads and/or prospects known to your clients, that you must ask for. The opportunity to ask for leads can present itself on at least three occasions during the selling process—at the close, upon completion and 30 days after completion when you call to follow up.
revenue	Income derived from sales of primary products or services sold by the business, such as kitchen cabinets, countertops, bathroom vanities, or an entire remodeling job.
spreadsheet (electronic)	A computer worksheet which allows you to work with and manipulate numbers; handy for preparing budgets.
target market	That segment of the market you will focus your efforts to reach and sell to. These are buyers whom you will educate to the value of using the services of a kitchen and bathroom professional.

Chapter 3

UNDERSTANDING FINANCIAL REPORTS

The sea, washing the equator and the poles, offers its perilous aid, and the power and empire that follow it..."Beware of me," it says, "but if you can hold me, I am the key to all the lands."
- Ralph Waldo Emerson

To help you more closely relate to the financial information presented, this chapter will introduce you to the financial statements of a one-year-old kitchen and bathroom business. For the purposes of relating how each financial report is used to manage for success, we will follow the financial management of this business throughout the book. From the information found in these statements, you will see what impact they have, what they indicate and how you can implement them as a guide in your business.

THE BUSINESS

The business is owned by a couple just completing a successful first year. They are proud of their achievements and the network of clients and tradespeople who will provide them with referrals in the future. Yet, for all their early success, they haven't been entirely free of worry over the true progress in learning what forces are at work within the business.

THE OWNERS

They are a skilled and talented team; she is a professional designer and he is an experienced contractor and installer. Neither have a formal background in financial management. They have just opened their year-end financial statements mailed to them by their financial advisor, who is a certified public accountant, recommended by a business acquaintance. The accountant has a number of other remodeling contractors as clients and has helped them lay out a comprehensive plan to keep more of what they earn sheltered from their corporate tax liabilities. However, the owners feel they should know more about the inner workings of their business on a day-to-day basis. As they look over the Income and Expense Statement, the Balance Sheet and the Cash Flow Statement, it occurs to them that they are really unprepared to understand the full impact of what these reports are telling them.

Certainly, they know what their assets are and, because they must write checks almost every day, they are very familiar with their liabilities. They bought a computerized accounting package last year and, since using it, they are convinced they have given themselves a distinct advantage. Where they would formerly rely on their bookkeeper to take their information each month and produce their financial reports, they can now produce their own. They have realized a savings, and they can get the results more easily at the close of each month. However, they know that they can and should have a better appreciation of what is really going on within their business. For instance, while they have the financial reports in front of them, they really don't understand how the money actually flows through the business. The accountant has told them that the information that appears on the Balance Sheet does not appear on the Income and Expense Statement and that the Cash Flow Statement is used to explain their liquidity. But, in their own minds, it appears there is some kind of missing link that should provide them with a better understanding of the information actually available from these reports, and they wonder what actions they should take in response.

As you read the next section of this chapter, refer to the financial statements for this company's first year in business found at the end of this chapter.

THE FINANCIAL STATEMENTS

In order to insure that there is a smooth flow of information between the statements we are about to discuss, I felt it might be helpful to start with an appreciation of the terms used in describing the proper use of these reports, beginning with the reports themselves and the function of each. You will see that many of the terms tend to flow across all three reports. If you understand the importance of the terminology and its use within each report, you will have a better understanding in the interpretation of all your financial statements.

Income and Expense Statement

The Income and Expense Statement has at various times been referred to as the Income Statement, the Profit and Loss Statement or just a P&L. Its primary function is to answer the question, "Did my income exceed my expenses during this given period of time?" (be it a month, a quarter or a year). Because a lot can happen in the course of a short time, the more frequently an Income and Expense Statement is prepared and used, the more reliable your information will be. The Income and Expense Statement is essentially a temporary depository for this information until such time (usually at the end of the accounting period) when it will be summarized and the information transferred to the Balance Sheet.

According to *generally accepted accounting principles* (GAAP), adopted by the accounting profession as a whole, the most accurate and reliable method of gathering such economic information is one called the *accrual method* of accounting. With this method, the information you will be looking at on the Income and Expense Statement, the recording of cash in and out of the business (the credits and debits to the various accounts), will be based on when the money was earned rather than when it was actually received. Likewise, expenses will be recognized as they are incurred, not necessarily as they are paid.

When we talk about *Revenues from Sales*, we are referring to revenues generated from the operation of the business, which are the primary sales of products and services, i.e., the revenues from a kitchen project. One might ask what other types of sales there could be? How about the revenues generated from the sale of an asset? For instance, there may be an old piece of equipment sitting in the back of the shop which no one really uses any longer. You're determined to clean the shop so you will have more usable space. You instruct your employees to move this equipment out to the storage shed, since it really is not a functional piece of equipment used in the operation of the business. When you decide to sell this piece of equipment you will have to recognize those revenues, in some form.

However it was generated (not as a result of the primary operation of the business, but through the sale of an asset), we need to categorize this income as something other than *Revenues from Sales*, or we are being less than accurate. Furthermore, as we get to a discussion of ratios later in the book, the way you apply this information to your business will play a significant role in how you are judged as a manager. Segregating these funds into *Other Income* as listed below *Earnings from Operations* on the Income and Expense Statement, we still report the income, but we do not distort our ratios.

Cost of Goods Sold represents the expense of the materials (cabinets, appliances, tile, dry wall, lumber, etc.) labor, and subcontracts (electrical, plumbing, painting, etc.) used in completing a project. These, I feel, you are most familiar with, for you deal with them on a daily basis. Another way to recognize these costs is that you wouldn't have them if you didn't have any work. Subtracting the costs of these items leaves us with your *Gross Profit Margin*.

I realize that many people refer to this as their gross profit, however, since we have yet to deduct your *Operating Expenses* (rent, utility bills, insurance, advertising or the salaries of office staff), this is really not a profit at all. Rather, we hope that after deducting these expenses you are left with a margin of profit.

Depreciation Expense is not really a cash outlay, but rather a recognition of the loss of an asset's value due to time and wear on items such as display products. This would be one way in which you could expense the funds you laid out to build your showroom.

After subtracting your *Operating Expense* and *Depreciation Expense* from the *Gross Profit Margin*, you arrive at your *Earnings from Operations* (before *Interest* and *Taxes*). Why is that figure so important? It must be large enough to cover the other two items we have yet to account for, *Interest Expense* and *Taxes*. This figure must provide a cushion to cover both these items if you expect to show a profit. *Interest Expense*, by the way, is not really an operating expense. For example, the interest you are paying to finance the purchase of the company vehicle, generally, is not attributed to the cost of producing the completed project. The value of the *asset* (truck) owed to your creditors is offset on the Balance Sheet by the *debt* or obligation incurred (*the long-term note*).

However, if you look closely, you will notice the balance in that account does not include the interest. That portion is handled as an expense attributed to a liability and not as a result of the primary operation of the business. It is broken out here in the same way *Other Income* is treated. When you subtract the *Interest Expense* from *Earnings from Operations*, you are left with *Earnings before Income Tax*, which is the number the Internal Revenue Service (IRS) is interested in. It is on the basis of this number that your *Income Tax Expense* is calculated. Subtract the *Income Taxes* from this figure and you have arrived at the bottom line, or your *Net Income*. This number then is representative of your ability to create a profit.

We have looked at how money was generated by the business by studying the Income and Expense Statement, the first of our three financial worksheets. As stated earlier, however, the Income and Expense Statement is essentially a temporary depository for this financial information. It must now be summarized and transferred to the Balance Sheet.

BALANCE SHEET

The *Balance Sheet* can be thought of as a snapshot taken in time, of where this particular business stood as of a particular date. It is essentially a record of who owned what portion of the business on any given date. Where we spoke of credits and debits as the language of the Income and Expense Statement, assets and liabilities are the language of the Balance Sheet. The basic Balance Sheet equation, which says that: Assets = Liabilities + Owner's Equity, reminds us of its purpose and, in order for it to be accurate, this equation must be in balance at all times. So to begin with, an *Asset* is property, both tangible (your display units including the walls, lighting, cabinets, countertops, etc., in the showroom) and non-tangible (proprietary knowledge such as copyrights, photography, patents, formulas, etc.) that may be employed at some later date, to produce income. Some typical examples of these assets will include *cash*, *investments*, *accounts receivables* (the final payment a customer promised to pay you by the end of next week for a job you completed last month), *inventory* and *prepaid expenses*.

A *Liability* then represents your creditor's claims against those assets (the value they say they have invested in those assets). *Accounts Payable* (money you owe the electrical contractor for a job), *Notes Payable* (the payments you are making on that new CAD station for the next 90 days), and *Accrued Expenses* (services or products you have received and haven't yet been billed for), are all examples of liabilities.

Finally we have *Owner's Equity*, which is your claim as the owner (or owners in the cases of corporations and partnerships) against these same assets. The value of any physical assets you may have contributed to the business, such as a personal computer or a drafting table are some examples. Certainly any cash investments you make to the business will also be included here.

A very helpful tool for properly maintaining the various accounts for your business is a structure or listing, referred to as a Chart of Accounts. I have included a sample for your use at the end of this chapter; however, keep in mind that this is generic, and your accountant or bookkeeper may choose to use her or his own, or may modify this one. Most accounting software packages will not provide you with a template specifically for the kitchen and bathroom industry, so those usually have to be modified for your own purposes. As you study the Chart of Accounts, you can see that there is a natural flow to the information which makes it easy to enter, retrieve and analyze.

As you can see, the Chart of Accounts is broken out into five sections. Upon the close of the accounting period, the information contained in the first three sections, *Assets*, *Liabilities* and *Owner's Equity*, is used to compile the Balance Sheet, and the information from the remaining sections, *Income* and *Expenses*, is used to prepare the Income and Expense Statement.

Think of it as a map or index of where to find the various types of accounts. Whenever you don't quite understand where to debit or credit a particular account, this chart may prove helpful in how to proceed.

ASSETS		=	LIABILITIES		+	OWNER'S EQUITY	
Debit for Increases	Credit for Decreases	=	Debit for Decreases	Credit for Increases	+	Debit for Decreases	Credit for Increases

Remember that any entry you make to one side of the equal sign in the above equation must be offset by making an entry on the other side of the equal sign, so that the basic balance sheet equation remains in balance. You may find the following information helpful by looking at the account balance to see if its Normal Balance matches the table below, once you have posted your entry to the account.

	INCREASE	DECREASE	NORMAL BALANCE
BALANCE SHEET ACCOUNTS			
Asset Accounts	A Debit Entry	A Credit Entry	A Debit Balance
Liability Accounts	A Credit Entry	A Debit Entry	A Credit Balance
Owner's Equity Or Stockholder's Equity			
Capital			
Capital Stock	A Credit Entry	A Debit Entry	A Credit Balance
Retained Earnings	A Credit Entry	A Debit Entry	A Credit Balance
Draws			
Dividends	A Debit Entry	A Credit Entry	A Debit Balance
INCOME AND EXPENSE STATEMENT ACCOUNTS			
Revenue	A Credit Entry	A Debit Entry	A Credit Balance
Expense	A Debit Entry	A Credit Entry	A Debit Balance

The *Net Income* (your bottom line on the Income and Expense Statement) will eventually surface on your Balance Sheet in one of several forms. This value, or wealth, may be distributed directly to the owners, as *Cash Dividends to Stockholders* or as *Income to the Owner or Partners* in those scenarios. The entry entitled *Capital Stock* is the value of the owner(s) investment of capital in the business. The other alternative is that all or some of that *Net Income* could also be retained by the business in order to meet or reduce its obligations. In other words, that money would in effect become *Retained Earnings* under *Owner's Equity*. Why are *Retained Earnings* a form of *Owner's Equity*? Precisely because they are not removed from the business. Such earnings might be earmarked for new capital outlay, such as the purchase of a new building or new equipment *(Property, Plant and Equipment)*, or to retire some of your debt both in the form of *Short-Term Notes Payable* (short term obligations, usually under one year) and *Long-Term Notes Payable* (such as notes over one year and mortgages). By using the retained earnings this way, the value of an owner's existing equity is increased.

In addition to recording new purchases (e.g., that new laser color printer with 1200 dpi capability, that you will use for design presentations) as *Property, Plant and Equipment*, you would have met with your accountant and summarized all the depreciation you have written off for the preceding accounting period (in this case the past year) and recorded it as *Accumulated Depreciation*.

Since we are talking about Assets and Liabilities, it would seem to make sense to discuss some of the other money which went into the business, but never made it to the bottom line.

Cash and *Accounts Receivable* represent both liquid and not-so-liquid consideration for the products and services you provided to your customers. As many of these funds came into the business, you used them to pay for, among other things, *Inventory* and *Operating Expenses*, thereby reducing your *Accounts Payable*, the funds owed to your suppliers and vendors. There is also the probability that you paid some *Pre-Paid Expenses*, such as the rent and insurance. There are still other expenses that you incurred, but have not paid off as of the close of the accounting period. More than likely you have not been billed for them, and yet you are aware you have received them and will have to pay for them in the future. These you will recognize as *Accrued Expenses* and can include such things as *Operating Expenses* and *Interest Expense*. No doubt some of that *Cash* and *Accounts Receivable* went to pay for labor costs and you would also use those funds to reduce your tax liability under *Income Tax Payable*. The money received and used within the business is always important to managers, and lenders and investors, as well. It is one important measure of how well these funds are being used to pay obligations and deliver a return to the owners. However, because the information that appears on the Income and Expense Statement does not appear on the Balance Sheet, we don't really get a very good picture of the disposition of these funds during the course of the accounting period.

STATEMENT OF CASH FLOW

In 1986, the Financial Standards Accounting Board (FSAB), a watchdog of the accounting industry, recognized that it was a major shortcoming to rely solely on the Income and Expense Statement and Balance Sheet. Accordingly, they recommended that a Statement of Cash Flow be prepared along with the Income and Expense Statement and Balance Sheet, to better serve the needs of business owners and managers who must make decisions based on the information contained in these statements. Essentially, the Statement of Cash Flow is used to develop profiles for the purpose of projecting future activity. This one statement provides the missing interpretive link between all the financial statements regarding the generation and disbursement of these funds during the course of the past accounting period. However, as we shall see later, it also offers invaluable service as a tool to project both your short-term and long-term needs for capital.

With these three reports in place, you now need some kind of link or bridge between them. In order to provide a clear understanding of the flow of money through this business, I have modeled a sample worksheet entitled **BRIDGING YOUR FINANCIAL WORKSHEETS**, after one used in John A. Tracy's book entitled, *How To Read A Financial Report*. Should you care for a further explanation of how to use these reports, I encourage you to read his book.

INCOME AND EXPENSE STATEMENT - FIRST YEAR
Fictional Business

			As % of Sales
Revenue From Sales		$529,500	100.00%
Cost of Goods Sold (Direct & Indirect)		297,053	56.10%
Gross Profit Margin		$232,447	43.90%
Operating Expense	190,168		35.91%
Depreciation Expense	9,833	200,001	1.86%
Earnings From Operations (Before Interest & Taxes)		$32,446	6.13%
Interest Expense		10,371	1.96%
Other Income		0	
Earnings Before Income Tax		$22,075	
Income Tax Expense		3,311	
Net Income		$18,764	3.54%

U.S. FEDERAL TAX RATES FOR CORPORATIONS

Taxable Income Over	But Not Over	Your Tax Is...	+		Of The Amount Over	Amount of Tax
$0	$50,000	$0.00	+	15%	$0	$3,311
$50,000	$75,000	$7,500.00	+	25%	$50,000	$0
$75,000	$100,000	$13,750.00	+	34%	$75,000	$0
$100,000	$335,000	$22,250.00	+	39%	$100,000	$0
$335,000	$10,000,000	$113,900.00	+	34%	$335,000	$0
$10,000,000	$15,000,000	$3,400,000	+	35%	$10,000,000	$0
$15,000,000	$18,333,333	$5,150,000	+	38%	$15,000,000	$0
$18,333,333				35%		$0
					Total Tax Due	$3,311

BALANCE SHEET - FIRST YEAR
Fictional Business

Cash		$18,539
Accounts Receivable		50,915
Inventory		79,500
Prepaid Expenses		9,775
Property, Plant & Equipment	$115,504	
Accumulated Depreciation	(9,833)	105,671
Total Assets		**$264,400**
Accounts Payable		
Inventory	$26,500	
Operating Expenses	9,567	$36,067
Accrued Expenses		
Operations	$14,663	
Interest	1,729	$16,392
Income Tax Payable		331
Short Term Notes Payable		37,714
Long Term Notes Payable		65,999
Owner's Equity		
Capital Stock	$89,133	
Retained Earnings	18,764	107,897
Total Liabilities & Owner's Equity		**$264,400**

> Federal Income Tax represents 10% of annual corporate taxes. By law 90% must be paid during the year in order to avoid penalties. Sample assumes no state income taxes are due.

CASH FLOW STATEMENT - FIRST YEAR
Fictional Business

Cash Flows From Operating Activities

Net Income	$18,764	
Accounts Receivable Increase	(50,915)	
Inventory Increase	(79,500)	
Prepaid Expenses Increase	(9,775)	
Depreciation Expense	9,833	
Accounts Payable Increase	36,067	
Accrued Expenses Increase	16,392	
Income Tax Payable Increase	331	($58,803)

Cash Flows From Investing Activities

Purchase of Property, Plant & Equipment		(115,504)

Cash Flows From Non-Operating Activities

Other Income		0

Cash Flows From Financing Activities

Short-Term Borrowings	$37,714	
Long-Term Borrowings	65,999	
Capital Stock Issue	89,133	
Cash Dividends To Stockholders	0	192,846
Net Increases In Cash During Year		$18,539

BRIDGING YOUR FINANCIAL WORKSHEETS

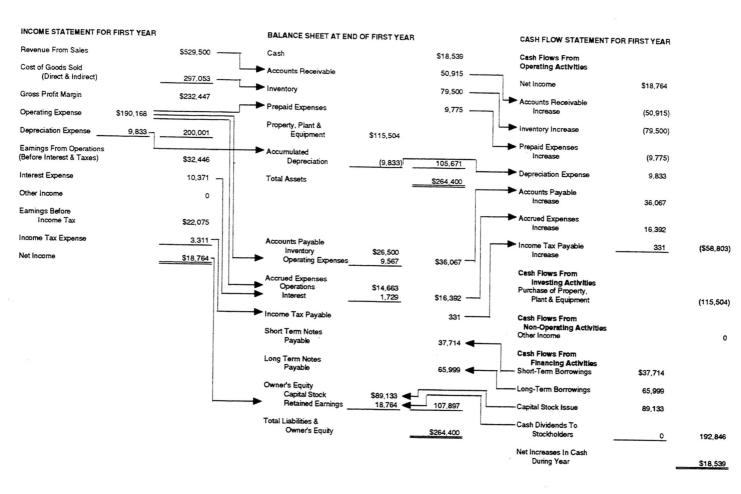

CHAPTER 3

Reference Information—Charts And Terms

CHART OF ACCOUNTS

(Typical for Kitchen and Bathroom Dealer)

Account Number	Description

ASSETS

100	Petty Cash
110	Bank Deposits
110.10	General Bank Account
110.20	Payroll Bank Account
110.30	Project Bank Account
120	Accounts Receivable
120.10	Notes Receivable
130	Deferred Receivables
	(Your project contracts are charged to this account, being diminished by progress payments as received. This account would be offset by Account 480, Deferred Income)
140	Property, Plant and Equipment
140.10	Real Estate and Improvements
140.20	Leasehold Improvements
144	Motor Vehicles
144.01	Repairs, Parts and Labor
144.02	Tire Repairs or Replacement
144.20	Fuel
144.25	Oil, Lubricants, Filters
144.30	Licenses and Fees
144.40	Depreciation
144.50	Insurance
145	Power Tools
145.01	Repairs, Parts and Labor
146	Office Furniture
147	Office Equipment
147.01	Repairs, Parts & Labor
147.02	Insurance
148	Computer Equipment
148.01	Repairs, Parts and Labor
148.02	Insurance
170	Inventory of Materials and Supplies
170.10	Cabinets
170.20	Countertops
170.30	Hardware
170.40	Plumbing Fixtures
170.50	Electrical Fixtures
	(These accounts show the values of all expendable materials and supplies. Charges against these accounts are made by authenticated requisitions showing project where used.)

CHART OF ACCOUNTS, continued
(Typical for Kitchen and Bathroom Dealer)

Account Number	Description
180	Returnable Deposits
180.10	Plan Deposits
180.20	Utilities
190	Prepaid Expense
190.10	Insurance
190.20	Bonds

LIABILITIES

400	Accounts Payable
410	Subcontracts Payable
420	Notes Payable
430	Interest Payable
440	Contracts Payable
450	Taxes Payable
450.10	Old-Age, Survivors and Disability Insurance (withheld from employee's pay)
450.20	Federal Income Taxes (withheld from employee's pay)
450.30	State Income Taxes (withheld from employee's pay)
460	Accrued Expenses
460.10	Wages and Salaries
460.20	Old-Age, Survivors and Disability Insurance (employer's portion)
460.30	Federal Unemployment Tax
460.40	State Unemployment Tax
460.51	Payroll Insurance (public liability and property damage)
460.52	Payroll Insurance (worker's compensation)
460.60	Interest
470	Payrolls Payable
480	Deferred Income
490	Advances by Clients

OWNER'S EQUITY

500	Capital Stock
510	Earned Surplus (Retained Earnings)
520	Paid-In-Surplus

INCOME

700	Income Accounts
700.101	Project Income
700.102	Project Income
700.103	Project Income
700.20	Cash Discount Earned
700.30	Profit or Loss from Sale of Capital Assets
700.40	Interest Income

CHART OF ACCOUNTS, continued
(Typical for Kitchen and Bathroom Dealer)

Account Number	Description
EXPENSES	
800	Project Expense
800.100	Project Work Accounts
800.700	Project Overhead Accounts
810	Office Expense
810.10	Office Salaries
810.11	Insurance on Property and Equipment
810.20	Donations
810.21	Utilities
810.22	Telephone and Other Communication
810.23	Postage
810.30	Repairs and Maintenance
820	Departmental Expense
830	Departmental Expense
840	Departmental Expense
850	Cost of Equipment Ownership
850.10	Depreciation
850.20	Interest
850.30	Taxes and Licenses
850.40	Insurance
850.50	Storage
860	Loss on Bad Debit
870	Interest
900	Expense on Office Employees
900.10	Worker's Compensation Insurance
900.20	Old-Age, Survivors and Disability Insurance
900.30	Employees Insurance
900.40	Other Insurance
900.50	Federal and State Unemployment Taxes
910	Taxes and Licenses
910.10	Sales Taxes
910.20	Compensating Taxes
910.30	State Income Taxes
910.40	Federal Income Taxes

CHAPTER 3
SUMMARY OF TERMS

TERM	DEFINITION
accounts payable	Money you owe your suppliers and other creditors for purchases you have made and charged to your account.
accounts receivable	Revenues from sales which you have agreed to accept on a delayed payment schedule.
accrual method	Recognizes income as it is earned rather than as received, and expenses as they are incurred, rather than when they are actually paid. These are your accounts receivables and accounts payables.
accrued expenses	Services or products you have received, yet have not been billed for, as of the close of the accounting period. An example would be your cabinets that arrived yesterday from your supplier, yet the bill may not arrive for another 2 or 3 days.
accumulated depreciation	That portion of an asset's value which has been written off to date.
assets	Any type of property possessed by the business which may be of some future financial benefit. This could be tangible property (buildings, land, equipment, etc.) and non-tangible property (patents, copyrights, formulas, designs) valued on your balance sheet.
balance sheet	A financial report designed to accurately represent the ownership and debt of the business.
cash dividends to stockholders	A return of a portion of the net income to the stockholders of a corporation for their sharing in the risk of the operation of the business; i.e., the quarterly earnings; the annual return to investors of a corporation.
certified public accountant	An individual recognized for educational and professional achievement and licensed in the state in which he or she practices.
chart of accounts	A structure of the various accounts your business uses to account for all its financial transactions.
depreciation expense	A non-cash outlay; a recognition of the loss of an asset's value due to time and wear, such as depreciation on a kitchen and bathroom dealer's showroom display unit.
Financial Standards Accounting Board (FSAB)	A watchdog committee recognized by the accounting profession to establish guidelines and principles.
generally accepted accounting principles (GAAP)	Industry standards adopted by the accounting profession.
income and expense statement	A financial report designed to determine whether or not the business' income exceeded its expenses or vice versa during a given period of time.
income tax payable	The amount of income taxes due to either the federal or state governments based upon the earnings of the business in the prior accounting period. This is based on the Net Profit before Taxes amount reflected on your Income and Expense Statement.
inventory	Materials, parts and products sold by the business and maintained on hand, such as cabinets, countertops, hardware and laminates.
liabilities	The creditors' claims against the assets of the business, i.e., accounts payable, accrued expenses, payroll taxes payable.
long-term notes payable	Obligations of the business with a duration in excess of the next 12 months. This appears on your Balance Sheet as the Long-Term Liabilities such as Notes Payable, Mortgages.
net income	Also known as the bottom line, this figure is a measure of your ability to create wealth. It is arrived at only after you have subtracted all costs, expenses and taxes associated with the operation of your business. The is the Net Profit amount reflected on your Income and Expense Statement.

CHAPTER 3
SUMMARY OF TERMS

notes payable	Payments owed against a note held by one of your creditors; reflected as the Notes Payable amount on your Balance Sheet.
owner's equity	Also known as partner's equity or stockholder's equity, this is direct (Investments) or indirect (Retained Earnings) accounting of the owner's claims against the assets of the business. This appears on your Balance Sheet.
prepaid expenses	Those expenses which the business must pay in advance, such as rent and insurance premiums.
ratios	Relationships between financial calculations which allow for meaningful interpretations of management's abilities, including profit ratios, leverage ratios and turnover ratios.
retained earnings	A portion of the net income used to satisfy some of the outstanding debt of the corporation, or to be invested in other capital expenditures, in either case increasing the value of the stockholder's existing investment. This is the amount reflected on your Balance Sheet under Owner's Equity.
short-term notes payable	Short-term obligations of the business, meaning they are due and payable within the next 12 months.
statement of cash flow	A financial report designed to assess both the short- and long-term obligations of the business.

Chapter 4

THE INTEGRITY OF PROFIT

How happy the lot of the mathematician! He is judged solely by his peers, and the standard is so high that no colleague or rival can ever win a reputation he does not deserve. No cashier writes a letter to the press complaining about the incomprehensibility of Modern Mathematics and comparing it unfavorably with the good old days when mathematicians were content to paper irregularly shaped rooms and fill bathtubs without closing the waste pipe. - W.H. Auden

Financial information is essential to the operation of a profitable business. As the business matures, new and ever-widening requirements will become a reality. A business must be able to depend on the integrity of its financial reporting in order to make informed and intelligent decisions. The most widely accepted systems in place today are those based on industry standards, meaning those adopted by the accounting profession as a whole. Virtually all computerized accounting software used in business today adheres to these principles and guidelines. By employing this uniform approach, you, your banker, your lender, your investors and your insurance company, can all be certain of the design and methodology of gathering the information. Hopefully, this will provide meaningful results for comparative purposes.

WHAT IS THE ROLE OF FINANCIAL STATEMENTS IN BUSINESS?

There are many different types of financial statements available to the small-business person; however, the three most commonly employed by small businesses are the Balance Sheet, the Statement of Cash Flow and the Income and Expense Statement. Each of these financial statements serves a distinct function, and, if you understand those functions, you will be better able to appreciate the information contained in them, and how others will interpret that information. It is not my purpose to teach accounting, but rather to explain the significance of this information and how you can use it to manage for profit.

As a result of their first year in business and the information contained in the statements presented in the previous chapter, our fictional owners have projected their second-year reports as a basis for decision-making for the coming year. These second-year projections are used as a base reference throughout the remaining chapters in the book.

THE BALANCE SHEET

The Balance Sheet summarizes the assets of the business (i.e., anything of value owned by the business, or anything possessing a service potential or future benefit to the business), a reconciliation of the creditors' claims against the assets of the business (referred to as the liabilities of the business), and a determination of the residual value of the business or equity in the business (which is the owner's claim against the assets of the business). (See **BALANCE SHEET, Second Year,** at the end of this chapter.) Where the Income and Expense Statement gives us information concerning the business during some period of time, the Balance Sheet is prepared as of a particular date. It is a snapshot of where that business stands as of that date. The name of this financial statement is derived from the function of the basic balance sheet equation which states that:

Assets = Liabilities + Owner's Equity

No matter which of these entities you are trying to determine, that basic equation must remain in balance. If we look closely at the Balance Sheet, we find that, with respect to those assets, there are several distinct categories: *Current Assets, Long-Term Assets, Fixed Assets and Other Assets*. *Current Assets* represent the cash and those resources of the business that could readily be converted to cash within 12 months of the date of the Balance Sheet. *Cash* on hand or in the bank, *Accounts Receivable*, *Inventory*, *Pre-Paid Expenses* and *Short-Term Investments* are some examples of *Current Assets*. *Long-Term Assets* are typically interest-bearing investments or investments capable of producing dividends for the business.

Businesses will typically maintain these types of investments in their portfolio for longer than one year. Some typical examples might include stocks, bonds, savings accounts, etc. *Fixed Assets* represent the fixtures and equipment utilized for daily operations, which, as such, are not available for resale as a normal part of the operation of the business. *Other Assets* are resources held by the business, such as proprietary knowledge, including secret formulas, patents or trademarks owned by the business.

BALANCE SHEET - SECOND YEAR
Projected for December 31, 1996

ASSETS

Current Assets:
Cash	$26,531
Accounts Receivable	4,715
Inventory	130,642
Prepaid Expenses	8,307
Other Current Assets	0
Total Current Assets	**$170,195**

Net Fixed or Plant Assets:
Buildings	71,300	
Equipment & Machinery	25,637	
Vehicles	14,950	
Other Fixed Assets	22,957	
	$134,844	
Accumulated Depreciation	(9,833)	
Total Net Fixed Assets		125,011

Other Assets	0
Total Assets	**$295,206**

LIABILITIES & OWNER'S EQUITY

Current Liabilities:
Accounts Payable	37,080
Accrued Expenses	2,551
Income Taxes Payable	1,047
Short Term Notes Payable	0
Total Current Liabilities	**$40,678**

Long-Term Liabilities:
Installment Debt Payable	$98,968
Mortgage Payable	0
Other Long-Term Liabilities	0
Total Long-Term Liabilities	**$98,968**
Total Liabilities	**$139,646**

Owner's Equity
Paid-In Capital	$89,133
Retained Earnings	66,427
Total Owner's Equity	**$155,560**
Total Liab & Owner's Equity	**$295,206**

Liabilities = Assets - Owner's Equity

As with assets, the liabilities of the business may also be categorized. *Current Liabilities* are those obligations or debts that will become due and payable sometime within the 12-month period following the preparation of the Balance Sheet. Accounts Payable, Notes Payable, Interest Payable, Taxes Payable, the current portion of Long-Term Debt, and salaries and wages currently owed, would all be examples of *Current Liabilities*. *Long-Term Liabilities*, less the current portion, represent the outstanding debt that is to be carried by the business for longer than the next 12 months.

Assets - Liabilities = Owner's Equity

Equity, also referred to as the net worth of the business, represents the owner's claims against the assets of the business. *Equity*, which may be expressed as: *Owner's Equity*, *Partner's Equity* or *Stockholder's Equity*, will generally consist of the following breakdown: the owner's initial investment and subsequent investments in the business along with the *Retained Earnings* of the business, which, in the case of a corporation, are the *Accumulated Earnings to Date*, less any *Dividends* paid, from the time the corporation was founded.

Many of the figures reflected in the Balance Sheet are used by potential investors and lenders to determine the business' financial stability and performance. Successful owners and managers will also know how to interpret these numbers as a means of determining the future direction of the business. These are called financial ratios, and will be examined more closely in Chapter 9.

THE INCOME AND EXPENSE STATEMENT

The Income and Expense Statement, also referred to as the Income Statement, the Statement of Income and Expenses, the Profit and Loss Statement or the P&L, should be of concern to every manager or business owner, for it is essentially the business' report card with respect to what it has achieved over a given period of time. It basically answers the question, "Did my income exceed my expenses during this given time period, or vice versa?" That period of time can be as infrequent as once a year, or it can be done every quarter or every month. One of the real advantages of computerized accounting packages is that, provided it is used as it should be, on a daily basis, it allows you to walk into your office each morning and know exactly where you stand, at the stroke of a key.

Think of what kind of an edge that can give you with respect to your competition. You will:

1. Eliminate most of the guesswork and have substantial facts on which to base your decisions for the day.
2. Know what you have spent with respect to any given project, as well as what you should have invoiced for to date.
3. Have the ability to accurately assess your immediate needs for additional funds.
4. See how effectively your marketing plan is working.
5. Use the information to decide whether to cut back on overtime or hire additional people.

6. Know whether you need to increase your inventory levels or your most basic supplies.
7. Determine whether or not you must undertake a new advertising campaign in order to create more sales.
8. Perceive whether there is an upward spiral or a downward trend in your business.

The following **INCOME AND EXPENSE STATEMENT** also provides that essential window on the true costs and expenses of your business operation. With that information, you can properly forecast and plan for your own profitability. The information produced from the Income and Expense Statement will be utilized in conjunction with additional information contained on your company's Balance Sheet to calculate the financial ratios that potential lenders and investors will use to assess your company's performance. To be of significant value, the information contained on your Income and Expense Statement should be compared either with figures from a prior period or the current year's budget. Used this way, it will afford you some meaningful feedback.

Revenues - Cost of Sales = Gross Margin
and
Gross Margin - Operating Expenses = Net Profit Before Taxes

This equation explains the function of the Income and Expense Statement. But, let's take a closer look at what this document can really do for us. It provides us with a significant amount of feedback, provided we learn to use it correctly and frequently. Before we examine the different sections on the Income and Expense Statement more closely, you should know that it can and should be used on a routine basis to check your progress in accordance with your initial strategy. Many businesses also use it to make comparisons to some previous period, such as the prior month, or the same period during the prior year. This one shows year-to-date progress in relation to the projected or budgeted performance.

INCOME AND EXPENSE STATEMENT
Period Ending December 31, 1996

	1995 (Actual)	1996 (Projected)	(Y-T-D)
Revenues From Sales	$529,500	$635,400	
Cost of Sales			
Direct Costs			
Labor	76,672	92,362	
Equipment Rental	2,125	3,500	
Materials	189,751	201,000	
Sub-Contracts	51,787	40,500	
Indirect Costs			
License Fees	5,500	8,300	
Training Fees	1,500	2,500	
Sales Commissions		12,963	
Contingency Fees	7,943	9,531	
Total Cost of Sales	$335,278	$370,656	
Gross Margin	$194,223	$264,744	
Operating Expenses			
Administrative Salaries	$18,225	$31,350	
Payroll Taxes	6,891	8,562	
Rent	37,065	36,000	
Telephone & Utilities	4,050	4,200	
Insurance	11,040	12,000	
Advertising	23,061	20,000	
Maintenance & Repairs	1,544	2,200	
Gas & Oil	3,716	3,900	
Depreciation	9,833	9,833	
Travel & Entertainment	2,979	1,750	
Non-Income Taxes	367	450	
Owner's Compensation	39,202	40,000	
Other Operating Expenses	1,328	1,200	
Total Operating Expenses	$159,301	$171,445	
Net Operating Income	$34,921	$93,299	
Interest Expense	10,371	10,468	
Other Income	0	0	
Net Income Before Taxes	$24,550	$82,831	
Income Tax Expense	3,311	16,404	
Net Income	$21,239	$66,427	

INCOME AND EXPENSE STATEMENT
Percent of Sales

	1995 (Actual)	1996 (Projected)	(Y-T-D)
Revenues From Sales	100.00%	100.00%	
Cost of Sales			
Direct Costs			
Labor	14.48%	14.54%	
Equipment Rental	0.40%	0.55%	
Materials	35.84%	31.63%	
Sub-Contracts	9.78%	6.37%	
Indirect Costs			
License Fees	1.04%	1.31%	
Training Fees	0.28%	0.39%	
Sales Commissions	0.00%	2.04%	
Contingency Fees	1.50%	1.50%	
Total Cost of Sales	63.32%	58.33%	
Gross Margin	36.68%	41.67%	
Operating Expenses			
Administrative Salaries	3.44%	4.93%	
Payroll Taxes	1.30%	1.35%	
Rent	7.00%	5.67%	
Telephone & Utilities	0.76%	0.66%	
Insurance	2.08%	1.89%	
Advertising	4.36%	3.15%	
Maintenance & Repairs	0.29%	0.35%	
Gas & Oil	0.70%	0.61%	
Depreciation	1.86%	1.55%	
Travel & Entertainment	0.56%	0.28%	
Non-Income Taxes	0.07%	0.07%	
Owner's Compensation	7.40%	6.30%	
Other Operating Expenses	0.25%	0.19%	
Total Operating Expenses	30.09%	26.98%	
Net Operating Income	6.60%	14.68%	
Interest Expense	1.96%	1.65%	
Other Income	0.00%	0.00%	
Net Income Before Taxes	4.64%	13.04%	
Income Tax Expense	0.63%	2.58%	
Net Income	4.01%	10.45%	

REVENUES

Revenues, or *sales*, form the basis for the validity of the other numbers that appear on the Balance Sheet. The interpretation placed on these numbers will rely primarily on your total sales from the primary operation of the business. Too many entrepreneurs have learned the hard way that you cannot afford to place too much emphasis on these numbers alone. There must be some balance between these and your levels of profitability. High sales volume is not necessarily an indicator of profitability. Your volume may be disproportionate to your profit if you are not charging enough for your goods or services. This is where managing for profit comes into play. From year to year, there should also be some indication that the business is not stagnating, but rather mirroring a healthy reflection of management's commitment to growth and prosperity.

MONTHLY BUDGETS

Now, look at the following budget which can be broken down on a month-to-month basis, so that it becomes a regular management tool. As early as you can, you will want to track the sales volume of your business on a month-to-month basis. This information will afford you a more realistic approach to developing future budgets, and it will accurately reflect the peaks and valleys the business is likely to encounter in the course of each month's activity. This should be a meaningful source of information with respect to the management and decision-making processes you must use.

For example, when there is a pattern of a significant drop in business during a given period of time, referred to on the budget as *Adjustments*, it might indicate the appropriate time to schedule vacations, complete inventories, accomplish in-house work and generally avoid situations involving additional expenditures. Similarly, the ability to look ahead to peak periods should allow you to reconsider your buying patterns, your staffing requirements and your advertising budgets.

MONTHLY BUDGETS - Initial Version
Projected for Second Year

Annual Sales $635,400

	Month Adjustment	JAN 5.6%	FEB 5.7%	MAR 7.3%	APR 9.6%	MAY 13.2%	JUN 14.7%	JUL 18.7%	AUG 6.5%	SEP 3.3%	OCT 3.8%	NOV 5.6%	DEC 6.0%	Totals 100.0%
Revenues From Sales		$35,582	$36,218	$46,384	$60,998	$83,873	$93,404	$118,820	$41,301	$20,968	$24,145	$35,582	$38,124	$635,400
Cost of Sales														
Direct Costs														
Labor		$5,172	$5,265	$6,742	$8,867	$12,192	$13,577	$17,272	$6,004	$3,048	$3,510	$5,172	$5,542	$92,362
Equipment Rental		$196	$200	$256	$336	$462	$515	$655	$228	$116	$133	$196	$210	$3,500
Materials		$11,256	$11,457	$14,673	$19,296	$26,532	$29,547	$37,587	$13,065	$6,633	$7,638	$11,256	$12,060	$201,000
Sub-Contracts		$2,660	$2,708	$3,468	$4,560	$6,270	$6,983	$8,883	$3,088	$1,568	$1,805	$2,660	$2,850	$47,500
Indirect Costs														
License Fees		$465	$473	$606	$797	$1,096	$1,220	$1,552	$540	$274	$315	$465	$498	$8,300
Schedules, Reports & Shop Drawings		$140	$143	$183	$240	$330	$368	$468	$163	$83	$95	$140	$150	$2,500
Sales Commissions		$0	$0	$1,067	$1,403	$1,929	$2,148	$2,733	$950	$482	$555	$818	$877	$12,963
Contingency Fees		$534	$543	$696	$915	$1,258	$1,401	$1,782	$620	$315	$362	$534	$572	$9,531
Total Cost of Sales		$20,423	$20,788	$27,689	$36,413	$50,069	$55,758	$70,930	$24,655	$12,517	$14,414	$21,241	$22,758	$377,656
Gross Margin		$15,160	$15,430	$18,695	$24,585	$33,804	$37,646	$47,889	$16,646	$8,451	$9,732	$14,341	$15,366	$257,744
		42.60%	42.60%	40.30%	40.30%	40.30%	40.30%	40.30%	40.30%	40.30%	40.30%	40.30%	40.30%	
Operating Expenses														
Administrative Salaries		$2,613	$2,613	$2,613	$2,613	$2,613	$2,613	$2,613	$2,613	$2,613	$2,613	$2,613	$2,613	$31,350
Payroll Taxes		$814	$814	$814	$814	$814	$814	$814	$814	$814	$814	$814	$814	$9,762
Rent		$3,089	$3,089	$3,089	$3,089	$3,089	$3,089	$3,089	$3,089	$3,089	$3,089	$3,089	$3,089	$37,065
Telephone & Utilities		$350	$350	$350	$350	$350	$350	$350	$350	$350	$350	$350	$350	$4,200
Insurance		$1,000	$1,000	$1,000	$1,000	$1,000	$1,000	$1,000	$1,000	$1,000	$1,000	$1,000	$1,000	$12,000
Advertising		$1,667	$1,667	$1,667	$1,667	$1,667	$1,667	$1,667	$1,667	$1,667	$1,667	$1,667	$1,667	$20,000
Maintenance & Repairs		$183	$183	$183	$183	$183	$183	$183	$183	$183	$183	$183	$183	$2,200
Gas & Oil		$325	$325	$325	$325	$325	$325	$325	$325	$325	$325	$325	$325	$3,900
Depreciation		$819	$819	$819	$819	$819	$819	$819	$819	$819	$819	$819	$819	$9,833
Travel & Entertainment		$146	$146	$146	$146	$146	$146	$146	$146	$146	$146	$146	$146	$1,750
Non-Income Taxes		$38	$38	$38	$38	$38	$38	$38	$38	$38	$38	$38	$38	$450
Owner's Compensation		$4,167	$4,167	$4,167	$4,167	$4,167	$4,167	$4,167	$4,167	$4,167	$4,167	$4,167	$4,167	$50,000
Other Operating Expenses		$100	$100	$100	$100	$100	$100	$100	$100	$100	$100	$100	$100	$1,200
Total Operating Expenses		$15,309	$15,309	$15,309	$15,309	$15,309	$15,309	$15,309	$15,309	$15,309	$15,309	$15,309	$15,309	$183,710
Net Operating Income		($150)	$121	$3,386	$9,276	$18,495	$22,336	$32,580	$1,337	($6,858)	($5,578)	($968)	$56	$74,034

WHAT IS THE DIFFERENCE BETWEEN GROSS PROFITS AND NET PROFITS?

Refer to the Income and Expense Statement earlier in this chapter, and note that, while it is accepted practice to refer to *Gross Profits*, I have chosen to refer to *Gross Margin* instead. I truly believe *Gross Profits* is a misnomer, and often confusing to the uninformed. *Gross Margin* reflects the total funds that remain after having subtracted *Cost of Sales* from *Total Revenues*. It does not represent what you get to keep! If there is any profit to be realized from your hard work and the investment of your time and resources, it is yet to be determined. That is what *Net Profit after Taxes* is all about; but, you must still determine whether or not you have realized a *Profit before Taxes*. You can do that by subtracting your *Operating Expenses* from the remaining *Gross Margin*. If the value of what remains is a positive one, then you have a *Net Profit before Taxes*. If it is a negative, you have suffered a loss, and this should be a sign you need to reevaluate your strategies and your position.

Questions to ask of yourself and of your business as you evaluate poor performance:

1. How accurate have I been in our estimating practices?
2. Do I thoroughly understand the bidding process? What don't I understand about it?
3. Is more training required for our employees or me?
4. Does everyone in the company fully comprehend our relationship with our subcontractors, or between our customers and ourselves?
5. Have I been bidding our jobs simply because our competition bids them that way, or because I know we are making a profit?
6. Have I properly identified all our expenses?
7. Was there anything that had to be redone because it was performed or supplied incorrectly in the first place?
8. Whose fault was that?
10. Is there a communication problem?
11. What can I do differently in the future?
12. Ask probing questions. We learn from our mistakes!

WHAT IS THE DIFFERENCE BETWEEN DIRECT COSTS AND INDIRECT COSTS?

You may also have heard references made with respect to *Direct Costs* and *Indirect Costs* and not fully understood the differences. First of all, we are talking about costs, not expenses. Costs are those things you associate with the finished product or service you sell or offer, either directly or indirectly.

Direct Costs

Direct costs may represent the labor you employ, the subcontract you entered into, the equipment you must rent to complete the job or the materials required to build or complete the finished products or services you sell.

Indirect Costs

Indirect costs may include such things as consultant fees, job training fees, work items and training related to worker safety and the cost of permits and fees associated with your work. If there are multiple projects or products you offer, there may be a means of spreading your *Indirect Costs* over a portion of each, rather than having them all fall on one customer or product. Proper planning may allow you to maximize your management efforts with respect to *Indirect Costs*, thus allowing you to exercise control in these areas. Some people intentionally leave out some of these costs in an effort to be more competitive, and, while this may help them win the job, one has to wonder at what price. **To be truly competitive, you cannot leave anything out.**

You must be competitive at every level. Perhaps we could characterize this next item as an example of a hidden cost, but, I believe it should properly be classified as an example of an *Indirect Cost* or part of your *Cost of Sales*—a part that should be highly visible so that you won't overlook it

Have you ever done a job that was completed exactly as you envisioned it, especially a remodeling job? If you are being honest, you know that it is almost impossible, and, not necessarily because you made a mistake in your original assessment of the work. The customer may change his or her mind about something; there is some previously unknown problem that suddenly emerges or there are other unforeseen delays. Whatever the reason, it is your business that is suffering, not your customer.

HOW TO HANDLE HIDDEN COSTS - CONTINGENCY FEES

You could and should build in a small *Contingency Fee* for each job you do in an effort to offset these added expenses of doing business. I want to caution you here. I am not suggesting that you gouge your customers for services you don't render. Rather, this must be viewed as a sort of insurance policy that permits you to spread the expense of such delays over all your work. Failing to take the opportunity to add such a *contingency fee* into each job you do will eventually have a telling effect, for it will result in your taking less time to provide that outstanding customer service that distinguishes you and your firm.

If you understand that mistakes will happen, but that you don't have to shoulder the cost alone, you should be able to devote more attention to the needs of your customers, without having to rush them or cause them to make decisions they will later regret.

Understand that I am not recommending this *contingency fee* as another profit center, but, rather, as a method of legitimately recouping lost earnings as a result of unforeseen or unknown obstacles which you will routinely encounter in the normal course of your work. It should be spread out over each job you do to help offset the costs of these unknown factors. Some businesses and projects may be more susceptible to these costs than others, so you will have to decide individually what these amounts or percentages should be for each job. Whatever amount you choose, it must be realistic, and even that may not be sufficient to prevent you from losing some jobs.

Collectively then, both *Direct Costs* and *Indirect Costs* are referred to as the *Cost of Sales, Cost of Revenues*, etc. When you subtract them from your *Revenues*, you arrive at your *Gross Margin*.

WHAT ARE EXPENSES?

Here is where many owners and managers get themselves in trouble. Whereas they can usually identify *costs* rather easily because they work so closely with many of these items, *expenses* are usually acknowledged as something the bookkeeper or accountant is responsible for. Nothing could be further from the truth! This is a major reason why so many small businesses fail. Because these are things most managers or even owners don't deal with on a day-to-day basis, they tend to lose sight of these issues, and, as the old saying goes, "out of sight, out of mind." To the extent that these issues are not addressed head on, they are missed in the bidding processes, and, as a result, they eat up profits that might otherwise have been realized.

Examples of *Expenses* would be:

1. Salaries of Office Staff
2. Rent
3. Utilities
4. Advertising
5. Travel
6. Telephone
7. Owner's Compensation
8. Autos and Trucks

WHAT IS THE BOTTOM LINE?

How much do you actually get to keep? Unfortunately, you can't expect to get to this point if you don't fully comprehend what stands between you and your business objectives. Yet that is exactly what so many do. Every time you bid a job without covering all your costs and expenses, you are, in fact, setting yourself and your business up to lose, not profit, from your efforts.

Dun & Bradstreet's findings point to insufficient funds as the number two cause for most business failures. If, after deducting what the business owes, you don't have sufficient profits to grow with and beyond your competitors, if you don't have sufficient profits to satisfy the needs and wants of your customers as those needs and wants change, how long can you continue to remain in business? If, after deducting taxes, you cannot convince prospective lenders or investors of your potential to pay them back, how will you be able to reach for new goals or dreams? The bottom line is not some figment of your imagination. It is a very real and measured testimonial to your management and entrepreneurial skills. It is what others who can help you or hurt you will judge you by.

STATEMENT OF CASH FLOW

The Statement of Cash Flow is the financial statement you, as the owner or manager of a kitchen and bathroom firm, want to become most familiar with. It is the one you can use most effectively to guide your business through the maze of hidden costs. I am referring to the devastating penalty and interest assessments your business will incur if you don't pay your bills and taxes on time, or, if you bid on a job based on a discounted price for materials, and then fail to take advantage of that discount because you don't have the funds available. Too often, people confuse cash flow with profits, and they are not the same thing. You may operate your business unprofitably for a long time before you realize you are in trouble, because there is a steady cash flow through the business. On the other hand, you may also operate a business with a profit from the first day, but you may be out of business at the end of the first 30 days if you don't have sufficient cash flowing into the business. Insufficient capital or cash flow is one of the single, most devastating causes of small-business failures.

The Statement of Cash Flow really amounts to a calendar or schedule whereby you plot the payments that must be made within a very specific time frame, and, at the same time, you try to anticipate which funds will be available to meet those obligations. Arrangements are then made to offset any expected shortfalls. By doing this ahead of time to avoid any penalty assessments or interest charges, you will avoid such hidden charges which systematically eat away at your profit margins.

Examine the initial version of the following **STATEMENT OF CASH FLOW, Initial Version**. Our fictional kitchen and bathroom business owners prepared this statement with their accounting program. Needless to say, it got their attention when they looked at the last few months of the year and noticed the serious threat to their flow of cash. They went to work on finding ways to pare down some of the expenses and costs associated with their ambitious plans for the coming year. Much of the anticipated growth they are expecting stems from a project already committed to for the months of May through July. They have been contacted by one of their previous clients, a custom-home builder, who wants them to design and install the bathrooms, kitchens and laundry rooms in several custom homes.

Now that the owners have viewed this original draft, they realize they must rethink their strategy to get them through this second year. They decide to take another hard look at their proposed monthly budgets to determine where they might further reduce their costs of sales and expenses.

You should know something about their business and how they want to conduct it. The couple resides in a town that is essentially a bedroom community to a large city about 45 minutes away. Most of the homes are between 20- and 50-years old, and more young families are moving in to raise their families. The town has grown steadily over the past 5 years, and, while the growth in new housing may level off, a population shift toward younger, more professional families should continue. There is a mass merchandiser located 10 miles from the town, but our couple has identified a need for someone who can provide both the products and services they plan to offer and the talents and skills that they possess.

STATEMENT OF CASH FLOW - Initial Version

Expenses, Cost of Sales (COS) and Cash on Hand for January are based on Balance Sheet figures from first year. COS excluding weekly payroll & commissions is calculated in the following month. Deposits are based on figures for the following month.

Initial Version

	2nd Year	Jan.	Feb.	Mar.	Apr.	May	Jun.	Jul.	Aug.	Sep.	Oct.	Nov.	Dec.
Monthly Adjustments		5.6%	5.7%	7.3%	9.6%	13.2%	14.7%	18.7%	6.5%	3.3%	3.8%	5.6%	6.0%
	Annual Budget												
Revenues	$635,400	35,582	36,218	46,384	60,998	83,873	93,404	118,820	41,301	20,968	24,145	35,582	38,124
# Weekly Payroll Periods		4	4	5	4	5	4	4	5	4	4	5	4
Gross Margin	40.56%												
As a % of Sales - Charge Sales	16%												
Cash On Hand		18,539	31,059	9,517	5,360	10,031	22,702	38,896	56,716	19,781	(2,964)	(17,264)	(27,721)
COS (excl. Comm. & Reg. Payroll)		(36,067)	(14,252)	(14,507)	(19,645)	(25,835)	(35,523)	(39,560)	(50,324)	(17,492)	(8,881)	(10,226)	(15,070)
Cost of Sales (Weekly Payroll)		(6,640)	(6,640)	(8,300)	(6,640)	(8,300)	(6,640)	(6,640)	(8,300)	(6,640)	(6,640)	(8,300)	(6,640)
Cost of Sales (Commissions)		0	0	(1,067)	(1,403)	(1,929)	(2,148)	(2,733)	(950)	(482)	(555)	(818)	(877)
Cash Sales	533,736	25,406	25,860	33,118	43,553	59,885	66,690	84,837	29,489	14,971	17,240	25,406	27,221
Charge Sales	(101,664)	(4,839)	(4,926)	(6,308)	(8,296)	(11,407)	(12,703)	(16,159)	(5,617)	(2,852)	(3,284)	(4,839)	(5,185)
++ Accounts Rec.	131,757	50,915	4,452	4,919	6,198	8,137	11,158	12,599	15,883	6,460	3,073	3,249	4,715
Purchase of CAD Equipt.		0	(12,160)	0	0	0	0	0	0	0	0	0	0
Operating Expenses		(16,392)	(15,309)	(15,309)	(15,309)	(15,309)	(15,309)	(15,309)	(15,309)	(15,309)	(15,309)	(15,309)	(15,309)
Short-term Debt + Interest	(40,351)	(3,363)	(3,363)	(3,363)	(3,363)	(3,363)	(3,363)	(3,363)	(3,363)	(3,363)	(3,363)	(3,363)	(3,363)
Long-term Debt + Interest	(13,415)	(1,118)	(1,118)	(1,118)	(1,118)	(1,118)	(1,118)	(1,118)	(1,118)	(1,118)	(1,118)	(1,118)	(1,118)
Customer Deposits @	15.00%	4,618	5,914	7,777	10,694	11,909	15,150	5,266	2,673	3,079	4,537	4,861	4,778
Cash in flow		99,478	67,284	55,332	65,804	89,962	115,699	141,598	104,761	44,291	21,885	16,252	8,992
Cash out flow		(68,419)	(57,767)	(49,972)	(55,773)	(67,260)	(76,803)	(84,882)	(84,980)	(47,255)	(39,149)	(43,973)	(47,561)
(Cash Shortfall)**		31,059	9,517	5,360	10,031	22,702	38,896	56,716	19,781	(2,964)	(17,264)	(27,721)	(38,569)

++ Used Average Collection Period of 36 days, 92% collected within 30 days balance collected in the following month.

** Profit and Cash Flow are not the same thing.

They have formulated the following strategy:

1. They encourage their customers to use the full design capabilities of the business and their custom-crafted product line for a finished project that will reflect an upscale lifestyle with a more personalized touch.
2. They offer free in-home consultation service, not to be confused with free design, and, in order to make their business more attractive, they encourage sales through a long-term financing plan.
3. In an effort to build sales and customer loyalty as rapidly as possible, they run extensive advertising to make their presence in the market a viable alternative.
4. Understanding the referral value of offering personalized service, they have implemented an extensive customer service program.

As you examine the cash flow statements, you will notice that it is part of their plan to purchase new CAD equipment in the early part of the year. They will need approximately $12,160 to purchase the CAD equipment and software. They plan to add a commission salesperson in March to free up the designer/owner.

As you look at the numbers included in both the initial **MONTHLY BUDGETS** and the **STATEMENT OF CASH FLOW**, keep in mind that these are only projections. They may never be achieved; however, after taking the time to prepare these calculations on their accounting package, it is prudent to work with these numbers as they are the closest thing the owners have to a blueprint for building the success of this business.

We have applied the accounts receivable funds in the following fashion: An average collection period of 36 days was used with 92 percent being collected within 30 days and the balance collected within the following month. Our owners have worked in the industry for a number of years and appreciate that there is a downward trend in business during the latter part of each year, due, in large part, to a seasonal factor associated with the local economy.

The row entitled *Monthly Adjustments* reflects this seasonality factor based upon their appreciation of the local market and last year's performance. These percentages reflect that portion of annual revenues they expect to earn. Our kitchen and bathroom professionals would like to know when the business will require cash, as well as how much will be needed, to meet operating requirements. This type of information, tracked routinely by our owners over the years, will eventually give them a major advantage in developing a realistic profile about their business. Knowing when the peaks and valleys occur in a business can be very advantageous when making management decisions, as we will see later.

Their plans call for them to increase their sales volume to approximately $635,400 in the second year. A significant key to making them competitive in the marketplace is going to be their ability to offer financing, preferably long-term, to their clients. They intend to encourage their customers to take advantage of credit cards for smaller purchases and third-party financing for the larger purchases. Here is where that old adage, "use other people's money," comes into play. Our business owners are not bankers, and simply cannot afford to carry their customers' purchases long term, nor should they attempt this for the short term.

This was a strategy which they realized needed to be changed during the first year of business, so they have already aligned themselves with a financial lending institution and are ready to offer these services to their clients.

CORRECTIVE OPTIONS

A business that is essentially a cash business may be able to continue to stumble along for quite some time without a profit, but eventually it catches up. A business that produces a profit, but experiences a cash shortage, may be out of business in no time at all, unless corrective steps are taken immediately. Our business here is a prime example of this. What might our owners consider doing about this predicament? Their original strategy may be a good one, if this issue of cash flow can be addressed quickly. One primary target as we have already discussed, is the owners' decision to arrange for some means of providing their customers both long- and short-term financing.

The options we just mentioned will allow the owners to move significant sums from the *Charge Sales* to the *Cash Sales* account on a monthly basis. With credit card purchases, they will pay a merchant fee or discount, but, they will have the cash available to them on a regular basis. There will still be some instances where our fictional kitchen and bathroom professionals may feel compelled to extend credit to one or more of their clients, if they want their business. This will be especially true when dealing with commercial accounts, such as builders and large corporations, where the jobs may run over extended periods of time.

Our owners currently work with several builders, and their business is represented by the charge sales they carry on their books. They do require a 15 percent deposit on the jobs they do for these people, and they don't believe requiring more is going to make a significant difference, especially in the months concerned. Remember, the local economy is affected by some seasonality factors, and these builders also try to work around them.

A number of considerations do come into play here. One of these accounts is a builder who is retiring in the coming year, and closing his business. Our owners feel that while they don't want to shut off this source of business, they could offer shorter terms, say 15 days, and still keep this customer. Because of these factors, they expect to see their charge sales reduced by about 25 percent, but more importantly they hope to collect their money sooner.

WHAT ADDITIONAL OPTIONS ARE OPEN TO THEM?

They decide to look at their *Costs of Sales*. Maybe there is something here they have overlooked or could reconsider. One of the owners feels that with the additional work they are committed to, their labor costs are really in line with the volume of work they hope to accomplish. So, while he does not intend to cut back, he does believe that between himself and some of the new personnel they will hire, they could take up some of the slack and cover about $7,000 of the work he originally thought he would subcontract out. Something else they consider is the fact that time is money, and, accordingly, they have always attempted to turn their work around quickly. In fact, they make every effort to complete the entire process of consultation, design, selection, delivery and completion of the project, within a maximum of

30 days, and sooner whenever possible. Because they require deposits and payments scheduled to coincide with these events, and the financing is now in place, they believe they will have the ability to pay some of their own payables (about 65 percent of them) earlier and realize on average a 2 percent discount on their purchases. While it may not seem like much, it will reduce their cash outlay by $3,528 during the year. Outside of those potential savings, they really don't see room for much else to contain in the area of *Costs of Sales*. These changes impact their overall *Costs of Sales* and improve their *Gross Margin* to 41.67 percent of *Revenues*.

EXPENSE REVIEW

After reviewing their expenses, our professionals find two alternative options here as well. He realizes he could empty out and dispose of a storage building they have been renting. Over the past year, he had used it to store cabinet doors, moldings, pieces of laminates, tile and odds and ends that were left over from jobs, with the expectation they would use them at a later opportunity. Those later opportunities have never arrived, and it now costs them in excess of $83 a month to store them. By eliminating the storage facility, they will reduce their annual expenses by $1,065 for the year.

In a further attempt to improve their cash flow position, our business owners agreed they would find a way to live on $40,000 between the two of them, instead of taking out the $50,000 they feel they were entitled to.

Even with this corrective option they realize they will not totally resolve their expected shortfalls. The suggestion to reduce their compensation was made at his insistence, because he doesn't like to be in debt. Part of their plan has been to reduce their debt as quickly as possible. She, however, believes they must reconsider this strategy. She correctly believes that if this business is ever to grow, they will have to incur some debt. Their responsibility, then, is to manage and use it to their maximum benefit, and not to allow it to steal their future earning potential. Looking back at their initial **STATEMENT OF CASH FLOW**, you will note that they have both some short-term and long-term debt which they are paying off. The short-term debt is a note in the amount of $37,714, which they are paying off at 12.67 percent and has 12 months to go. The long-term obligation is a seven-year instrument for $65,999, which they are paying off at 10.65 percent. The combined monthly obligation on these notes is $4,481. They do not have the cash to purchase the new CAD system outright, and, while they could borrow the funds against their credit card, that would cost them 13.125 percent, and add an additional $1,087 per month to their obligations, for the next 12 months.

One of the owners has noticed an advertisement that came with the monthly bank statement advertising new lower rates. She suggests they consider rolling all this debt into one note at the reduced rate. He however doesn't want to be in debt for any longer than they have to be. She goes to the amortization program that came with their accounting package. If approved, they could roll all this debt into one loan at the rate of 9.75 percent, which is what the bank is currently offering and will be able to pay the entire amount off within 60 months.

Interestingly, they can save $436.27 in interest over the life of the loan, while lowering their combined monthly payments to just $2,447.73. This consolidation will allow them to purchase the CAD system and reduce the demand on their cash flow. (See the following **STATEMENT OF CASH FLOW, Modified Version**.)

Further computations would reveal that this exercise of going back through their *Costs of Sales* and *Expenses*, would yield an even more positive effect. It accounted for a $19,265 difference in *Net Profits before Taxes*. (See the next example, **MONTHLY BUDGET, Modified Version**.) That information in itself would make for a more convincing argument as to why they could use the loan.

STATEMENT OF CASH FLOW - Modified Version

Modified Version

	2nd Year Annual Budget	Jan. 5.6%	Feb. 5.7%	Mar. 7.3%	Apr. 9.6%	May 13.2%	Jun. 14.7%	Jul. 18.7%	Aug. 6.5%	Sep. 3.3%	Oct. 3.8%	Nov. 5.6%	Dec. 6.0%
Monthly Adjustments													
Revenues	$635,400	35,582	36,218	46,384	60,998	83,873	93,404	118,820	41,301	20,968	24,145	35,582	38,124
# Weekly Payroll Periods		4	4	5	4	5	4	4	5	4	4	5	4
Gross Margin	41.67%												
As a % of Sales - Charge Sales	12%												
Cash On Hand		18,539	33,299	27,565	27,119	35,694	52,557	73,248	95,811	63,469	44,350	33,470	26,531
COS (excl. Comm. & Reg. Payroll)		(36,057)	(13,860)	(14,108)	(19,134)	(25,163)	(34,599)	(38,531)	(49,015)	(17,037)	(8,650)	(9,960)	(14,678)
Early Payment Discounts		198	201	258	339	466	519	660	229	116	134	198	212
Cost of Sales (Weekly Payroll)		(6,640)	(6,640)	(8,300)	(6,640)	(8,300)	(6,640)	(6,640)	(8,300)	(6,640)	(6,640)	(8,300)	(6,640)
Cost of Sales (Commissions)		0	0	(1,067)	(1,403)	(1,929)	(2,148)	(2,733)	(950)	(482)	(555)	(818)	(877)
Cash Sales	559,152	25,406	25,860	33,118	43,553	59,885	66,690	84,837	29,489	14,971	17,240	25,406	27,221
Charge Sales	(76,248)	(4,839)	(4,926)	(6,308)	(8,296)	(11,407)	(12,703)	(16,159)	(5,617)	(2,852)	(3,284)	(4,839)	(5,185)
++ Accounts Rec.	131,757	50,915	4,452	4,919	6,198	8,137	11,158	12,599	15,883	6,460	3,073	3,249	4,715
Purchase of CAD Equipt.		0	0	0	0	0	0	0	0	0	0	0	0
Operating Expenses		(16,392)	(14,287)	(14,287)	(14,287)	(14,287)	(14,287)	(14,287)	(14,287)	(14,287)	(14,287)	(14,287)	(14,287)
Short-term Debt + Interest		0	0	0	0	0	0	0	0	0	0	0	0
Long-term Debt + Interest		(2,448)	(2,448)	(2,448)	(2,448)	(2,448)	(2,448)	(2,448)	(2,448)	(2,448)	(2,448)	(2,448)	(2,448)
Customer Deposits @	15.00%	4,618	5,914	7,777	10,694	11,909	15,150	5,266	2,673	3,079	4,537	4,861	4,778
Cash in flow		99,675	69,726	73,637	87,901	116,090	146,073	176,610	144,086	88,096	69,333	67,183	63,456
Cash out flow		(66,376)	(42,161)	(46,518)	(52,208)	(63,534)	(72,825)	(80,798)	(80,617)	(43,746)	(35,864)	(40,652)	(44,115)
(Cash Shortfall)**		33,299	27,565	27,119	35,694	52,557	73,248	95,811	63,469	44,350	33,470	26,531	19,341

++ Used Average Collection Period of 36 days, 92% collected within 30 days balance collected in the following month.

** Profit and Cash Flow are not the same thing.

MONTHLY BUDGETS - Modified Version
Projected for Second Year

		JAN	FEB	MAR	APR	MAY	JUN	JUL	AUG	SEP	OCT	NOV	DEC	Totals
Annual Sales	$635,400											Modified Version		100.0%
Month Adjustment		5.6%	5.7%	7.3%	9.6%	13.2%	14.7%	18.7%	6.5%	3.3%	3.8%	5.6%	6.0%	
Revenues From Sales		$35,582	$36,218	$46,384	$60,998	$83,873	$93,404	$118,820	$41,301	$20,968	$24,145	$35,582	$38,124	$635,400
Cost of Sales														
Direct Costs														
Labor		$5,172	$5,265	$6,742	$8,867	$12,192	$13,577	$17,272	$6,004	$3,048	$3,510	$5,172	$5,542	$92,362
Equipment Rental		$196	$200	$256	$336	$462	$515	$655	$228	$116	$133	$196	$210	$3,500
Materials		$11,256	$11,457	$14,673	$19,296	$26,532	$29,547	$37,587	$13,065	$6,633	$7,638	$11,256	$12,060	$201,000
Sub-Contracts		$2,268	$2,309	$2,957	$3,888	$5,346	$5,954	$7,574	$2,633	$1,337	$1,539	$2,268	$2,430	$40,500
Indirect Costs														
License Fees		$465	$473	$606	$797	$1,096	$1,220	$1,552	$540	$274	$315	$465	$498	$8,300
Schedules, Reports & Shop Drawings		$140	$143	$183	$240	$330	$368	$468	$163	$83	$95	$140	$150	$2,500
Sales Commissions		$0	$0	$1,067	$1,403	$1,929	$2,148	$2,733	$950	$482	$555	$818	$877	$12,963
Contingency Fees		$534	$543	$696	$915	$1,258	$1,401	$1,782	$620	$315	$362	$534	$572	$9,531
Total Cost of Sales		$20,031	$20,389	$27,178	$35,741	$49,145	$54,729	$69,621	$24,200	$12,286	$14,148	$20,849	$22,338	$370,656
Gross Margin		$15,552	$15,829	$19,206	$25,257	$34,728	$38,675	$49,198	$17,101	$8,682	$9,998	$14,733	$15,786	$264,744
		43.71%	43.71%	41.41%	41.41%	41.41%	41.41%	41.41%	41.41%	41.41%	41.41%	41.41%	41.41%	
Operating Expenses														
Administrative Salaries		$2,613	$2,613	$2,613	$2,613	$2,613	$2,613	$2,613	$2,613	$2,613	$2,613	$2,613	$2,613	$31,350
Payroll Taxes		$714	$714	$714	$714	$714	$714	$714	$714	$714	$714	$714	$714	$8,562
Rent		$3,000	$3,000	$3,000	$3,000	$3,000	$3,000	$3,000	$3,000	$3,000	$3,000	$3,000	$3,000	$36,000
Telephone & Utilities		$350	$350	$350	$350	$350	$350	$350	$350	$350	$350	$350	$350	$4,200
Insurance		$1,000	$1,000	$1,000	$1,000	$1,000	$1,000	$1,000	$1,000	$1,000	$1,000	$1,000	$1,000	$12,000
Advertising		$1,667	$1,667	$1,667	$1,667	$1,667	$1,667	$1,667	$1,667	$1,667	$1,667	$1,667	$1,667	$20,000
Maintenance & Repairs		$183	$183	$183	$183	$183	$183	$183	$183	$183	$183	$183	$183	$2,200
Gas & Oil		$325	$325	$325	$325	$325	$325	$325	$325	$325	$325	$325	$325	$3,900
Depreciation		$819	$819	$819	$819	$819	$819	$819	$819	$819	$819	$819	$819	$9,833
Travel & Entertainment		$146	$146	$146	$146	$146	$146	$146	$146	$146	$146	$146	$146	$1,750
Non-Income Taxes		$38	$38	$38	$38	$38	$38	$38	$38	$38	$38	$38	$38	$450
Owner's Compensation		$3,333	$3,333	$3,333	$3,333	$3,333	$3,333	$3,333	$3,333	$3,333	$3,333	$3,333	$3,333	$40,000
Other Operating Expenses		$100	$100	$100	$100	$100	$100	$100	$100	$100	$100	$100	$100	$1,200
Total Operating Expenses		$14,287	$14,287	$14,287	$14,287	$14,287	$14,287	$14,287	$14,287	$14,287	$14,287	$14,287	$14,287	$171,445
Net Operating Income		$1,265	$1,542	$4,919	$10,970	$20,441	$24,388	$34,911	$2,814	($5,605)	($4,290)	$446	$1,498	$93,299

If these numbers can be supported by the overall strategy, and a convincing argument can be made as to why these additional funds are necessary, now is the time to ask for them, not after they are in trouble. At that point, it can send the wrong message. Cash is to the business what blood is to your body. It is the vehicle of all the nutrients, essential chemicals, oxygen and stimuli your body functions with. Cut off the supply and you are in trouble. A shortage of cash will have the same effect upon your business.

THE STATEMENT OF CASH FLOW AS A MANAGEMENT TOOL

The more you use this report, the more you will learn how much flexibility it has to offer. It is a management tool that is unsurpassed in its value to you in your efforts to maximize the flow of cash through a project or business.

Look at the row entitled *Monthly Adjustments* on the **CASH FLOW STATEMENT, Modified Version**. Here, we see what one might describe as the peaks and valleys of this business. Based on their own experience with this market, we can see the projections which illustrate the impact of seasonality adjustments in the local economy. From a management perspective, what kind of feedback does this provide?

SEASONAL CYCLES

We know from this report that their slow period begins in September and continues pretty much through February. On the other hand, their busy period is from April through August. With what types of management decisions might this information assist the owners? They would probably do well to explain to their employees that no vacation time is available during the busy period. That is when their talents and skills are required the most. Their staff needs to plan extended leaves of absences and vacations during slow months.

Before deciding to hire more full-time people in June or July, they might instead consider bringing in some part-time help, or even some temporary or seasonal help. They may consider subcontracting out some of this work.

While each state and province is different, if you lay off employees, you are likely to see an increase in your unemployment compensation rates. Realizing that you are entering the slow time of year for your business, you may not want to incur the increased liability.

PURCHASE DECISIONS

How will you respond if your favorite supplier shows up on your doorstep in mid-July with an unbelievable offer? He can sell you an entire trailer-load of sinks, solid-surface materials, laminates or cabinets at 60 percent off, if you will order from him today! The offer is tempting, because you use these products every day and, if you increase your sales, you would have a very attractive offer for your customers and a profit for yourself. If you have a Statement of Cash Flow available, you can ask your supplier a simple question that will allow you to make an enlightened decision: "When can I expect delivery?" If the answer is 4 to 6 weeks, you will probably end up storing this inventory until next spring, since you will have already hit your slow period. Couldn't you put that cash to better use, rather than having it sit on your shelf, costing you money?

DON'T USE THE CASH FLOW STATEMENT TO YOUR DISADVANTAGE

For most small businesses, the Cash Flow Statement should show salaries for owners from the start of the business. Not doing this is unrealistic, and is generally used only for the purpose of showing profitability early on. Bankers, lenders and investors will not be impressed by this. They want the facts as they really are, so produce your Cash Flow Statements showing a salary for you, and showing the periods when you are both profitable and unprofitable. Some businesses don't become profitable for quite some time, and astute lenders and investors already know where to find that information. Prepare two statements; one reflecting your cash position which shows where it really stands before any bank loans or investments, and a second version which shows the impact of the loan(s) and your ability to repay them within the limits of your projected revenues and cash flows.

Managing cash flow includes responsibilities with respect to the management of a firm's current assets:

1. *Make deposits in a timely and routine fashion.* If they are not in the bank, you will not be able to take advantage of early payment discounts, and, furthermore, you may be subjecting your business to unnecessary fines and penalties.

2. *Invoice in a timely fashion.* If you employ a charge system for your clientele, you need to ensure that they are billed as quickly as possible. At this point, they are using your money, and good cash management dictates that you convert your receivables to cash as quickly as you can.

3. *Work your aged receivables.* The faster you can turn your receivables into cash, the more quickly you can pay your own bills and avoid fines and penalties. You will also increase your ability to pay your bills early and take advantage of early payment discounts. Perhaps most important of all, you will increase the chances of collecting your money without hassle. If your customers are aware of how serious you are about collecting your money, you will no doubt get paid first. Remember, the squeaky wheel gets the grease.

4. *Keep inventory levels low, but profitable.* You must have inventory on hand to sell when customers are prepared to buy, otherwise they will shop elsewhere. The problem is that, too often, a business will buy a fairly large amount of inventory in order to get the best possible price and terms.

    In order to effectively manage the business, you need as much flexibility as possible when it comes to your current assets, and, while inventory is certainly recognized as a current asset, it is the least flexible in terms of its liquidity. Be sure you maintain enough on hand to meet your requirements, but not so much that you tie up the firm's ability to meet its short-term obligations.

Look at the information we can turn up by using the Statement of Cash Flow. What did it cost us? A little bit of time and energy. There was no loss of money or other precious resources. It was a simple, inexpensive tool we could use to foresee the need for cash within a business. If used properly, and on a weekly basis, it can allow you to plan, judge and be proactive in your management style, not to mention add profits to your bottom line.

Similarly, think of the advantage you have afforded yourself by reviewing your monthly budgets. You have developed a much better appreciation of your business and how it operates. You now have a fairly clear idea of when you can expect to be busy and profitable. This should allow you to plan for the off-peak periods. For instance, it might allow you to better schedule not only vacation times, but also training and research time, for you and your employees. The discovery and use of this information has allowed you to make better use of your resources by planning in advance. Since such information is different and critical to the function of any business, you are in a position to tailor the use of it and your planned response in such a manner that it is now your *trade secret*.

WHERE IS THE BREAK-EVEN POINT?

Refer to *Exhibit A* of the following **BREAK-EVEN ANALYSIS** worksheets. One of the reasons to set out a goal or budget for yourself is to provide some direction and encouragement, so that you can ask yourself better questions about your strategies.

Another important tool in this quest would be an understanding of where you have to be in order to break even. After all, how can you be sure you are headed for a profit without knowing where you are? Your break-even point is that point at which you have met all your *Fixed Expenses*. Any revenues in excess of the resulting *Costs of Sales* contribute to your profitability. Is there some way you can pinpoint that occurrence with some degree of accuracy? Definitely, assuming you have done a thorough job of compiling your expenses and costs, and are on target to achieve your revenue projections within your given time frame.

Retailers can tell you how many units they must sell of an item before they break even. Manufacturers will be able to tell you how many units they must produce before they break even. Although you are not strictly a retailer or a manufacturer, there is a way to determine how a **cust**om**er service provider** breaks even.

FORECASTING

From your Annual Budget (if you are attempting to forecast this information), or from your Income and Expense Statement (if you are trying to determine what it actually was), you can extract the dollar amounts for the following:

- Revenues from Sales
- Total Costs of Sales
- Gross Margin
- Total Operating Expenses
- Net Operating Income
- Interest Expense
- Other Income
- Net Income before Taxes

In this example, we have used our fictional business figures for the second year of operation. You will need to calculate what percentage of sales each of these entities represents.

I recommend that you round off at the second number after the decimal point. In case you have forgotten how to arrive at these percentages, I would suggest using a calculator and entering the dollar amount of the item and dividing it by the dollar amount of the revenue figure.

Dollar Amount of Item ÷ Dollar Amount of Revenue Figure

Calculate what percentage of *Revenues from Sales* your *Gross Margin* represents, by referring to the *Revenues* in the **BREAK-EVEN ANALYSIS** worksheets.

BREAK-EVEN ANALYSIS

Step 1 Using *Exhibit A*, enter $264,744, the *Gross Margin* figure and divide that by $635,400, the *Revenues from Sales* figure. The resulting answer on your calculator will be .41665722.

Multiply that by 100 percent and round two decimal places. Your answer is 41.67 percent and represents your *Gross Margin* as a percent of *Revenues from Sales*. You can calculate each of these items the same way, always dividing the item by the *Revenues from Sales*.

Step 2 Once you have that information available, you can determine the break-even point for this particular period. That figure is arrived at by dividing your *Fixed Expenses* by your *Gross Margin* expressed as a percent of *Revenues from Sales*. (If you use 41.67 percent, you will not arrive at the exact figure in this case, but, if you round off to eight decimal places, you arrive at exactly the correct number—.41665722. We are using large numbers and rounding them off.)

Step 3 $411,477 represents your production zone, or the volume required to break even. Does that mean everything in excess of that figure represents profit? No! It does mean that each dollar you have earned to date would be sufficient to cover your *Cost of Sales* and the overhead you must cover for that particular period. It also means that each dollar you earn over and above that figure falls into the contribution zone.

Step 4 Referring to *Exhibit B*, a portion of each of these dollars contributes directly to your bottom line before taxes. In order to know what that amount is, you must subtract your *Sales to Break Even* from *Revenues*, and apply your same overall *Cost of Sales* (expressed as a percent of *Revenues*) to this figure.

Steps 5 and 6 The apparent difference between the $82,831 and the *Net Income before Taxes* can be explained by the *Interest Expense* and *Other Income*. Otherwise, these numbers are in balance, proving the validity of this approach.

This break-even analysis is an essential tool to understanding your business profitability. It only takes a few minutes to prepare, but it provides you with valuable information when establishing past performance or preparing your monthly and annual budgets.

Exhibit C of the **BREAK-EVEN ANALYSIS**, shows a completed version of the analysis and *Exhibit D* is a blank copy of the **BREAK-EVEN ANALYSIS**, that you may use to practice with in the everyday operation of your business.

FINANCIAL REPORTS—A SENSE OF DIRECTION

If you will focus your attention on the three reports we have just looked at, the Balance Sheet, the Income and Expense Statement and the Statement of Cash Flow, you will come to a much greater appreciation of the workings of your business. Because operating a business depends on so many different elements, you, as the owner or manager, must have an overview of how it is to function properly. How else can you ever expect to guide and direct it to growth and prosperity? These three financial statements provide you with that overview.

BREAKEVEN ANALYSIS
Service Business
Exhibit A

Objective: To find the breakeven point in revenues from sales.

Step #1 - Extract the following figures from your Annual Budget if you are trying to *forecast* this information, or from your most recent Income & Expense Statement if you are trying to determine what it actually was.

Look up:	Revenues From Sales	$635,400
	Total Cost Of Sales	$370,656
	Gross Margin	$264,744
	Total Operating Expenses	$171,445
++	Net Operating Income	$ 93,299
	Interest Expense	$ 10,468
	Other Income	$ 0
	Net Income Before Taxes	$ 82,831

Step #2 - Determine the percent of Revenues From Sales, each of these items represents. To do that, divide each of those numbers by the figure for Revenues From Sales: (Calculation #1)

	Revenues From Sales	100.00%
	Total Cost Of Sales	53.88%
**	Gross Margin	41.67%
	Total Operating Expenses	26.98%
	Net Operating Income	10.45%

** To be completely accurate you would have to carry this number out to 0.41665722 or eight decimal places. Because the numbers are large we will find a difference of $42, as we calculate the breakeven point. This is due to rounding off.

Step #3 - Breakeven Analysis (Calculation #2)

Enter the Operating Expenses	$171,445
Divide by Gross Margin (as a decimal)	÷ .4167
The resulting answer equals	**$411,477**

your Breakeven point in Revenues From Sales. Think of this as your **Production Zone**, meaning the dollar volume required to Breakeven.

Calculation #1

Entry #1: 370656
Entry #2: ÷ 635400
Entry #3: = 41.67%

Sample Calculation of percentage for Gross Margin

Calculation #2

Entry #1: 171445
Entry #2: ÷ .4167
Entry #3: = 411477

BREAKEVEN ANALYSIS
Service Business
Exhibit B

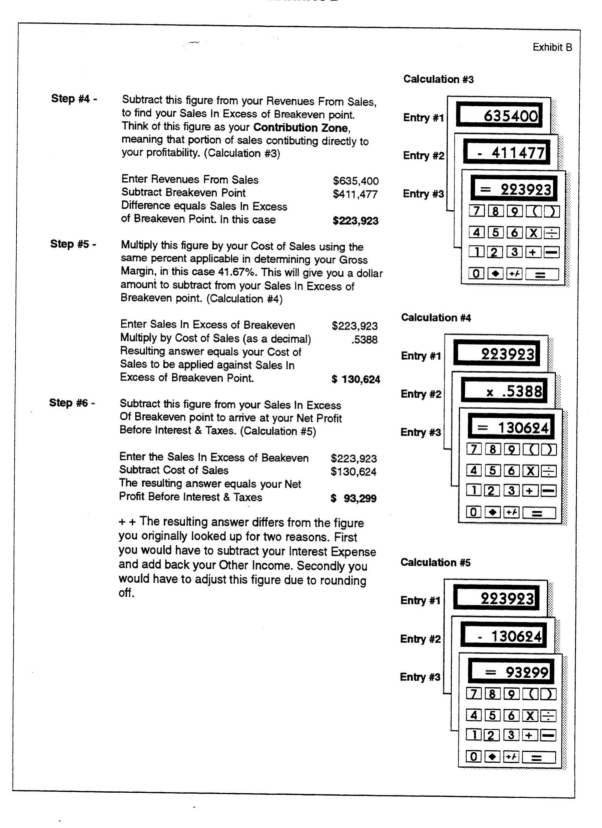

Step #4 - Subtract this figure from your Revenues From Sales, to find your Sales In Excess of Breakeven point. Think of this figure as your **Contribution Zone**, meaning that portion of sales contibuting directly to your profitability. (Calculation #3)

Enter Revenues From Sales	$635,400
Subtract Breakeven Point	$411,477
Difference equals Sales In Excess of Breakeven Point. In this case	**$223,923**

Step #5 - Multiply this figure by your Cost of Sales using the same percent applicable in determining your Gross Margin, in this case 41.67%. This will give you a dollar amount to subtract from your Sales In Excess of Breakeven point. (Calculation #4)

Enter Sales In Excess of Breakeven	$223,923
Multiply by Cost of Sales (as a decimal)	.5388
Resulting answer equals your Cost of Sales to be applied against Sales In Excess of Breakeven Point.	**$ 130,624**

Step #6 - Subtract this figure from your Sales In Excess Of Breakeven point to arrive at your Net Profit Before Interest & Taxes. (Calculation #5)

Enter the Sales In Excess of Beakeven	$223,923
Subtract Cost of Sales	$130,624
The resulting answer equals your Net Profit Before Interest & Taxes	**$ 93,299**

+ + The resulting answer differs from the figure you originally looked up for two reasons. First you would have to subtract your Interest Expense and add back your Other Income. Secondly you would have to adjust this figure due to rounding off.

BREAKEVEN ANALYSIS
Exhibit C

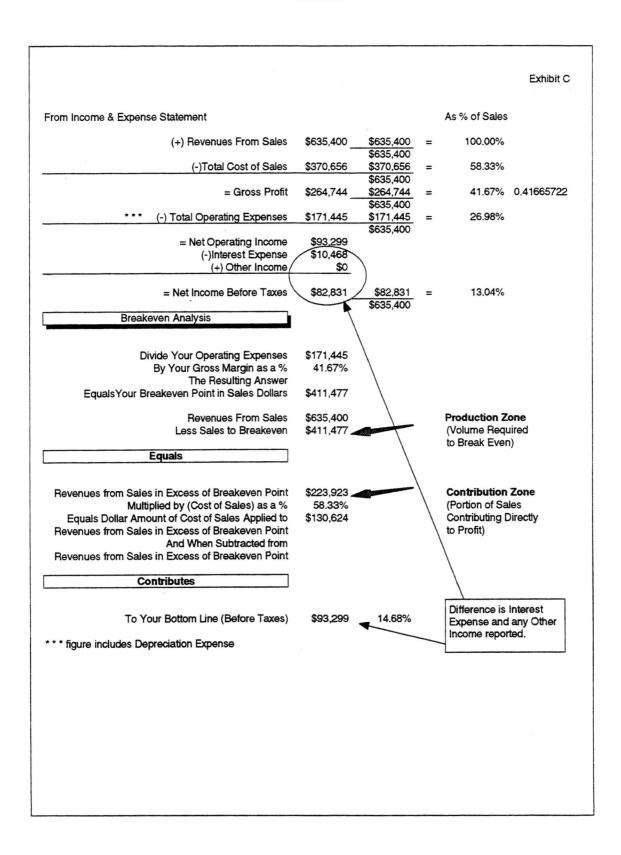

BREAKEVEN ANALYSIS
Exhibit D

Exhibit D

From Income & Expense Statement   As % of Sales

(+) Revenues From Sales _____ _____ =

(-) Total Cost of Sales _____ _____ =

= Gross Profit _____ _____ =

*** (-) Total Operating Expenses _____ _____ =

= Net Operating Income _____
(-) Interest Expense _____
(+) Other Income _____

= Net Income Before Taxes _____ _____ =

Breakeven Analysis

Divide Your Operating Expenses _____
By Your Gross Margin as a % _____
The Resulting Answer
Equals Your Breakeven Point in Sales Dollars _____

Revenues From Sales _____
Less Sales to Breakeven _____   ← **Production Zone** (Volume Required to Break Even)

Equals

Revenues from Sales in Excess of Breakeven Point _____
Multiplied by (Cost of Sales) as a % _____   ← **Contribution Zone** (Portion of Sales Contributing Directly to Profit)
Equals Dollar Amount of Cost of Sales Applied to _____
Revenues from Sales in Excess of Breakeven Point
And When Subtracted from
Revenues from Sales in Excess of Breakeven Point

Contributes

To Your Bottom Line (Before Taxes) _____

*** figure includes Depreciation Expense

Difference is Interest Expense and any Other Income reported.

CHAPTER 4

Reference Information—Formulas And Terms

SUMMARY OF FORMULAS

Basic Balance Sheet Equation

As a kitchen and bathroom dealer, the value of your tools, investments, inventory and showroom should be equal to the value of what is owed to your creditors plus the amount you, as the owners and investors, have contributed to the business.

Assets = Liabilities + Owner's Equity

Basic Income and Expense Statement Equation

This equation produces what we have entitled this chapter, namely, *The Integrity of Profit*. It simply states that the income you have produced from the primary operation of your kitchen and bathroom business, which is referred to as Revenues is your starting point. After subtracting your Cost of Sales from Revenues, you are left with your Gross Profit Margin. From this number, subtract your Operating Expenses and you arrive at your Net from Operations, or the earnings strictly from the operations. At this point, you add back in any Other Income (such as that generated through the sale of an asset) and subtract your Interest Expense, in order to reveal whether or not you have earned a Net Profit Before Taxes.

Revenues - Cost of Sales = Gross Profit Margin

Gross Profit Margin - Operating Expenses = Net from Operations

Net from Operations + Other Income - Interest Expense = Net Profit Before Taxes

Break-Even Analysis

As a service business, and not strictly a retailer nor manufacturer, you, as a kitchen and bathroom dealer, require an alternative approach to determine where your break-even point lies. Our example provides you with a reliable approach. If you take your fixed Operating Expenses and divide those by your Gross Profit Margin (as a percentage of sales) the resulting answer equals your break-even point for the period.

Operating Expenses ÷ Gross Profit Margin = Break-Even Point in Revenues

CHAPTER 4 SUMMARY OF TERMS	
TERM	**DEFINITION**
adjustments	As they apply to the budget process, these might certainly apply to seasonality factors or influences on the local economy, thus impacting your own business performance. Possibilities include regions subject to extremes in weather, tourism shifts, areas heavily dependent on manufacturing and their accompanying business cycles.
aged receivables	Generally, a reference to the older and dated accounts receivables.
basic balance sheet equation	This equation is used to insure Balance Sheet is in balance. assets = liabilities + owner's equity
break-even point	That point at which a business can expect their efforts to contribute directly to their bottom line, usually as measured in dollars or units of production.
charge sales	Sales made to customers who choose a payment method you offer, other than immediate cash payment, such as credit card sales and third-party financed projects.
contingency fees	Remuneration necessary to assist you in offsetting some of the contingency costs.
current assets	Those assets which can typically be converted to cash within the next 12 months. They may be cash, securities, accounts receivable, inventory or checking account.
direct costs	Costs attributed directly to the production of a finished project, such as a remodeling project's directly related costs of sales (cabinets or countertops).
forecasting	Also called budgeting, attempts to predict where and how the business will perform in the future, generally by looking at past performance and analyzing it.
indirect costs	Those costs attributed indirectly to your producing a finished project, such as unique training, shop drawing, long-distance phone calls.
long-term assets	Those assets, also known as fixed assets, which are usually expected to have a service life of some future time frame, such as the physical plant, property or equipment you own and use in your business.
long-term financing	Third-party financing available to your customers in order to accommodate large and expensive purchases such as a kitchen and bathroom remodeling project. This would be provided by credit card companies, commercial lenders and banks.
monthly budgets	Projections of the financial operations of the business during future monthly periods. This is an annual budget broken down into monthly units in order to provide management with an idea of its responsibilities in a more timely fashion.
net worth of the business	Your assets minus your liabilities equals owner's equity which is another way of determining the net worth of a business.
other assets	These assets are tangible or non-tangible in nature, however, they possess some future potential value to your business. They might include patented processes or designs as well as secret formulas, copyrights or other proprietary knowledge.
shortfalls	A cash shortfall refers to a cash position relative to what must be paid out, or when there's less in the bank than what you must pay out.
short-term financing	Third-party financing available to your customers in order to accommodate less-expensive purchases, such as individual components in a remodeling project. This would be provided by credit card companies, commercial lenders and banks.
strategy	A game plan or concept of how you will conduct your business in order to achieve the mission of the business.
trade secret	A business advantage that is yours because you thoroughly understand how your business operates, which gives you an edge over your competition, or perhaps you possess some unique information that benefits your firm

Chapter 5

PRICING FOR PROFIT

Success is more dangerous than failure, the ripples break over a wider coastline. - Graham Greene

You may believe your primary control for profit is pricing. Large numbers of people in service businesses do not understand that there is a significant difference between markup and profit, and, accordingly, they unconsciously underprice their work. There is also a distinct difference between pricing your work as a retailer and pricing it as a **customer service provider**. The true retailer is trying to create a profit by turning over as much inventory as many times as possible within a given period or cycle. The strategy is to sell volume. Your role as a **customer service provider** requires a different strategy. You want to sell value, not simply price.

VALUE

Capitalize on your ability to make yourself worth more; in other words—add value. You can carve out your own niche in the market. Identify yourself as the expert in the field, and then work at communicating your message to the client who will buy your services and products.

COMMUNICATE

Part of that communication process is pricing, but it's only one part of the whole. Your customer's perception of the quality you are offering is the essential ingredient to success here. The price you ask can either reinforce or destroy that perception. If customers don't see a correlation between what you say you will provide and the price you charge, you will probably end up losing the sale, or worse, not earning a referral. This is why it is so important to listen to your prospects, ask plenty of probing questions and satisfy yourself that you have a real appreciation for what they want, rather than selling them what you think they want or need. First, though, you must consider the mechanics of pricing your work in order to make the profit margin you desire.

Following are three examples, each of which serves a distinct purpose. The exhibits and the detailed explanations that follow will help to clarify them.

- The first example, under the heading **Profit And Markup Are Not The Same Thing**, is used to show the mechanics of how to correctly price and sell something, in order to achieve the desired profit margin.

- The second example, under the title, **Steps For Pricing**, explains pricing a job with a straight across-the-board mark-up of 15 percent. Here I will also introduce you to a contingency fee and how to arrive at it. For many that may work very well.

- For others, our **Alternative Pricing Approach**, will be more in line with what you are currently doing. This method recognizes that in your market, your customer base is already comfortable with the *manufacturer's suggested retail price* (MSRP) of your various product lines, and I am not suggesting you depart from that approach as it relates to products. However, I would like you to use this method for the proper pricing of your other *costs of sales* items and your *overhead*.

Give each example an opportunity, in the order given, as each one carries over to the next.

THE DIFFERENCE BETWEEN PROFIT AND MARKUP

To distinguish between *profit* and *markup*, review the examples. This does not tell you how much profit you should be charging, there are too many variables that should be addressed before making that decision. These percentages are used only for purposes of illustration.

1. PROFIT AND MARKUP ARE NOT THE SAME THING

Step 1 Assume your costs of sales are $830 on this particular job, and you have allocated $170 in operating expenses for a total of $1,000 in combined costs and expenses. You want to make a 30 percent pre-tax profit based on the selling price, so that you can put aside a 30 percent profit before taxes for the business. How do you do it?

Step 2 If you figured that you must take your combined cost of sales and expenses and multiply that sum by 1.3 to arrive at the correct selling price of $1,300 ($1,000 + $300), you are mistaken. What you made was a $300 profit based on what your costs were. But, this is not the same thing as earning a 30 percent profit on what you sold it for. Take that $300 profit and divide it by the $1,300 selling price and see what kind of a profit you actually made.

Step 3   You made a 23 percent profit, not a 30 percent profit as you originally planned. In order to have sold your goods or services at a 30 percent profit based on your selling price, you must sell them for $1,428.57. That's a difference of $128.57 more than the $1,300 ($1,000 + $300) price you were prepared to charge. If you have been struggling to maintain your profitability, this may very well be one of the reasons why.

If your pricing was considerably higher than $1,428.57, it may be the reason you don't sell some jobs—you are overpricing your work! You have been using a retail method of pricing your goods or services that really doesn't apply in your situation. You were applying a 30 percent markup based on costs, but you were not making a true 30 percent profit. Not only have you lost the opportunity to earn the correct profit in a single transaction, but think in terms of what it will now cost you to make up that difference.

PROFIT AND MARK-UP ARE NOT THE SAME THING

Objective - Price your work so that you will earn a 30% profit based on the price you will charge for it.

Step #1 - Summarize your Cost Of Sales and correct allocation of Operating Expenses for this job.

Total Cost Of Sales	$830.00
Operating Expenses	$170.00
Determine Total Costs & Expenses	**$1,000.00**

Step #2 - Determine profit you need and apply correct markup.

Most people will take the Total Costs & Expenses and multiply that figure by 1.30 in order to arrive at a selling price of $1,300.00 which is not correct. With this method you have priced your work to make only a 23% profit based on what it has cost you. (Calculation #1)

$300 ÷ $1,300.00 = 23%

Use the following method, profit based on the **Selling Price** to arrive at the correct price.

Costs	+	Markup	=	Selling Price
$1000	+	30% of SP	=	100% of SP

$1000	=	100% of SP - 30% of SP
$1000	=	70% of SP
$1000 ÷ 0.70	=	SP

You have determined that you require a 30% profit on this particular job, therefore your Costs plus 30% of the Selling Price equals the Selling Price or 100%. The difference between the Selling Price and the Markup is 70% of the Selling Price. Divide the Costs entered in Step #1, by this figure. (Calculation #2)

Step #3 - The resulting answer, is the correct Selling Price, in order to realize a profit of 30% before taxes.

In this case   **$1428.57**

$428.57 ÷ $1,428.57 = 30%

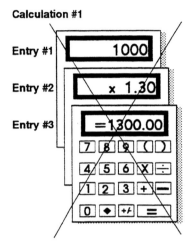

Calculation #1

Entry #1 1000
Entry #2 x 1.30
Entry #3 =1300.00

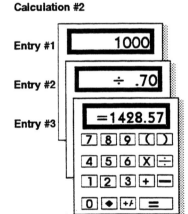

Calculation #2

Entry #1 1000
Entry #2 ÷ .70
Entry #3 =1428.57

TRUE PROFIT PICTURE

Take a look at the following example, entitled **True Profit Picture**. There is a difference between pricing your goods or services based on the costs, as opposed to pricing them at a profit based on their selling price. But, there is more to this story.

In this example, our correct pricing based on the selling price should have been $1,428.57. But, if we had priced it according to our costs, we would have only charged $1,300, a difference of $128.57. That effectively amounts to a 9 percent discount ($128.57 ÷ 1,300 = .0989). What should really be an eye opener, however, is how much it now requires in increased sales to make up that amount of profit!

You must now find an additional job worth $612.24 just to make up the $128.57, assuming you are using the same profit margin. And that $612.24 job is only to replace the amount you originally left on the table, there is no additional return on your investment for this second job.

TRUE PROFIT PICTURE

	Profit Based on Costs	Profit Based on Selling Price
Cost Of Sales	$830.00	$830.00
Overhead	$170.00	$170.00
Profit	30.00%	30.00%
Selling Price	$1,300.00	$1,428.57
Cash Profit	$300.00	$428.57
Difference		$128.57

REST OF THE STORY

Correct Price	$1,428.57
Effective Discount	9.0%
Incorrect Price	$1,300.00
Cost of Sales + Overhead	$1,000.00
Required Increase In Sales	42.9%
** Additional Sales Required	$612.24

** These additional sales will only provide you with the difference which you failed to pickup in the first place. It does not give any additional return on your investment in this sale.

How much will you get to keep?

Remember we are talking about pre-tax profits here. Dollars that must be used to offset losses due to errors in judgement, technical mistakes, mathematical errors, as well as cash shortfalls.

MAKE YOURSELF WORTH MORE—BUT HOW MUCH MORE?

As a **custom**er service provider, you need to make yourself worth more by selling value instead of price. But how much more? Reconsider that *Effective Discount* of 9 percent that appears in the previous illustration, **TRUE PROFIT PICTURE**, under *Rest of the Story*. Since that is essentially the difference between the two methods, in this scenario, that is the added difference in the price you seek. Is there any question in your mind that, collectively, you and your staff can't tap into your creative abilities and make yourselves worth 9 percent more? You shouldn't worry about what you hear others say about their profit margins, as long as you understand yours. Theirs may have no bearing on yours, whatsoever, unless you know how they arrived at it.

Secondly, consider that while you may ordinarily target a specific profit margin for most jobs, you do not set that percentage in stone. I would suggest that you consider a floor or limit that you will not go below. How much higher you go over and above your target markup should depend on several factors. Foremost will be what your market will bear, but factors such as risk, distance, time restraints, etc., should all enter into your decision-making process.

The selling price of your goods or services should be equal to the cost of those goods or services, plus a markup sufficient to cover your overhead and provide a comfortable profit. That definition is one I have seen used many times, and, while I have no argument with the statement itself, I have found that many people misinterpret it or use it without analyzing it properly. Generally, it is the operating expense portion that most people stumble over.

That may sound a little incongruous, but, since many business owners leave these for the bookkeeper to take care of, they are not familiar with what their actual expenses are, and consequently may fail to cover them. On the other hand, if you do your own design work or remodeling, you generally have a fair idea of what must go into a job—namely your cost of sales. You work with these items every day. The operating expenses simply don't get the same attention to detail, and, unfortunately, "out of sight," frequently means, "out of mind." Far too often, many of these expenses are either overlooked or under-compensated for. This is especially true in smaller businesses, where a bookkeeper is not employed and the owner is constantly playing catch up with the paperwork. This again is where the importance of a budget comes in, so that you know what those expenses are, and can reasonably spread them over every job you will do in the coming year.

RETAIL VS. SERVICE BUSINESS

One of the problems observed with respect to most textbooks or articles written on this subject is that, in almost every case, the examples used are predicated on either a manufacturing or a retail situation, and those examples are simply not adequate for most service businesses such as kitchen and bathroom firms.

Take a look at the work you do. It frequently involves discussion, planning and custom designing, not to mention special ordering, subcontracting, and some retail selling as well. As a kitchen and bathroom professional, you are not selling something by the gross. Almost every job you do is custom, with none being alike. You are selling your talents, your skills and your time. How do you put a price on those? The estimating process, especially if it involves considerable planning and preparation, is not an exact science, making your job even more difficult.

As you rely on others, you also assume a responsibility for their work. Their accuracy and dependability must also be a consideration as you prepare proposals. As mentioned earlier, these are some of the reasons you want to be able to include some type of a contingency fee in your jobs.

CALCULATING EXPENSES

Assuming you have defined and refined your estimating methods, and are convinced you have been as accurate and thorough as you can be in identifying your true costs for a job, your next step is to be just as accurate in assessing a portion of your expenses to the project. With a budget in place, you should know what expenses you must cover. What portion of time or budgeted revenues will the job cover? If this job is going to cover a span of several weeks, possibly overlapping over several months, you need to cover the *fixed expenses* in your quote. But what method will you use?

At this point, you should estimate your *costs of sale* for the particular project. Provided you have completed an annual budget, you should be able to use your *budgeted annual cost of sales* and your *budgeted annual fixed expenses* to help you arrive at a figure which will cover your *fixed expenses* for the job. This is when knowing where you want to go can pay off. With these three items available, you should be able to establish a relationship or ratio and solve the equation for that portion of operating expenses you must charge with the job.

The ratio would be expressed as follows:

$$\frac{\text{estimated costs of this sale}}{\text{budgeted annual cost of sales}} = \frac{\text{operating expense of this sale}}{\text{budgeted annual operating expense}}$$

Plug in your numbers to solve the unknown value, which, in this case, is the *operating expense of this sale*. The next step in the solution to your problem will equate to:

$$\frac{\text{budgeted annual operating expenses} \times \text{estimated costs of this sale}}{\text{budgeted annual cost of sales}} = \text{operating expense}$$

Multiplying your *budgeted annual operating expenses* by your *estimated costs of this sale* and dividing the resulting number by your *budgeted annual cost of sales* will give you the figure you are looking for here. Namely, the amount you will charge for *operating expenses* relative to this job.

Using these equations in the examples, you will understand how and why I arrived at the *fixed expenses* I will be assessing in the scenarios given. However, my approach is based on the fact that I am using an annual budget. I have established two separate numbers; my *budgeted cost of sales* for the year and my *fixed* or *operating expenses* for the year. They can also be stated in relationship to one another. In the first example, the *Budgeted Fixed Expense* is $171,445. If you were to divide that number by the *Budgeted Cost of Sales* figure of $370,656 you would arrive at a figure of 46.25 percent. Assuming your budget does not change during the year, you could simply determine your *cost of sales* for each job and take 46.25 percent of that figure to arrive at the correct assessment of *fixed expenses* for that job. It saves a lot of math if you use this method. It may not always come out to the penny, but it is close enough. Be sure you adjust the percentage at the beginning of each new year for all work, and employ this approach using the annual figures. Monthly budgets will not work because of seasonality factors along with a host of other variables.

2. STEPS FOR PRICING

Looking at the worksheets entitled **STEPS FOR PRICING**. *Exhibit A* shows you the completed worksheet and *Exhibit D* is provided as a guide to use in your business. *Exhibits B* and *C* take you through the actual steps of pricing a job where you are looking for a straight profit across the board.

Step 1 You are preparing an estimate for a client, and, reviewing the details of what the project contains, you have calculated and summarized your *Cost of Sales* at $13,086.92 for this particular project. To that, you add your subcontractors' estimates of $3,027.68 for a total *Cost of Sales* on this job of $16,114.60. How much must you invoice this client in order to cover your *Operating Expenses* or *Overhead*, in relation to the time and resources invested in this job? If, as we have previously discussed, you have prepared a valid budget, then you have some idea of what your *Annual Budgeted Cost of Sales* and *Annual Budgeted Operating Expenses* are.

Step 2 Looking at *Exhibit A*, and using these three variables, *Cost of Sales* (this job), *Annual Budgeted Cost of Sales*, and *Budgeted Operating Expenses*, you can now proceed to set up a ratio or proportion in order to determine what you will charge to cover your operating expenses on this job. As you can see, that amount comes to $7,453.72. At this time you can total your *Costs of Sales* and *Operating Expenses* to arrive at your total costs of $23,568.32.

Step 3 Assuming you want to make a 15 percent profit based on your *Selling Price*, you can now use the formula:

Costs + Markup = Selling Price

In this case, we take $23,568.32 and add 15 percent of the *Selling Price*. That is the same as saying the *Selling Price* is equal to 100 percent. 100 percent less the 15 percent is equal to 85 percent. Following that step, divide $23,568.32 by .85 which gives us the estimated initial *Selling Price* of $27,727.44.

Step 4 One final calculation I am recommending is the *Contingency Fee*. When we discussed the annual budget, I suggested to you that contingencies are a fact of life. You have to recoup those costs somewhere along the line, and I recommend that this is the time and place. The same logic and approach we just used for determining the *Estimated Selling Price* should again be applied to producing a *Selling Price* which includes a *Contingency Fee* of 1.5 percent. Subtract the 1.5 percent from 100 percent and that is equal to 98.5 percent. Now divide your *Estimated Selling Price* of $27,727 by .985 and you will have your *Selling Price* of $28,149.69.

You have just completed a worksheet for in-house use. This is simply one way to arrive at your pricing. In this example, you are assured of a 15 percent profit clear across the board on everything. You can customize and fine tune this in any way you wish to, but, keep in mind that you need to consider what the market will bear.

With regard to the *contingency fee*, the actual percentage rate you establish should be based on your past performance and experience. No one can tell you what that should be.

STEPS FOR PRICING
Service Business - Approach 1
Exhibit A

COSTS OF SALES

Complete a quantity take-off
Locate unit cost per item
Multiply quantity by unit costs
Complete estimate summary for total costs $13,086.92
Add Subcontract Costs $3,027.68
Add Equipment Rental Costs
Add Job Indirect Costs   _____

COSTS OF SALES (This job) $16,114.60

FIXED EXPENSES

Estimated Cost of Sales (This job) $16,114.60
Budgeted Cost of Sales (Annual) $370,656.00

Estimated Fixed Expenses (This job)   ?
Budgeted Fixed Expenses (Annual) $171,445.00

Set up a ratio or proportion between these two sets of numbers.

$$\frac{\$16,114.60}{\$370,656.00} = \frac{?}{\$171,445.00}$$

Isolate and solve for the unknown

$$\$171,445.00 \times \frac{\$16,114.60}{\$370,656.00} = \$7,453.72$$

FIXED EXPENSES (This job)   ? = $7,453.72

SELLING PRICE

Costs of Sales $16,114.60
Fixed Expenses $7,453.72
Total Costs $23,568.32

Profit Margin required as a % of selling price   15.0%

Costs   +   Markup   =   (Initial) Selling Price

$23,568.32   +   0.15SP = SP
$23,568.32 = SP - 0.15SP
$23,568.32 = 0.85SP

$$\frac{\$23,568.32}{0.85} = \$27,727.44$$

Use the same formula to arrive at the correct Selling Price with a Contingency Fee (See Exhibit C)   = $28,149.69

STEPS FOR PRICING
Service Business
Exhibit B

Objective -
1. Calculate the proper allocation of Operating Expenses.
2. Calculate the correct Selling Price for a job you are bidding on.
3. Calculate a Contingency Fee to be included in your final price.

Given:**
- Estimated Cost of Sales for this job $16,114.60

***
- Annual Budgeted Cost of Sales $370,656.00
- Annual Budgeted Operating Expense $171,445.00
- Desired Profit Margin   15%
- Desired Contingency Fee   1.5%

** Estimated Cost of Sales for this job include all Labor, Materials, Subcontracts and Equipment Rentals, Etc., used in producing the finished project.

*** Look up these amounts from your Annual Budget.

Step # 1 - Objective # 1. Establish a ratio or proportion between your Cost of Sales for this job and your Annual Cost of Sales, and also between your Operating Expenses for this job and your Annual Operating Expenses.

$$\frac{\text{Cost of Sales (This Job)}}{\text{Cost of Sales (Annual)}} = \frac{\text{Oper. Expns (This Job)}}{\text{Oper. Expns (Annual)}}$$

$$\frac{\$16{,}114.60}{\$370{,}656.00} = \frac{?}{\$171{,}445.00}$$

Isolate and solve for the unknown value:

$$\frac{\$171{,}445.00 \times \$16{,}114.60}{\$370{,}656.00} = ?$$

Make the following 5 entries into your calculator: (Calculation # 1)

#1 Enter 171,445
#2 Enter x16,114.60
#3 You will see the answer = 2762767597
#4 Divide by 370,656
#5 You will see the answer = 7,453.72

$$\$7{,}453.72 = ?$$

This number represents the amount of Operating Expenses to be charged with this job.

Step # 2 - Total your combined costs for this job: (Calculation # 2)
- Cost of Sales $16,114.60
- Operating Expenses $ 7,453.72

                Total Costs   **$23,568.32**

Calculation #1

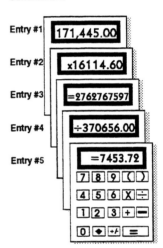

Entry #1: 171,445.00
Entry #2: x16114.60
Entry #3: =2762767597
Entry #4: ÷370656.00
Entry #5: =7453.72

Calculation #2

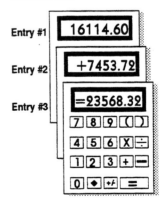

Entry #1: 16114.60
Entry #2: +7453.72
Entry #3: =23568.32

STEPS FOR PRICING
Service Business
Exhibit C

Step # 3 - Objective #2. Use the following method, profit based on the **Selling Price** to arrive at the initial Selling Price **without** the Contingency Fee: (Calculation # 3)

```
Costs         + Markup      = Selling Price
$23,568.32    + 15% of SP=    100% of SP
                $23,568.32  = 100% of SP-15% of SP
                $23,568.32  = 85% of SP
                $23,568.32 ÷ 0.85 = $27,727.44
```

You have determined that you require an 15% profit on this particular job, therefore your Costs plus 15% of the Selling Price equals the Selling Price or 100%. The difference between the Selling Price and the Markup is 85%. Divide the Total Costs calculated in Step # 2, by this figure. (Calculation # 3)

So your initial Selling Price   =   **$27,727.44**

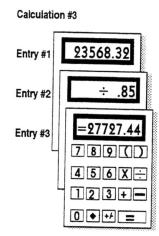

Calculation #3

Entry #1 23568.32
Entry #2 ÷ .85
Entry #3 =27727.44

Step # 4 - Objective #3. Use the following method to determine what the Selling Price **with** your desired Contingency Fee at 1.5% should be: (Calculation # 4)

```
Initial Selling Price + Contingency Fee = Selling Price
$27,727.44 + 1.5% of SP    = 100% of SP
             $27,727.44    = 100% of SP-1.5% of SP
             $27,727.44    = 98.5% of SP
             $27,727.44 ÷ 0.985 = $28,149.69
```

You have determined that you require a 1.5% Contingency Fee on this particular job, therefore your initial Selling Price plus 1.5% of the Selling Price equals the Selling Price or 100%. The difference between the Selling Price and the Contingency Fee is 98.5%. Divide the initial Selling Price calculated in Step # 3, by this figure.

So your Selling Price   =   **$28,149.69**

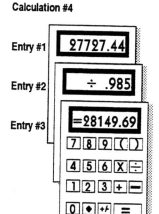

Calculation #4

Entry #1 27927.44
Entry #2 ÷ .985
Entry #3 =28149.69

At this point you have properly calculated your Operating Expenses as they should be allocated to this job. You have properly priced it for a 15% profit using the method based on the Selling Price, and finally you have added in the Contingency Fee.

STEPS FOR PRICING WORKSHEET
Exhibit D

Exhibit D

COSTS OF SALE	Costs	Markup	Selling Price	Notes
Materials				
	_____	_____	_____	
	_____	_____	_____	
	_____	_____	_____	
	_____	_____	_____	
	_____	_____	_____	
Subcontract Costs				
	_____	_____	_____	
	_____	_____	_____	
	_____	_____	_____	
	_____	_____	_____	
Indirect Costs				
	_____	_____	_____	
	_____	_____	_____	
	_____	_____	_____	
Equipt. Rental				
	_____	_____	_____	
	_____	_____	_____	
Labor Costs				
	_____	_____	_____	
	_____	_____	_____	
Totals	(a.) _____		(b.) _____	

FIXED EXPENSES
Estimated Cost of Sales (This job)   (a.) _____
Budgeted Cost of Sales (Annual)   _____

Ratio Format

Estimated Fixed Expenses (This job)   ?

$$\frac{\text{Est. COS (This job)}}{\text{COS (Annual)}} = \frac{\text{Est. Fixed Expenses (This Job)}}{\text{Fixed Expenses (Annual)}}$$

Budgeted Fixed Expenses (Annual)   _____

Set up a ratio or proportion between these two sets of numbers. (See Exhibit A or E) ⟶

_____ = _____?

Isolate and solve for the unknown   _____ x _____ = ?

FIXED EXPENSES (This job)   ? =

SELLING PRICE OF IN-HOUSE COSTS OF SALES ITEMS & FIXED EXPENSES

Subtotal of COS In-House items only from (a.) _____
Fixed Expenses _____
Total Costs

Profit Margin required as a % of selling price _____

Costs	+	Markup	=	(Initial) Selling Price
_____	+	_____ SP	=	SP
		_____	=	SP - SP
			=	SP
				(Initial) SP
		_____	=	_____

CALCULATION OF TOTAL SELLING PRICE WITH CONTINGENCY FEE

Contingency Fee required as a % of selling price _____
Costs equal (b.) + Initial SP

Costs	+	Markup	=	Selling Price
_____	+	_____ SP	=	SP
		_____	=	SP - SP
			=	SP
				Selling Price
			=	_____

3. ALTERNATIVE PRICING APPROACH

You may already be getting a higher markup on your cabinet lines, appliances and hardware, using the MSRP, than you would charge for the markup of your *costs of sales* associated with equipment rental and material or even your overhead. You might be charging a markup of 35-50 percent using the MSRP, whereas you believe that as far as your *overhead* is concerned, you require a 15 percent markup.

Take a look at the exhibits marked *E* through *H*. Here is an *Alternative Approach* in which you price your work using the MSRP for some of the items in your *cost of sales*, different markups for other suppliers or subcontractors and your 15 percent markup for other items in your *cost of sales* as well as your *fixed expenses*. In *Exhibits F* through *H*, we will walk through the individual steps. I have used the same numbers and breakdown for both approaches. However, with the *Alternative Approach*, we arrive at a higher selling price, which now offers you some additional challenges.

At this point you must have some idea of whether or not you are still competitively priced. Don't automatically assume you have to lower the price for this job. If you must reduce the price, you have the opportunity of deciding which options to employ. Here again is where you get the chance to define your own approach. Had you taken the time to price this job both ways, and you knew the price difference between these methods, you might decide on any one of several options and perhaps some others I am not considering here. Once you understand the mechanics, you can then tailor this system to meet your needs.

It may not be apparent yet, but, assuming you are successful in reaching your budgeted sales volume early in the year, what will you do with the fixed expense portion of your jobs for the remainder of the year? Continue to invoice for it anyway. Your reputation will suffer and you will lose credibility with your customer base if you merely charge lower prices near the end of the year because you have met all your fixed expenses. Think of those funds as a sort of bonus which will contribute directly to your bottom line. These are funds which you earned as a result of your skillful personnel and business management.

STEPS FOR PRICING
Alternative Approach
Exhibit E

	Your Costs	+	Calculation of markup @	=	MSRP or Selling Prices

COSTS OF SALES

Cabinets	$4,878.99		MSRP	$6,586.64
Countertops	$786.00		30%	$1,122.86
Appliances	$1,625.92		MSRP	$2,167.89
Subcontract Costs	$3,027.68		25%	$4,036.91

Other Costs of Sales

Labor	5246.01	(a)	+
Drawings & Permits	$250.00	(b)	
Other Materials	$300.00	(c)	
COSTS OF SALES (This job)	$16,114.60		SP of Other COS Items &
(See Calculations Below)			Expenses = $15,587.92
			(Initial) SP = $29,502.22

Selling Price with a Contingency Fee = $29,951.49
(See Step 8 Exhibit H)

FIXED EXPENSES

Estimated Cost of Sales (This job) $16,114.60
Budgeted Cost of Sales (Annual) $370,656.00

Estimated Fixed Expenses (This job)   ?
Budgeted Fixed Expenses (Annual) $171,445.00

Set up a ratio or proportion between these two sets of numbers.

$$\frac{\$16,114.60}{\$370,656.00} = \frac{?}{\$171,445.00}$$

Isolate and solve for the unknown $\$171,445.00 \times \frac{\$16,114.60}{\$370,656.00} = \$7,453.72$

FIXED EXPENSES (This job)   ? = $7,453.72

SELLING PRICE OF IN-HOUSE COSTS OF SALES ITEMS & FIXED EXPENSES

Other Costs of Sales
Items a + b + c above $5,796.01
Fixed Expenses $7,453.72
Total Costs $13,249.73

Profit Margin required as a % of selling price   15.0%

				(Initial)
Costs	+	Markup	=	Selling Price
$13,249.73	+	0.15SP	=	SP
		$13,249.73	=	SP - 0.15SP
		$13,249.73	=	0.85SP
				(Initial) SP
		$\frac{\$13,249.73}{0.85}$	=	$15,587.92

STEPS FOR PRICING
Alternative Approach
Exhibit F

Objective -
1. Calculate the correct Selling Price for your work so that you will earn a desired profit based on the price you will charge for it, while using the MSRP for some Costs of Sales items.
2. Calculate the proper allocation of Operating Expenses for this job.
3. Calculate a Contingency Fee to be included in your final price.

Given:
** Annual Budgeted Cost of Sales $370,656.00
*** Annual Budgeted Operating Expense $171,445.00
      Desired Profit Margin   15%
      Desired Contingency Fee   1.5%
** Estimated Cost of Sales for this job include all Labor, Materials, Subcontracts and Equipment Rentals, Etc., used in producing the finished project.
*** Look up these amounts from your Annual Budget.

Step # 1 - Just as you would for any other situation, always complete a quantity take-off. Locate the unit costs per item and multiply the quantities by the unit costs. Complete the estimate summary for total costs, by each category.

Step # 2 - Summarize your Cost of Sales and calculate their correct MSRP or selling price based on your markup for this job. (Calculations 1, 2 and 3)

	Your Costs	+ Calculation of markup @	= MSRP or Selling Price
Cabinets	$4,878.99	Using MSRP	$ 6,586.64
Countertops	786.00	30%(Calc.#1)	1,122.86
Appliances	1,625.92	Using MSRP	2,167.89
Subcontract Costs	3,027.68	25%(Calc.#2)	4,036.91
Other Costs of Sales	(Calc.#3)		+
Labor	5246.01		
Drawings & Permits	250.00		
Other Materials	300.00	SP of Other COS Items &	
Costs of Sales (This Job)	$16,114.60	Expenses = (Initial SP) =	? ?
	Selling Price w/Contingency Fee =		?

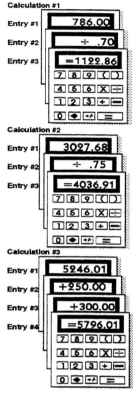

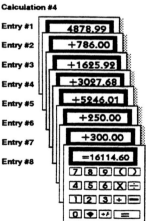

Step # 3 - Determine your costs of sales, including those items you for which you will use the MSRP. Total these costs to find your Costs of Sales (This Job). (Calculation #4). You will need this figure to calculate the corresponding Fixed Expenses you must charge with this job.

STEPS FOR PRICING
Alternative Approach
Exhibit G

Step # 4 - Establish a ratio or proportion between your Cost of Sales for this job and your Annual Cost of Sales, and also between your Operating Expenses for this job and your Annual Operating Expenses.

$$\frac{\text{Cost of Sales (This Job)}}{\text{Cost of Sales (Annual)}} = \frac{\text{Oper. Expns (This Job)}}{\text{Oper. Expns (Annual)}}$$

$$\frac{\$16,114.60}{\$370,656.00} = \frac{?}{\$171,445.00}$$

Isolate and solve for the unknown value:

$$\frac{\$171,445.00 \times \$16,114.60}{\$370,656.00} = ?$$

Make the following 5 entries into your calculator: (Calculation # 5)

#1 Enter 171,445
#2 Enter x16,114.60
#3 You will see the answer = 2762767597
#4 Divide by 370656
#5 You will see the answer = 7453.72

$$\$7,453.72 = ?$$

This number represents the amount of Operating Expenses to be charged with this job.

Step # 5 - Total your combined costs for this job: (Calculation # 6)
Other Cost of Sales (Calc.#3) $ 5,796.01
Operating Expenses   7,453.72

Total Costs $13,249.73

Step # 6 - Use the following method, profit based on the **Selling Price** to arrive at the initial Selling Price **without** the Contingency Fee:

Costs	+	Markup	=	Selling Price
$13,249.73	+	15% of SP=		100% of SP
		$13,249.73	=	100% of SP-15% of SP
		$13,249.73	=	85% of SP
		$13,249.73 ÷ 0.85	=	$15,587.92

You have determined that you require a 15% profit on this particular job, therefore your Costs plus 15% of the Selling Price equals the Selling Price or 100%.

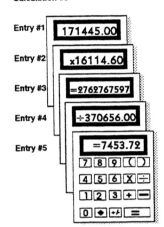

Calculation #5

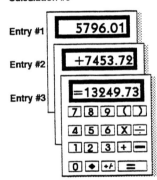

Calculation #6

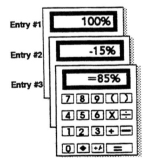

Calculation #7

STEPS FOR PRICING
Alternative Approach
Exhibit H

The difference between the Selling Price and the Markup is 85%. (Calculation # 7) Divide the Total Costs calculated in Step # 5, by this figure. (Calculation # 8)

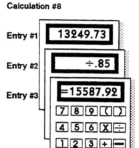

The resulting answer you have calculated is your initial Selling Price for these items, without a Contingency Fee, = **$15,587.92**

Step # 7 - Add this figure to your list of MSRP or Selling Prices you have calculated in Step 2, (Calculation # 9) and you arrive at your initial SP for the job.

	Your Costs	+	Calculation of markup @	=	MSRP or Selling Price
Cabinets	$4,878.99		Using MSRP		$ 6,586.64
Countertops	786.00		30%(Calc.#1)		1,122.86
Appliances	1,625.92		Using MSRP		2,167.89
Subcontract Costs	3,027.68		25%(Calc.#2)		4,036.91
Other Costs of Sales	(Calc. #3)				+
Labor	5,246.01				
Drawings & Permits	250.00		SP of Other		
Other Materials	300.00		COS Items &		
Costs of Sales (This Job)	$16,114.60		Expenses (Initial SP)	= =	$15,587.92 $ 29,502.22

Selling Price w/Contingency Fee = ?

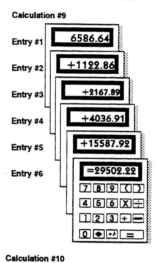

Step # 8 - Finally, we use the following method to determine what the Selling Price **with** your desired <u>Contingency Fee</u> at 1.5% should be: (Calculation # 10)

Initial Selling Price + Contingency Fee = Selling Price
$29,502.22 + 1.5% of SP = 100% of SP
            $29,502.22 = 100% of SP-1.5% of SP
            $29,502.22 = 98.5% of SP
$29,502.22 ÷ 0.985 = $29,951.49

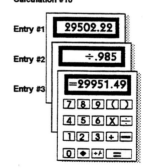

You have determined that you require a 1.5% Contingency Fee on this particular job, therefore your initial Selling Price plus 1.5% of the Selling Price equals the Selling Price or 100%. The difference between the Selling Price and the Contingency Fee is 98.5%. Divide the initial Selling Price calculated in Step # 7, by this figure.

So your correct Selling Price including the contingency fee for this job, using this alternative method:
= **$29,951.49**

MAXIMIZING PROFIT

Would you be willing to pay more taxes, assuming you didn't have to work any harder than you are now and could still take more profit out of your business? That's exactly what you may be able to do when you use the *profit based on selling price* method of marking up your goods and services. Look at the following sample worksheet, entitled **RESULTS OF MAXIMIZING PROFITS.**

In this particular worksheet, I have used the tax consequences for a corporation in the United States for illustration purposes only. My point is to illustrate the impact on your earnings when you use the *profit based on selling price* method instead of the *profit based on costs* method, assuming it doesn't put you in a higher tax bracket. I have indicated that we are using the same dollar value for *cost of sales* and for *overhead* in both cases.

We use the same d*esired profit margin* in both cases, with different results in terms of the *revenues* produced. That means a difference in our g*ross margin*, as well as a difference in our *net profit before taxes*. This also results in a different tax obligation, but, more impressively, a difference in earnings.

We realize an extra $9,567 in after-tax profits, or 16.83 percent more using *the profit based on selling price* approach. Yet, for every $1,000 of purchases, your customer paid only about 2.16 percent more.

As you can see from what we have covered in this chapter, proper pricing is critical to your profitability. If there is any part that isn't clear, be sure to read it again. Review this with anyone else within your organization who is responsible for pricing work. If you don't use consistent pricing methods, you are going to create confusion and some very angry customers.

RESULTS OF MAXIMIZING PROFITS

	Pricing Based On Costs	% of Revenues	Pricing Based On S.P.	% of Revenues
Cost Of Sales	$370,656	59.62%	$370,656	58.34%
Overhead	$171,445	27.58%	$171,445	26.98%
Total Costs & Expense	$542,101		$542,101	
Desired Profit Margin	15%		15%	
Revenues	$621,681		$635,374	
Gross Margin	$251,025	40.38%	$264,718	41.66%
Depreciation Expense	$9,833		$9,833	
Interest Expense	$10,468		$10,468	
Net Before Taxes	$69,113	11.12%	$82,805	13.03%
Taxes	$12,278		$16,404	
Net Profit	$56,835	9.14%	$66,401	10.45%
Difference	**16.83%**		**$9,567**	
Difference in Revenues	$13,692			
Sales Volume in Thousands	635			
Additional cost to customer per $1,000.00	$21.55	or	2.16%	

Comparison of Taxes For Each Method Using
U.S. FEDERAL TAX RATES FOR CORPORATIONS

Cost Method
Taxable Income $69,113

From	To	Base	Rate	Over	Tax
$0	$50,000	$0.00 +	15%	$0	$0
$50,000	$75,000	$7,500.00 +	25%	$50,000	$12,278
$75,000	$100,000	$13,750.00 +	34%	$75,000	$0
$100,000	$335,000	$22,250.00 +	39%	$100,000	$0
$335,000	$10,000,000	$113,900.00 +	34%	$335,000	$0
$10,000,000	$15,000,000	$3,400,000 +	35%	$10,000,000	$0
$15,000,000	$18,333,333	$5,150,000 +	38%	$15,000,000	$0
$18,333,333		$0.00	35%	$0	$0

Taxes Due $12,278

Selling Price Method
Taxable Income $82,805

From	To	Base	Rate	Over	Tax
$0	$50,000	$0.00 +	15%	$0	$0
$50,000	$75,000	$7,500.00 +	25%	$50,000	$0
$75,000	$100,000	$13,750.00 +	34%	$75,000	$16,404
$100,000	$335,000	$22,250.00 +	39%	$100,000	$0
$335,000	$10,000,000	$113,900.00 +	34%	$335,000	$0
$10,000,000	$15,000,000	$3,400,000 +	35%	$10,000,000	$0
$15,000,000	$18,333,333	$5,150,000 +	38%	$15,000,000	$0
$18,333,333		$0.00	35%	$0	$0

Taxes Due $16,404

HOURLY CHARGES

Large numbers of service businesses price their work solely on the basis of their time, charging for their services by the hour. What many may fail to understand is that their actual costs will change from day to day, unless they have done a detailed analysis of what their actual labor fees plus payroll burden is, and how accurate their assessment of their operating expenses is.

Far too many of these people are establishing their pricing structure solely by what the competition is charging. To compound matters, they rarely change their fees, for they are essentially concerned with what everyone else is doing. The response I frequently hear is, "You don't understand my market. These are prices, based on industry standards, that we are forced to live with."

First of all, where can you find these so-called industry standards in writing, that says you must follow them? No doubt there are typical hourly service charges, but, successful businesses realize that before they adopt those hourly charges, they must be assured of making a profit. That would seem to follow common sense and logic, wouldn't it? But, I can tell you from personal experience, that common sense and logic are not necessarily related.

After reviewing a client's financial system and showing him that he had actually lost $10,000 in the previous year, I recommended, among other things, that he consider charging more for his hourly service call and consider charging for travel time. He decided he couldn't do those things, because he would no longer be competitive. In other words, he felt compelled to let the competition dictate when and how he will eventually go out of business!

SERVICE WORK

There are two critical functions you must understand with respect to hourly charges for your service work. The first issue is billable hours. If your hourly charge is based on four 40-hour weeks each month, 160 hours total, and you have allocated a portion of your *fixed expenses* to each hour, you are losing money every day you work, and billing your customers less than 8 hours in the course of that day. Every unforeseen delay, mistake, redo or under-estimate has cost your business profits.

Look at the following worksheet, entitled **HOURS BILLED FOR THE MONTH**. If we took all your monthly operating expenses or overhead items, totaled them up and divided them by 160 hours (in this case $4,275 divided by 160), we arrive at a basic hourly fee of $26.72. You must charge each of those 160 hours just to keep the doors to your business open. If, in the course of the month, you bill for anything less than 160 hours, there will be a corresponding increase in those costs.

HOURS BILLED FOR THE MONTH

When Your Monthly Overhead = $4,275.00 and		Hours Actually Billed During Month Is	the	Hourly Charge Required To Cover Overhead
Monthly Expenses		160 hrs =		$26.72
Rent	$1,000.00	155		$27.58
Telephone	$200.00	150		$28.50
Utilities	$180.00	145		$29.48
Insurance	$300.00	140		$30.54
Fuel for Vehicles	$450.00	135		$31.67
Repairs & Maintenance	$175.00	130		$32.88
Leases	$65.00	125		$34.20
Office Expenses	$20.00	120		$35.63
Bank Loan	$345.00	115		$37.17
Travel & Entertainment	$40.00	110		$38.86
Owner's Compensation	$1,500.00			
Sub-Total	$4,275.00			

Assuming you had to cover those expenses in 160 billable hours during a single month, you would have to charge $26.72 per hour just to cover your overhead. Now that figure doesn't include any labor or burden and no profit has been calculated in that figure either. Above you can see what happens to your costs when you bill for anything less than 160 hours during the month; they can go up dramatically and quickly!

Below you can see the added impact that productivity has on your costs, again without the labor or profit added in.

Issue of Productivity   If Based on hourly cost of $26.72

Compensated time =	8			
Productive time =	6	or	75%	**True Hourly Cost To You**
	Hours Actually Billed		**Hours Actually Required**	
	160		200	$33.40
	155		194	$34.48
	150		188	$35.63
	145		181	$36.85
	140		175	$38.17
	135		169	$39.58
	130		163	$41.11
	125		156	$42.75
	120		150	$44.53

Your best source of information regarding productivity is your own job costing records from previous work. If you haven't started keeping them, begin today!

PRODUCTIVITY

The hourly issue would seem serious enough, but that isn't the end of it. We have yet to discuss an equally serious issue of productivity. If you haven't yet considered this, you might want to. What you pay an individual on an hourly basis usually has nothing to do with productivity. I appreciate the fact that you have good workers, but the U.S. Department of Commerce research would indicate that the average employee is only productive 5 to 6 hours for each 8-hour work day.

A closer look at the bottom half of the previous worksheet, **HOURS BILLED FOR MONTH**, under the section, *Issue of Productivity*, shows the added impact of productivity on your costs, beginning with a base cost of $26.72 per hour. You need to understand that, when your actual productivity is factored into the equation, there are dramatic increases in your true costs. Look once more at the differences between the estimated and actual time required to complete a job. Your true hourly cost is increased in direct proportion to the additional time actually required to complete the work. If you can prove, with your own detailed job-costing records, that your people are more productive, that's terrific. If such records are not available, then after you have completed your next job, compare this method with your results. Which one is more accurate?

On the following charts, entitled **HOURLY RATE CALCULATIONS**, look first at the section, *Calculations of Labor Charges,* and you will notice that, even as you prepare a bid for two separate jobs using your own personnel, your labor expense will differ. Not only are the hourly pay rates different, but there is also a good chance you are paying a different worker's compensation rate for each employee, depending on job classifications. Keep in mind that payroll burden can increase an employee's compensation package as much as 100 percent of his or her hourly pay. So you must understand what those burdens are and how they impact your payroll if you want to bid your work for profit.

HOURLY RATE CALCULATIONS
Labor Charges

Calculations of Labor Charges	Hourly Rate	Burden Factors	Hourly Costs	Weekly Reg. Hours	Weekly Reg. Pay	Weekly O.T. Hours	Hourly O.T. Costs	Weekly O.T. Pay	Total Payroll
Employee A	$6.50	1.4	$9.10	40	$364.00		$13.65	$0.00	$364.00
Employee B	$6.00	1.35	$8.10	40	$324.00		$12.15	$0.00	$324.00
Employee C	$7.50	1.4	$10.50	40	$420.00	5	$15.75	$78.75	$498.75
Employee D	$6.75	1.35	$9.11	40	$364.50		$13.67	$0.00	$364.50
Employee E	$7.00	1.42	$9.94	40	$397.60		$14.91	$0.00	$397.60
Employee F	$5.50	1.37	$7.54	30	$226.05		$11.30	$0.00	$226.05
Sub-totals			$54.29	230	$2,096.15	5	$81.43	$78.75	$2,174.90
Estimates For Bid Preparation Job #1									
Personnel Required									
Employee A	$6.50	1.4	$9.10	30	$273.00		$13.65	$0.00	$273.00
Employee D	$6.75	1.35	$9.11	13	$118.46		$13.67	$0.00	$118.46
Employee F	$5.50	1.37	$7.54	6.75	$50.86		$11.30	$0.00	$50.86
Job # 1 Bid Sub-totals			$25.75	49.75	$442.32	0	$38.62	$0.00	$442.32
Estimates For Bid Preparation Job #2									
Personnel Required									
Employee B	$6.00	1.35	$8.10	28	$226.80		$12.15	$0.00	$226.80
Employee C	$7.50	1.4	$10.50	32	$336.00	0	$15.75	$0.00	$336.00
Job # 2 Bid Sub-totals			$18.60	60	$562.80	0	$27.90	$0.00	$562.80

SCHEDULING

Scheduling is a very important consideration. Many people in service businesses grapple with the problem of travel time. It takes time to get from one job to another. It also takes fuel and maintenance on the vehicle, not to mention your employee's pay. If you will take a candid look at this issue, I'm sure you will realize you must address it in a fair and equitable manner. Look at *Estimates*, on the following **HOURLY RATE CALCULATION** worksheet.

Your true hourly costs differ by as much as 11.06 percent on these two jobs. This is not an indictment of hourly charges *per se*, but, unless your real job costs are prepared accurately, there is a good chance you are losing money and not even aware of it.

On this same worksheet, the large arrows indicate those items that are the variables you must consider when establishing your hourly rate. I realize *fixed expenses* don't appear to be much of a variable, but, to the extent you have a real handle on these, they can be the source of your competitive edge. The smaller arrows that point to the circles drawn around your *labor costs* and *fixed expenses* for each of these jobs indicate the numbers that will determine your true *hourly costs*.

Realize that, as I have broken them out here, these calculations do not include any markup or profit at this point. You need to look at what you are charging on an hourly basis, frequently making the necessary adjustments as required. I have found that people who use an hourly charge tend to establish it by what the competition is doing, regardless of what it is truly costing them, and they may use it for years without ever thinking about changing it.

We have covered a lot of numbers in this chapter, but, unless you appreciate the significance of this information, there is good reason to believe you may be undercharging, or overcharging for your work.

HOURLY RATE CALCULATIONS
Estimates

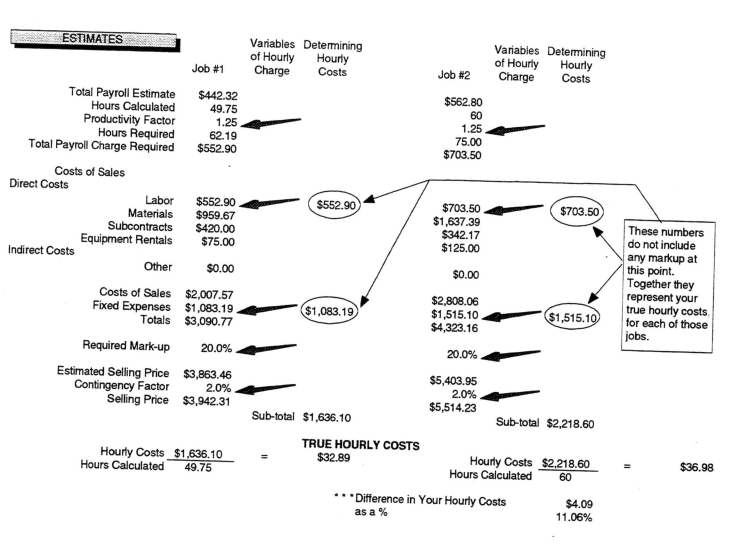

PRICING FOR PROFIT

CHAPTER 5

Reference Information—Formulas And Terms

SUMMARY OF FORMULAS

PRICING FOR PROFIT

$$\frac{\text{Cost of Sales + Operating Expenses}}{(100\% - \text{Desired Profit Margin})} = \text{Selling Price}$$

In order to arrive at the correct Selling Price, that will produce the desired Profit Margin before Taxes, you can employ the following formula:

> Take your Cost of Sales and add that to the amount of Operating Expenses you have allocated for this job. Divide that combined total by 100 percent minus the Desired Profit Margin.

ALLOCATING OPERATING EXPENSES FOR A PROJECT

$$\frac{\text{Estimated Cost of Sales (this project)}}{\text{Budgeted } \textit{Annual} \text{ Cost of Sales}} = \frac{\text{Operating Expenses (this project)}}{\text{Budgeted } \textit{Annual} \text{ Operating Expenses}}$$

When preparing an estimate, you can use this method to allocate the proper amount of money for Operating Expenses for this project. This method does assume you are using an Annual Budget, and therefore have some idea of what your estimated Cost of Sales and Operating Expenses are for the year. You probably have a reliable method of estimating your Cost of Sales for this job, and so, with these three variables in place, we can proceed to the next part of this formula which says:

$$\frac{\text{Budgeted } \textit{Annual} \text{ Operating Expense} \times \text{Estimated Cost of Sales (this project)}}{\text{Budgeted } \textit{Annual} \text{ Cost of Sales}} = \text{Operating Expense (this project)}$$

Essentially, we have established a ratio between these numbers, and, since we have three variables, we can solve for the unknown value, in this case the proper allocation of Operating Expenses for this project.

STEPS FOR PRICING (Approach 1)

$$\frac{\text{Cost of Sales + Operating Expenses}}{(100\% - \text{Desired Profit Margin})} = \text{Initial Selling Price}$$

As you may have realized, this part of this formula is exactly the same thing we discussed above in Pricing for Profit, however, there are two additional points here. This method applies to jobs in which you desire a straight across-the-board markup. In other words, the percentage of profit for Cost of Sales and Operating Expenses will be the same. In many cases, that won't work for a variety of reasons. Therefore, there is an Alternative Approach further along in this illustration. In addition, in virtually every remodeling job, there are Contingency Costs to be dealt with and, in the second part of this solution, we will address adding the Contingency Fee to your Initial Selling Price.

SUMMARY OF FORMULAS, continued

STEPS FOR PRICING, continued

Step 1   Initial Selling Price + Contingency Fee = 100% of Selling Price

Step 2   Initial Selling Price + (__% of SP) = 100% of Selling Price

Step 3   Initial Selling Price = 100% of Selling Price - (__% of SP)

Step 4 $\dfrac{\text{Initial Selling Price}}{100\% \text{ of Selling Price} - (\_\_\% \text{ of SP})}$ = Selling Price w/Contingency Fee

In order to arrive at the Selling Price with Contingency Fee, we begin with the Initial Selling Price established in the first part of this approach. You must establish for yourself how much of a Contingency Fee you require for each job and express it as a percentage of the Selling Price. That figure plus the Initial Selling Price is equal to 100 percent of the Selling Price (Step 2). In Step 3, you can see that the Initial Selling Price is equal to 100 percent of the Selling Price less the percent of Selling Price you have established in Step 2. Finally in Step 4 you can arrive at the Selling Price with Contingency Fee by dividing the Initial Selling Price by 100 percent of the Selling Price less the figure you established in Step 2.

STEPS FOR PRICING (ALTERNATIVE APPROACH)

Realistically, the only difference between this method and the previous method is that in this case you would determine the proper allocation of Operating Expenses as we indicated earlier. You would then apply your Desired Profit Margin as we calculated it, in Pricing for Profit. Then you would calculate separately all the individual items of work (Costs of Sale), with the required markup for all these elements, and total these to arrive at your Initial Selling Price. Finally, you would determine your Selling Price with Contingency Fee, just as we have in the previous example.

HOURLY RATE CALCULATIONS

While I have not exactly presented a formula, it is imperative that you recognize the impact that all the different variables can have on your True Hourly Costs. In the example I have included, those variables include a Productivity Factor, Labor (here I am referring to the different combinations of Hourly Pay based upon the teams you might assemble), the proper allocation of Fixed or Operating Expenses, and finally the application of the correct Markup and Contingency Fee. Please note that these differences occur internally to your organization.

CHAPTER 5 SUMMARY OF TERMS	
TERM	**DESCRIPTION**
estimating process	Method used by dealers to arrive at the cost of their products and services, which recognizes their expenses and calculates a margin of profit for their investment.
manufacturer's suggested retail price (MSRP)	A price which manufacturers deem to be competitive, based upon their own marketing research, and presumably on the product's features and benefits.
markup	The calculation of the correct amount of charges required to produce a selling price that will cover the seller's costs and overhead and provide the seller with a margin of profit.
operating expenses	Those expenses necessary to operate the business on a day-to-day basis, such as salaries of office staff, rent, utilities and insurance.
productivity	Output of goods or services, possibly listed by department or individual, and frequently based on some predetermined and standard measure. The output can also be listed by dollar volume of work, material installed or number of projects sold during a given period.
profit based on costs	A selling price arrived at by adding the percentage of profit to the costs associated with the finished project.
profit based on selling price	A selling price arrived at, after careful consideration of costs, expenses, the market and the desired return on investment. This is the price that will provide the desired profit margin after deducting all costs and expenses associated with delivering the finished project.
retailer	A person or business owner who conducts business, such as a department store or a mass merchandiser, by reselling that which others manufacture or make, and profit by the sheer volume,
scheduling	Designation of time, personnel and resources to insure the most productive and therefore profitable means of completing a project. Scheduling informs management, subcontractors and tradespeople of available time slots and delivery dates

Chapter 6

FINE TUNING FOR PROFIT

Mathematics may be compared to a mill of exquisite workmanship, which grinds your stuff to any degree of fineness; but, nevertheless, what you get out depends on what you put in; and as the grandest mill in the world will not extract wheat flour from peascods, so pages of formulae will not get a definite result out of loose data.
- Thomas Henry Huxley

Even the most conscientious have a problem with the hidden costs of operating a business. Those hidden costs can do tremendous damage if not recognized early on. Knowing what they are and learning how to spot them can make a big difference in ensuring your continued profitability. Unfortunately, time is not always on your side, so controls may have to be built into your system in order to alert you to the potential for such errors. Checklists, standard operating procedures and guidelines are some examples of such controls.

GOVERNMENT REGULATIONS, FINES AND PENALTIES

This category is more forgotten than hidden, and is frustrating to deal with, since there isn't much you can do about these once you do learn about them. Each time you fail to file a required form or report or pay a tax by a prescribed deadline, you expose your business to the threat of paying these fines and penalties. No one knowingly budgets fines and penalties into their working budget, so, when they are levied against your business, you can be assured they are coming out of any potential profits the business may make. You certainly don't want to get yourself into problems with the Internal Revenue Service (IRS), over the issue of withholding taxes from your employees. They are not very understanding, when it comes to this issue in particular, and with good reason. That money does not belong to you, and, furthermore, it represents taxes due to the IRS, and they apply hefty penalties if you don't comply.

PAYROLL TAX PENALTIES

For amounts not properly or timely deposited, the penalty rates are:

- 2 percent - Deposits made 1 to 5 days late
- 5 percent - Deposits made 6 to 15 days late.
- 10 percent - Deposits made 16 or more days late. Also applies to amounts paid to the IRS within 10 days of the date of the first notice sent to you by the IRS asking for the tax due.
- 15 percent - Amounts still unpaid more than 10 days after the date of the first notice sent to you by the IRS asking for the tax due, or the day on which you receive notice and demand for immediate payment, whichever is earlier.

ORDER IN WHICH TAX DEPOSITS ARE APPLIED

Tax deposits are applied first to satisfy any past due under-deposits for the quarter, with the oldest under-deposit satisfied first. So, if you make a payment and your previous payments were under-deposited, the new payments will be used to satisfy the past requirements and penalties, and the newest payment is now short, subjecting you to still more penalties. One method I know a number of people use is to write a check for the amount of the deposit on each payday, and set those funds aside immediately, so that you do not overlook and/or spend that money elsewhere. Be sure you make your deposits on time!

TAKING ADVANTAGE OF EARLY DISCOUNTS

Another way to look at early payment discounts is as self-imposed penalties. Your supplier is offering you the same advantage as is being offered to your competitors, but, if you fail to grasp it, you are, in a sense, imposing a penalty on yourself. Assume that both you and your competitor are preparing a proposal, and you both call the same vendor for a price on a truckload of cabinets for a builder client. You are both quoted a price of $20,000 and the terms are 2% 10 days net 30. If your competitor elects to take advantage of the 2 percent discount and you can't, how much of an edge will he or she have over you? If both of you mark up your purchase by 20 percent based on the selling price, your competitor can still make the same return on the money as you, but can also afford to pass close to a $500 savings along to the customer. That's a competitive advantage.

FAILING TO USE OTHER PEOPLE'S MONEY

You are not in the business of lending money. Don't offer to finance or carry the customer through to the completion of the project with your own money when working with a retail customer. No matter how lengthy or short the duration of the work, insist upon an initial deposit and incremental draws. This is often the reason why so many business people subject themselves to excessive interest charges and late fees. Your money is tied up supporting uncompleted projects, and you are then unable to pay your own bills, which can mean penalties, or missing out on early payment discounts.

If you have used a written proposal and contract, you should be able to convince your customers that this is the method you customarily use, and that it helps you to keep your costs down and thus be more competitive—something they can appreciate. Be specific within the terms of your agreement as to how much the entire job will cost, how much you are asking for as a deposit in order to get started, and at which points you will expect to be paid progress payments.

On the other hand, your clients are going to expect you to assist them with a payment schedule or financing program that they can use to help them make their purchase. There is such a wide variety of third-party programs available for retail customers that, with a little diligence on your part, you should be able to offer a plan that is equitable and easy to work with. This will free up your funds, and bring those larger purchases in line with your client's budget.

(For more information about point-of-purchase financing, see NKBA's publication, entitled **Leveraging Design: Finance and the Kitchen and Bathroom Specialist**, by Debi Bach.)

Don't overlook your suppliers. They have just as much interest in moving their inventory as you do, and can be approached for special terms and considerations. You will never know what they are willing to negotiate unless you ask. Granted, you don't have to risk hearing "No!" if you don't ask, but then you won't get a "Yes!" either. Such assistance doesn't necessarily have to be in the form of discounts or terms only. Manufacturers typically offer co-op funds for advertising to businesses who sell their products.

Check with your own suppliers, nationally, regionally and locally, and inquire as to what is available in your area. Reducing your current advertising expense might be justification for expanding your level of advertising in order to attract more customers. Or, you may be able to use those savings to create a unique in-store promotion to boost sales. Being on the lookout for new and untapped sources of savings regarding the use of other people's money leads us to another very important question.

SHOULD YOU BORROW IN ORDER TO DISCOUNT?

As any small-business person knows these days, one of the biggest issues of concern is cash flow, or perhaps, more succinctly, the lack thereof. Yet every month, people are offered discounts and savings incentives which are passed up. I am talking about the payment discounts your suppliers offer for paying your account early.

Probably the primary reason you don't pay these bills early and take advantage of these discounts is that you don't have access to the necessary cash. There is still another alternative. Look at the accompanying worksheet, entitled **SHOULD YOU BORROW TO DISCOUNT?** *Exhibit A* shows you an example of a completed worksheet used to make an evaluation. *Exhibits B* and *C* are designed to show you how to make the necessary calculations. In this example, you are faced with paying an invoice for some cabinets where the manufacturer is offering you standard terms of 2% 10 days net 30. This means it is actually encouraging you to save $253.08 on this invoice, if you will pay it within 10 days. Failing to take advantage of this early payment discount, you must still pay the invoice within 30 days.

However, if you don't have the cash, you can't take advantage of this potential savings opportunity. Your alternative is to consider borrowing the money from your lender. As this example shows, even at an 18 percent annual percentage rate (APR), if you borrow this money and pay it back by the due date of the invoice, you will pay just $122.31 for the use of those funds, and that results in a savings to you of $130.77. You will need to establish a line of credit with your banker, and, quite possibly, use your receivables as collateral, for the ability to access cash quickly, and thus afford yourself some savings opportunities. Such an arrangement will pay for itself many times over.

SHOULD YOU BORROW TO DISCOUNT?
Exhibit A

Early payment of invoice

Invoice Amount	$12,653.76			
Terms	%	Days	Net	
	2.0%	10	30	
Invoice Date	12/27/94			
Discount Date		06-Jan-95		
Due Date			26-Jan-95	
Early Discount		$253.08		
Remittance		$12,400.68	$12,653.76	

Cost to borrow from bank

	Interest	=	Principal	x	Rate	x	Time
Cost to Borrow	$122.31		$12,400.68		18%		20/365

Early Discount	$253.08
Cost to Borrow	$122.31
Savings	$130.77

SHOULD YOU BORROW TO DISCOUNT
Exhibit B

Objective: To determine whether or not it is cost effective for you to borrow money in order to take advantage of Early Payment Discounts on your purchases.

Step #1 - Determine how much money we can actually save by taking advantage of the 2% discount offered if this invoice is paid within 10 days. (Calculation #1)

Enter the full invoice amount Multiply this by the percent which is offered as the discount.	$12,653.76
	x.02
The resulting answer then represents the potential savings to the buyer, assuming they make the payment within ten days of the invoice date.	$253.08

Calculation #1

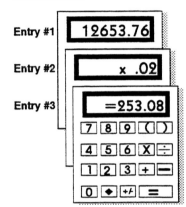

Step #2 - Determine the actual amount of money you will have to pay if you take advantage of the 2% savings. (Calculation #2)

Enter the amount of the invoice Subtract the potential savings at 2% or in this case	$12,653.76
	-253.08
The resulting answer then represents the amount you will actually have to pay in order to realize a 2% savings	$12,400.68

Calculation #2

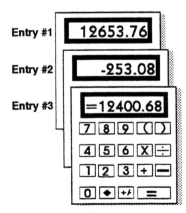

SHOULD YOU BORROW TO DISCOUNT
Exhibit C

Step #3 - Let us assume the money is not readily available and that you will have to borrow these funds to make the early payment. Furthermore it may take a full 20 days beyond the discount period to make good on this debt.

As an alternative, determine how much it will cost you in interest payments to borrow this money. (Calculation #3)

Enter the amount required to pay	$12,400.68
Multiply this by the percent which represents the rate the lender will charge to use these funds on an annual basis.	x.18
The resulting answer then represents the annual cost to the buyer, assuming they make the payment within 30 days of the invoice date. However since you are not going to use the money for that full time you need to determine the pro-rated amount of interest you will be charged to use the money for the 20 days before you can pay it back.	$2232.1224
Enter the annual amount Multiply that number by open parenthesis 20 divided by 365 close parenthesis	$2232.1224 x (20÷365)
The result is the amount you will be charged to use these funds for 20 days.	= $122.31

Calculation #3

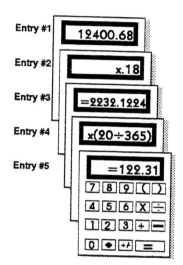

Step #4 - Determine the actual amount of money you will save by borrowing these funds early and taking advantage of the Early Payment Discount (Calculation #4)

Enter the amount of the discount	$ 253.08
Subtract the potential savings at 2% or in this case	-122.31
The resulting answer then represents the amount you will actually realize in a savings.	$ 130.77

Calculation #4

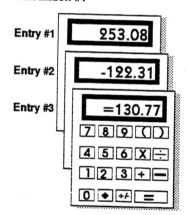

LABOR BURDEN AND PAYROLL COSTS

Here is where I find a significant number of people, even those who have been in business for a considerable time, do not understand the full impact of what it really costs them to carry an employee on the payroll. As a result, they frequently underbid their work because they are not charging an amount sufficient to cover their payroll burden.

Look at the following worksheet, entitled **FIRST YEAR COST FOR NEW EMPLOYEE**. I have attempted to show you the real cost of hiring an individual as a delivery driver in the United States—a position many businesses have. We have here an employee who is a single individual claiming two deductions. This person will be paid an hourly wage of $6.50. The worker's compensation rate for this individual's job description is $11.50 per $100 of compensation. I have calculated the cost to hire and train this individual at $2,000, based upon advertising for the position, time to conduct interviews, training and perhaps lost productivity while this individual learns all the responsibilities of the job. You also agree to pick up the group medical premium on an annual basis, at a cost of $1,500 per year, and you will pick up the cost of a week's paid vacation, $309.79. However, if that position is sensitive enough to your operation, it may mean you'll have to staff it while the employee is on vacation, which will cost you another $309.79. Federal Unemployment Tax (FUTA) is going to cost you an additional $56 over the course of the next year.

Taking all these expenses and allocating them over a 52-week period, you will spend $41.84 per week. During this particular pay period, the employee worked a total of 40 hours and did not have any overtime. That meant gross earnings for the week were $260. As the employer, you are responsible for paying regular compensation, as well as withholding federal income taxes, Medicare, social security taxes and state withholding taxes. You will also pay a State Unemployment Tax (SUTA) and FUTA, and the employer's share of matching amounts of both Medicare and social security taxes, in addition to whatever additional taxes might be applied locally.

In my example, I have calculated the gross pay, and, by using the 1995 Schedule E (Publication 15 IRS Code) for a weekly payroll period, I have been able to determine the amount of federal withholding ($18.00), Medicare ($3.77) and social security taxes ($16.12). After subtracting these amounts from the gross pay, we arrive at the employee's net pay of $222.11.

In the following step, I have calculated the payroll burden ($49.79) and added it to the gross earnings of $260, arriving at a total of $309.79. To this, I added the cost of the employee benefits for a true weekly cost of $351.63, which results in a true hourly figure of $8.79.

To be certain you understand the significance of that difference, I am going to ask you to take out your calculator and do some work with me. We are talking about a difference of $2.29 between the hourly figure we pay this individual and the $8.79 it is really costing us.

Divide the difference, $2.29, by $6.50 and see for yourself what it is really costing you over and above that hourly figure. A full 35 percent more! Remember, you are only talking about a worker's compensation rate in the range of 11 percent, which is very low by comparison to that of many of the skilled trades. In some businesses, these rates will run in excess of 100 percent of the worker's hourly figure.

Therefore, your true annual cost to employ this individual is $18,284.66, and, after adding in the cost to hire and train this employee, annual costs for this first year reach $20,284.66. Note that I have not included any sick pay, holiday, state unemployment or retirement contribution!

FIRST YEAR COST FOR NEW EMPLOYEE

(Based on Rates in 1995 Schedule E - Weekly Payroll)

Job Description - Delivery Driver

Employee Profile
Single employee, claims 2 deductions
Worker's Compensation rate for position $11.50

Cost to hire & train $2,000.00

Benefits Package
Group medical premium (annual)	$1,500.00
Annual Vaction (1 week)	$309.79
Replacement cost during vaction period	$309.79
F.U.T.A. @ .008% Of first $7,000	$56.00
Total Benefit Pkg Cost (annual)	$2,175.58
Allocated over 52 weeks	$41.84

Hourly Compensation

		Employer's Contribution	Employer's Deposit Requirements
Hourly Compensation Rate	$6.50		
O.T. Compensation Rate	$9.75		
Regular Hours	40		
Regular Pay	$260.00		
O.T. Hours	0		
O.T. Pay	$0.00		
Gross Pay	**$260.00**		
Less Federal Withholding	($18.00)		$18.00
Less Social Security (F.I.C.A.) @ 6.2%	($16.12)	$16.12	$32.24
Less Medicare Tax @ 1.45%	($3.77)	$3.77	$7.54
Net Pay	**$222.11**		
			$57.78
Worker's Compensation Premium		$29.90	
Sub-total of Payroll Burden		**$49.79**	
Gross Pay + Burden		$309.79	
Weekly Allocation of Benefits		$41.84	
True 1st Year Costs to Staff Position	$20,284.66		
True Annual Costs to Staff Position	$18,284.66		
True Weekly Costs		$351.63	
True Hourly Costs	**($8.79)**		

Additional Costs Not Included
Sick Pay As Used
S.U.T.A.
No Retirement Contribution

EMPLOYEE PRODUCTIVITY

Using your own figures, based on your payroll records and past performance from your own job-costing records, you need to do these calculations for every employee who works for you. (See the following **WEEKLY WAGE CALCULATION** worksheet.) There can't be any guesswork as you approach your bidding process. This worksheet allows you to see what your true hourly costs are, after factoring in some of your payroll burden from *Section A*. From this information, you can then produce a weekly, hourly or daily profile of what you are spending for your labor, as seen in *Section B*.

All of this information might be meaningless unless your crew's productivity is factored in. The U.S. Department of Commerce believes that most employers receive only 5 to 6 hours of productivity for every 8 hours of compensation they are paying. That is not necessarily an indictment of the labor force, but it is a reflection of how productive we really are.

The reasons for the disparity are many and varied. Time required on the telephone, time to clean up, time to stop work and unload deliveries, travel time, preparation time, changes necessitated by misplaced or undetected utilities, are but a few such examples.

What this means is that, unless your own job-costing records indicate otherwise, you are not as productive as you might think you are. If you have not been job costing, you should begin immediately, otherwise you may only be fooling yourself. For example, if in fact you are only achieving 5½ hours of production in the course of an 8-hour day, you must factor in an additional 31.25 percent of your actual labor costs, to cover the costs of labor on your work, and that is before the addition of any profit. (See *Section C*.) Since labor is such a large part of your costs of sales, this can be a very sensitive area as far as your productivity is concerned.

WEEKLY WAGE CALCULATION WORKSHEET

WEEKLY WAGE CALCULATIONS WORKSHEET

Regular Hours	40 Per employee							Section A	
EMPLOYEE	Hrly Rate	Gross Pay	Social Security 6.2%	Medicare 1.45%	Worker's Comp. Rate	Worker's Comp. Prem.	Actual Cost	Actual Hrly	Factor
Kevin Smith	$9.00	$360.00	$22.32	$5.22	21%	$75.60	$463.14	$11.58	128.65%
Danny Royce	$8.00	$320.00	$19.84	$4.64	19%	$60.80	$405.28	$10.13	126.65%
Judith Brown	$9.00	$360.00	$22.32	$5.22	17%	$61.20	$448.74	$11.22	124.65%
Mark Michaels	$7.00	$280.00	$17.36	$4.06	23%	$64.40	$365.82	$9.15	130.65%

Section B — Labor Costs

Per Week	$1,682.98
Per Hour	$42.07
Per Day	$336.60

'Productivity @ 1.3125

	$2,208.91
	$55.22
	$441.78

Section C

Productivity based on Dept. of Commerce findings that the average employee is only productive 5½ to 6 hours out of each 8 hour day. Your most accurate indicator would be your own job-costing records from previous work.

Thus to properly calculate your true production labor costs, if you are getting just 5½ hours of actual production time, you would have to factor in an additional 31.25% of your actual labor costs! These figures do not include any profit.

Additional Costs Not Included
Sick Pay As Used
F.U.T.A.
S.U.T.A.
No Retirement Contribution
No Benefits

Now that you have some idea of what your costs really are with respect to your employees, perhaps you will take a second look the next time you think you need to hire somebody. Is it worth the added expense? Will you have sufficient work to keep this individual employed, or will you be forced to lay him or her off, possibly raising your unemployment compensation rates? Would you be better off if you subcontracted out this work? Perhaps you should consider hiring part-time help or hiring temporary workers through an agency.

COMMISSION FOR SALESPEOPLE

One area many business owners find exasperating is how to compensate their salespeople fairly, while compensating themselves for their own risks. I am about to show you a program that does exactly that. Before I proceed, however, I would like to caution you: **You are now dealing with the people who can make your business grow and prosper**. You should make every effort to present this information in a positive fashion. Help your professional salespeople see this plan as a win/win situation for them and for your business. That is exactly what it is intended to be. (See the following **SALES COMMISSIONS WORKSHEET**.)

You are expected to know what kind of a profit margin you require to satisfy your investment, along with the associated risks and needs for future growth and development. The professional salesperson (someone who is strictly on a commission basis) is, in a sense, an independent businessperson. Yet, this person is using your resources and name to earn profits or commissions. Accordingly, I have set this up affording the owner the bigger slice of the pie, in compensation for those very risks we just talked about. The other element which is essential to understanding this plan, is that it is based on the profitability of the sale, not the sheer volume of sales.

SALES COMMISSION WORKSHEET

	Target Pricing {Before Contingency Fee}	Profit As %	Selling Price	Cash Profit	Commission As % Profit	Commission As $ Amt.	Owner's Share As % Profit	Owner's Share As $ Amt.
Section A		16.0%	$28,057.52	$4,489.20	39.0%	$1,750.79	61.0%	$2,738.41
Section B	This Job	15.0%	$27,727.44	$4,159.12	38.0%	$1,580.46	62.0%	$2,578.65
	Effective Discount/Bonus		($330.09)					
	Loss or Gain Split			($330.09) =		($170.33)		($159.76)

DATE	17-Jul-96
JOB #	1001331
SALESPERSON	B. Young
INVOICE #	R15463

Job Information		As % Of Sales	As % Of Profit	Section C	
Cost of Sales	$16,114.60	58.1%			
Allocation of Fixed Expenses	$7,453.72	26.9%			
Total Costs	$23,568.32	85.0%		*Total Costs* *To Owner*	
A Desired Profit Margin Of	15.00%				
Requires an Initial Selling Price Of	$27,727.44	100.0%		$23,568.32	
Realizing A Cash Profit Of	$4,159.12	15.0%		$1,580.46	
				$25,148.78	
It Also Produces A					
Sales Commission Of	$1,580.46	5.7%	38.0%		
Means A True Owner's Costs Of	$25,148.78	90.7%			
With Owner's Actual Share At	$2,578.65	9.3%	62.0%		
Plus An Allowance For					
A Contingency Fee Of	$422.25	1.5%			
Equals The Actual Selling Price Of	$28,149.68				

STRUCTURE THE COMMISSION

One of the loudest arguments I hear from business owners is that a salesperson who is paid a straight commission will often discount the price in order to get the sale, and the owner winds up with little or no profit. With the plan outlined here, you and the salesperson are sharing the profits and the discounts in such a manner that neither one will be hurt to the exclusion of the other. You will also know in advance how much of the profit you are actually forfeiting when you discount the price of the product or service.

This example is designed to be used in conjunction with any selling situation in which the salesperson has the right to exercise some discretion when setting the price. While it is used in this example, for someone on a straight commission, it can be applied to all compensation packages structured around a commission.

Section A

On the previous worksheet, you see the desired or *Target Pricing* which establishes a *selling price* of $28,057.52 delivering a 16 percent profit based on that selling price, or in terms of dollars and cents, $4,489,20. Furthermore, this profit is to be divided between the owner and the salesperson on the following basis: 39 percent of the profit or $1,750.79 as commission to the salesperson, and 61 percent of the profit or $2,738.41 as the owner's share of this sale. These percents are setup on a sliding scale and can be adjusted.

Section B

This is designed to show you the results when the job is sold for less than the target price. In this case, at 15 percent profit resulting in a selling price of $27,727.44, and a dollar profit of $4,159.12, to be divided on a different basis this time.

A commission to the salesperson of 38 percent of the profits or $1,580.46, and a return on investment to the owner of 62 percent of the profits in the amount of $2,578.65. There are a number of reasons why there is a difference in percents, but most notable is the fact that the owner, and not the salesperson, is taking the greatest risk. The time it will sit between the order process and the actual installation may cost the owner some money, which has not been factored in here, is one such example. At any rate, if this project or service is sold for the price in *Section B*, it results in a discount or loss of $330.09.

Why should the owner be the only one to bear the brunt of this loss? The ability of salespeople to sell should be measured by some standard, and that measure in this case is the revenues they bring in. If they only sell at a discount, there is a good chance they are becoming order takers, rather than professional salespeople. This plan allows them to see how much they are willing to give up. If they understand they are giving up $170.33 (almost 10 percent of their commission), out of their own pocket, they may be more inclined to sell value and not price.

Section C

We see an analysis of this sale, on the previous worksheet, again showing a complete breakdown as to how the profit will be divided. Notice that the *contingency fee* is applied after the calculation is completed. As stated earlier, the purpose of this fee is not to function as a profit center, but rather as an insurance policy, to be spread over all your jobs. No commission is calculated on this amount.

One issue I would also encourage you to think about and address is this: A sale is not consummated until full payment is received in exchange for the product or service the business has rendered. If you have clearly delineated areas of responsibility with respect to the collection of funds, adjustments, damages or returns, then there should be no disagreement between you and your salesperson about when compensation is due.

JOBS YOU DO JUST TO BREAK EVEN

You are not in business to break even. As a business owner or manager, your responsibility is to make sure there is enough work out there to keep your business busy and profitable. Otherwise, you are placing your business at tremendous risk without any hope of making a profit, and very possibly denying yourself an opportunity to find profitable work because you are too busy trying simply to break even. When you have employed a budget in the past, did you know where your break-even point was? If you did not, there is good reason to believe that not only were you not making a profit, you were actually losing money in the process when you agreed to do something, "just to break even."

If you set your goals using a budget, you can measure your progress from day to day, week to week and month to month. You will see how much more creatively and diligently you must work to find new opportunities for your business. It may mean you have not properly identified your own niche or that you need to spend more time marketing your services. It is also conceivable that you must broaden the range of services or products you can offer your customer base.

I would also ask you to seriously consider how you are placing your business at unwarranted risk by taking on unprofitable jobs. If you or one of your employees is injured on the job, what does that do to your chances of taking on another job that would be more profitable? Because you are not making a profit on such an undertaking, there is a good chance you or your employees will take a shortcut, either with respect to quality or service.

Consider what impact that might have to your own credibility and reputation, to say nothing of what it may do to your sense of integrity and level of ethical conduct you are trying to create within your business. What if there is a mistake? Will you be prepared to accept the responsibility and added cost, knowing it must come out of your own pocket? It is a situation none of us wants to be in, but, it is also one of those situations that can be avoided by utilizing all that we are talking about here, and developing strategies to assist you.

THE 80 - 20 SALES RULE

If you have developed a budget, you should be able to produce a marketing plan and separate marketing budget to help your organization identify and target new prospects in your market. When you go about the task of developing your marketing plan, don't forget the *80 - 20 rule*, which says that 80 percent of your business will come from 20 percent of your customers. Successful salespeople understand this and maximize their prospecting and marketing efforts accordingly. What can you do so that your investment in your marketing efforts will produce maximum results? Do you know which of your customers account for the 20 percent? How many more leads have you solicited them for?

REPEAT CUSTOMERS

Begin with making everyone aware of how important these *repeat customers* truly are. They come back primarily because they appreciate the service they receive and have come to expect. Solicit ideas and suggestions from your employees as to how these customers might better be served. Develop a survey of questions as to their inquiries and any possible suggestions of what they would like to purchase from you. Consider assigning account representatives to work with your commercial accounts if you have the need. Be certain they contact them on a regular basis, in order to tell them about the latest additions to your line.

REFERRALS

Teach your staff to ask for *referrals*. Your clients simply won't think about offering them. However, if you have done an outstanding job for them, there is no reason not to ask for referrals. Your previous customers know your organization on a firsthand basis, and they can be an excellent source of new business, but you must actively solicit their patronage.

MAKE CONTACT

Even your retail customers should be *contacted* on a regular basis (6 months, a year), so you can keep them informed about what is happening in your business. Some kitchen and bathroom professionals sponsor cooking classes in the showroom. Previous clients can be invited to attend and bring along a guest. In addition to good food ideas, they also see your entire line and how convenient and easy it is to function in a modern state-of-the-art kitchen.

FAILING TO UP-SELL

When you bring customers in the door, you and your staff may be missing a tremendous opportunity to increase sales by not taking advantage of their predisposition to buy from you. The best **customer service providers** in the business never let such an occasion pass without offering their customers the added value of their experience and service. They know that they can offer an idea or suggestion that may enhance the purchase, saving the customer time in the future.

Customers frequently overlook ancillary products until a professional salesperson takes the time to bring them to their attention. Thus, suggesting additional purchases can actually be a service that will entice customers to return and make additional purchases of their own. Train yourself and your staff not to be merely order takers, but rather professionals who encourage their clients to reveal their needs and who then satisfy those needs. Holding down your expenses and maximizing your ability to create additional sales, to *up-sell*, is one of the most cost-effective ways to operate a business.

LOW BIDDERS

Low bidders and customers who will buy only the lowest-priced work have always been around. Discount retailers have had a tremendous impact on the retail trade, as many former small-business owners can attest. Small businesses that attempt to capture their market by pricing alone are generally in for trouble. They don't have the sources of funding that the big competitors have, and, furthermore, they don't have any of the strategic plans or resources that many big businesses do.

Nevertheless, there are always going to be people who can only see price as the way to get a competitive edge. There may be competitors who are able to consistently and legitimately beat your prices, because they know what they are doing and run a profitable business. When you come up against someone like that, you want to learn as much as you can about their operation and what they are doing that makes them so successful. The low bidders I am referring to here are those who only know how to sell price, not value.

Wouldn't you agree that each bid you submit for a job has a price associated with it? You spend time, resources and sometimes even out-of-pocket money when you assemble a bid. If people underbid you consistently, this costs you money in the process. Develop a profile of your competition and learn how and where they are able to cut your prices. You may decide to avoid bidding against them, rather than paying for the privilege of doing so and then losing the bid. Strengthen your resolve to make yourself worth more and to redefine yourself within your market niche.

IMPROVED COMMUNICATIONS

In any organization, *communication* is the key to success. If you go back to the very beginning of this book and read it again, I think you will realize that communication is all that we have been talking about, in one way or another. Mistakes generally occur, not because of lack of intelligence, but because of a lack of awareness. Checklists help everyone to communicate ideas, policies and instructions to one another. Following the lead of many corporations, you can encourage personal employee responsibility in every part of your operation, by every person involved, to promote success in your business

However, we may still be missing one important factor. Successful corporations have realized the importance of what their employees are contributing. They understand that employees are their greatest asset, and the last thing they want to do is to stem the flow of ideas and suggestions for improving productivity and profitability.

In an effort to open the channels of communication, they have adopted what is referred to as a "no harm, implement policy." Simply stated, this policy says that, unless an employee's suggestion will have a detrimental effect on the business, the suggestion will be implemented. It has a two-fold purpose. It tells each employee that his or her ideas and suggestions are important to management, and it allows others to brainstorm with these suggestions and quite possibly expand upon them.

Unfortunately, far too many businesses adopt the attitude that, unless the employee can prove that the idea is cost effective in the first place, it is never even looked at. As a result, employees decide it's not worth the effort to submit their ideas, so they simply don't bother. You want to create an atmosphere where people can offer ideas and suggestions, as well as acknowledge responsibility for their mistakes. They must feel their input is valued by the business, and that they have an obligation to contribute to its future. Only an enlightened management can make that possible, but the payoff can be tremendous when you are successful.

JOB COSTING AS COMMUNICATION

Job costing is another form of communication designed to relate what is happening with your estimating and bidding skills. You wouldn't think it was a good idea to drive an automobile if none of the dials and gauges were operable. You wouldn't know if you were about to overheat your engine, run out of fuel, or have your battery die, without the vital information supplied by these necessary gauges.

Why is operating your business any different? Unless you are doing a thorough job of costing your projects, that is exactly what you are doing each time you submit a proposal and you don't use job costing to determine whether or not you are putting them together properly. You are simply repeating the same pattern of errors. Job costing does not have to be difficult. By analyzing the results you get from each job, you can tell where you must learn to be more accurate or to adjust your calculations.

JOB-COSTING ANALYSIS

Remember the job we calculated for the commissions of our salesperson? It turns out to be an excellent example of what we are discussing here. Our fictional business owners have completed a *Job-Costing Analysis* of this job, which is illustrated in the next worksheet. They were surprised to learn that they didn't fare as well as they first thought they had. To begin with, there was additional work. A bathroom valued at $7,517.24 was added to the original estimate, bringing the value of this job to $34,086.47. This extra work was calculated separately, but they still only realized a profit of $1,371.30 or 4.02 percent, and these were pre-tax profits not net-profits. What happened? Where did they go wrong? A look at the summary will help for starters.

Between the *redos and omissions*, there were approximately 10 hours of additional labor charged to this job by this crew. This sounds like more than a simple miscommunication. These are substantial hours for a job of this size. Part of this was for the time required to replace a door that had been installed incorrectly and had to be replaced. There was also time lost because the countertop was ordered, supplied and installed in the wrong material. Not only did the door and countertop have to be replaced, but some materials were overlooked altogether and others cost more ($46.72 more) than originally planned. A piece of rental equipment, which was not included in the original estimate, was used, costing an additional $75 plus tax. Apparently there was also a breakdown in communication between someone and the plumbing contractor, because he's charging $349.95 for the new hot-water heater he installed, after the owner, you and the plumber agreed, it should be done.

To add insult to injury, there was no provision for a contingency fee with the additional work. On top of all this, the sales commissions, $2,008.94, on both the original estimate and the extra work were not included. Now there is plenty of room for blaming, but it would be a waste of time. On the other hand, this job might provide an excellent example of how not to complete a project profitably. Exactly what might be learned from this experience?

Communication, especially at the project level, could be greatly improved if all the players knew what their roles and responsibilities encompassed. The salesperson was new to this business, and while that may explain some of the confusion surrounding this job, it doesn't justify it. The customers aren't looking for a scapegoat, but some acknowledgment that they were inconvenienced and, while they are pleased with the outcome of the work itself, they were less than enthusiastic with the process. The **ISSUES THAT INFLUENCE CLIENT PERCEPTIONS** checklist that was included at the end of the first chapter could make an excellent starting point to resolving many of these issues.

The *Summary* in the following worksheet would also seem to indicate that a better system is required for tracking changes and their appropriate charges. The purpose of the contingency fee, I might add, is not to compensate you for your mistakes. Rather, it is a means of covering some of the unforeseen problems that arise during the course of almost every job. In this particular case, about the only thing I could reasonably characterize that way might be the additional charges resulting from the price increases. Someone might have done a better job of asking about them in anticipation of these additional costs.

I am sure we could find a number of other problems and solutions by making better use of this *Job-Costing Analysis*, but that's not my purpose here. Without taking the time to complete such an analysis, you would probably not even realize how poorly this business performed during this project. With it, you can understand better some of the consequences of your performance as a whole. If this could happen to you, without planning for it, imagine how much more thoroughly you might be hurt, had you decided to do this job, "just to break even." You could very well have paid out of pocket for much of what your customer received.

JOB COSTING ANALYSIS

JOB #	Original Estimate	% of Sales	Changes	Adjusted Estimate	% of Sales	Actual Costs	Overages
1001331							
Revenues	$26,569.23	100.00%	$7,517.24	$34,086.47	100.00%		
Labor	5,246.01	19.74%	916.31	6,162.32	18.08%	6,590.14	427.82
Materials	7,840.91	29.51%	875.91	8,716.82	25.57%	9,653.41	936.59
Sub-Contracts	3,027.68	11.40%	2,722.43	5,750.11	16.87%	6,100.06	349.95
Equipt. Rentals	0.00	0.00%	0.00	0.00	0.00%	79.36	79.36
Costs of Sale	16,114.60	60.65%	4,514.65	20,629.25	60.52%		
Gross Margin	10,454.63	39.35%	3,002.59	13,457.22	39.48%		
Oper. Expens.	7,453.72	28.05%	1,875.00	9,328.72	27.37%	9,328.72	0.00
Contingency Fee	422.25	1.59%		422.25	1.24%	535.00	112.75
Commissions	1,580.46	5.95%	428.48	2,008.94	5.89%		
Net Before Tax	2,578.66	9.71%	699.11	3,277.77	9.62%		

S-U-M-M-A-R-Y

	Redo's	Ommissions	Price Increases
	199.57	228.25	
	786.00	103.87	46.72
		349.95	
		79.36	
		112.75	
Sub-totals	$985.57	$874.18	$46.72
Total	$1,906.47		
Profit	1,371.30		
As % Sales	4.02%		

Job costing is an effective management tool that can provide you with important information to improve your estimating skills for future jobs, and also to provide you with feedback on this particular job's profitability.

In the above example you will notice that the job was originally bid at a price of $28,149.69. At some point in the course of this job, the customer apparently decided on some additional work which you estimated at $7,517.24, thus bringing the total selling price of the job to $35,666.93.

Apparently, you believed that you would earn a profit in excess of 9% based on the combined prices, but as the job was completed, it turned out that you missed your target profit of $1906.47 or by about 5.6%. Without the benefit of this job cost report, you might never have understood exactly why and where you have lost money in relation to your bid on this particular job.

CHAPTER 6

Reference Information—Formulas And Terms

SUMMARY OF FORMULAS

COST TO BORROW

Interest = Principal x Rate x Time

The amount of Interest you will be charged on a loan is equal to the amount of Principal you will borrow, times the Annual Percentage Rate, times the Time (number of days divided by 365) you will use these funds for. To calculate the monthly charge, be sure to divide the Rate by 12, and use that number in your above calculation under the Rate.

EMPLOYER'S WAGE CALCULATION

Once again, I must point out that, while this is not a formula, it is in fact a critical piece of information when it comes to determining the profitability of your business. You cannot afford to overlook what your real labor costs are, not only on the basis of financial costs, but of productivity as well.

A FOUNDATION FOR SALES COMMISSIONS

Many small business owners express frustration at the thought of dealing with this issue, and, yet, it is certainly critical to hire, and fairly compensate, well-qualified people, who are directly responsible for creating sales. This method recognizes the risks inherent to both the salesperson and the kitchen and bathroom dealer, and compensates both equitably.

JOB COSTING

One of the best methods you can use to determine where you are productive, and therefore profitable, is to employ a Job-Costing Analysis of each project you take on. The sample we use summarizes your success with respect to managing your remodeling projects.

CHAPTER 6
SUMMARY OF TERMS

TERM	DESCRIPTION
checklists	An affordable, convenient tool everyone within an organization can use to make better use of time and resources. Some examples are: materials checklist, job sequence checklist, punch lists.
collateral	Security for a loan. This would be a physical asset that has some unencumbered equity remaining.
commission basis	Compensation plan for salespeople paid as a percentage of Gross Sales. A salesperson's commissions.
controls	A built-in system of checks and balances, such as checklists and standard operating procedures, that you can employ in your business to avoid problems.
co-op funds for Advertising	Advertising monies available to dealers through their distributors for products produced by various manufacturers, requiring compliance with their guidelines.
early payment discounts	Discounts offered by your suppliers as an incentive to pay early, such as 2% 10 days net 30.
Federal Insurance Contributions Act (FICA)	At present, this amounts to 6.2 percent on wages up to $62,700 for both the employee and the employer. These are social security taxes which are deducted from one's paycheck.
hidden costs	This refers to expenses not recognized until it is too late to avoid them, such as fines and penalties.
job costing records	The process of recording costs on the basis of job-by-job detail, in order to build a profile as to how your business operates.
line of credit	Prior arrangement for funds as needed, with a cap, through your bank or commercial lender.
Medicare	At present, this amounts to 1.45 percent on all wages for both the employee and the employer. These Medicare taxes are deducted from one's paycheck.
payroll taxes	Known also as federal or state withholding, these are income taxes assessed to the business or individual or both on the earnings for a given period.
sale	A transaction consummated when something of value is exchanged for something else of value, usually money. An example: A contract between you and your customer has been completed to your mutual satisfaction.
target pricing	Using the Profit Based on Selling method. Target pricing is the price to sell at, with the most competitive and profitable return. This would be the ideal price assuring customer value and business profit.
tax deposits	Federal and state income taxes that have been withheld; FICA and Medicare taxes plus the employer's share of matching amounts of FICA and Medicare. Also called 941 taxes.
up-sell	Recommending services or products that enhance and make more valuable your customer's purchases, such as appliances you sell with a remodeling job.
80 - 20 rule	Also called the Pareto Principle, this means that 80 percent of your business will come from 20 percent of your customers.

Chapter 7

YOUR REAL PROFIT CENTER—THE CUSTOMER

The mill will never grind with the water that has passed. - Sarah Doudney

Small businesses today face greater competition than ever before and should examine every option to promote themselves. A focused strategy directed at a specific market niche has far greater return on marketing dollars than one which is geared toward attracting anyone and everyone. There is a widespread misconception that every customer is price sensitive, and yet consumer-marketing studies would indicate that price is not the most critical factor to the majority of the buying public. Surprisingly, the numbers are fairly evenly divided with respect to buyer preferences identified. We find that there are five distinct categories of buyers:

- 17 percent of shoppers categorize themselves as "disenchanted shoppers" who have given up on the idea that shopping can be fun.
- 22 percent of shoppers are strictly "price hounds," and price is the only consideration affecting their buying decisions.
- 20 percent consider themselves "bargain hunters," generally seeking out specific name brands at discount prices.
- 19 percent of shoppers indicate they are most concerned with "quality of service."
- 22 percent see themselves as "low interest" shoppers; people who find shopping a bore and buy primarily from those who can supply what they want when they want it.

SERVICE PROVIDER

These numbers represent retail buyers, but they are probably indicative of the general attitude of all buyers in their buying practices. Remember, you are not an ordinary retailer, but, rather, a provider of customer service. If you have written a mission statement, I hope you have addressed, within the body of that statement, both customer and service concerns. I feel strongly that you cannot be a service provider and a discount retailer at the same time.

On the other hand, many service providers believe they should also be discounters, frequently losing sight of their purpose in their efforts to be all things to all people. Then they wonder why they are not making a profit. If you look closely at the words "customer service," you realize they convey the idea of a business that provides unique or custom service.

You are, in effect, telling the public that your business is not only capable, but willing to be judged on the basis of your performance of providing that service. The public's perception of the added value you deliver is expressed in its willingness to pay the price you ask for your services, as well as in the repeat business the customer brings you. Your role as a service provider is to provide service, not to discount your prices. Your objective is to sell added value, not to compete on the basis of selling volume.

The first thing that the discounters in the retail field do is eliminate unnecessary expenses or costs. Their marketing efforts revolve around providing a "self-serve" atmosphere conducive to impulse buying. If you're not convinced of this, just take a look at the supermarket business, which has a marketing concept that is the most highly structured or engineered in the world. The customers don't stand a chance from the moment they enter the front door. If they come in to purchase milk, there is a very good chance they will leave with several additional items. Why? Where is the milk case located? At the very rear of the store, so they are forced to pass numerous other impulse-type items. Do as the supermarket industry has done and learn to understand your potential customers and their buying patterns, without losing your own identity in the process.

You are a seller of value, not commodities. As a seller of value, you should be able to develop your own marketing strategies to reach those customers who will buy at your level of pricing. Pricing is a strategy to be used properly by retailers, not incorrectly by providers of service.

TYPES OF BUYERS

- The first category of *disenchanted shoppers*, poses a challenge. If you can sell them on the fact that you are going to make it easy for them to do business with you, they may be interested in having you do the work. If they sense that you are just a high-pressure salesperson, they will not be interested in doing business with you. If, however, they like your style, they can become loyal customers, as well as a good source of referrals.

- The second category of buyers are the *price hounds*; the ones you want to avoid. You will spend a disproportionate amount of time and energy trying to get their business, and you will no doubt have to lower your prices to get the work. They are usually a headache to work with, and their only loyalty will be to the lowest price, not to the good service you have provided in the past.

- The *bargain hunters* represent a mixed bag. They are interested in a specific brand at a discounted price. If you are selling a service or service-related product, you are, in effect, the brand. Your challenge, then, is to make them see the value you are adding to the work as the real bargain.

- The *quality of service* customers are going to represent your *bread and butter*. They are already predisposed toward buying from you. Make it simple and pleasurable for them to do this, and they will become loyal customers who are willing to recommend you to others.

- The *low interest* buyers present a different type of challenge in that your job is to make them feel comfortable with the idea of shopping, or, more specifically, with the idea of shopping with you. You need to show them that you are willing and able to uncover their every need and concern, relative to this sale. Become a partner in seeking a solution to their problems. You are offering consultive selling here, which will become the key to making the sale.

Which of these groups should you target as your potential market? Certainly, when you consider the *80 - 20 rule*, it makes more sense to target those customers who will give you repeat business. Allow the *price hounds* to put the competition out of business, not you!

ARE YOU WORTH MORE?

Perception plays a much bigger role in our business than many of us realize. Focus on the role perception plays with respect to profit. If you are going to charge more for your services, you must make yourself worth more. If you can envision yourself as a true professional, you can think and act like one. Never underestimate the intelligence of your customers, because the minute you do, they will remind you of it by taking their business elsewhere. If they perceive you as being less than professional in your approach, they may mistakenly conclude that there isn't any value to working with you.

People buy from you because they perceive you can offer them something of value. However, there are thousands of other businesses that compete with you daily in order to get those customers to spend their money with them. You need to distinguish yourself from the rest of the competition. If you have a lot of money, you might consider spending it on an expensive advertising campaign. Many large and successful corporations do this, but they generally have sources of substantial financial support.

Public relations, on the other hand, can be one of the most cost-effective methods of getting your story out, though this, too, requires some planning and preparation. The leading companies, large and small alike, have found outstanding customer service to be one of the most effective marketing tools available.

CUSTOMER SERVICE

Customers reward those businesses providing outstanding customer service.

1. Is your company active in community events, charities, social clubs, schools, etc.?
2. Do you have an active public relations program? Is someone on staff assigned to this responsibility?
3. Do you make it easy for consumers to do business with you? Do you offer financing?
4. Do you provide extended warranties beyond those supplied by the manufacturers of the products you sell?
5. Do you thank customers for their business? How?
6. Do you provide conveniences during the installation process?
7. Do you follow up before, during and after the project is completed? A year later? Years later?
8. Do your installers and subcontractors understand the *customer service* concepts you have created in the showroom, and extend them into the customer's home during the installation process?
9. Is buying a kitchen or bathroom from your company a positive experience?
10. Would you buy a kitchen from your firm?

Xerox Corporation disclosed studies that indicate a satisfied customer is more than six times as likely to do repeat business with you. Remember the *80 - 20 rule*. Think about how really cost effective it can be to work with this portion of your customer base. These people already know who you are and what you do. They are predisposed toward buying from you because they believe you offer them something of value. In cases like this, outstanding customer service can help you to foster a long and profitable relationship.

A U.S. Department of Commerce study done in the 1980s concluded that the average cost of attracting a new customer to a business runs as high as $3,000. The cost of keeping those you have is certainly far less than that, and is potentially far more profitable. Many people would claim that there is a high price attached to customer service, and I would be the first to agree. However, a higher price is paid by not providing outstanding customer service! Each business has its moment of truth, and that occurs any time your customers have an opportunity to make a judgment about the quality of the service you offer them.

Have you ever stopped to think about that, and how it relates to your business? What are some of those occasions, and how might they negatively influence your customers? As a consumer, one of my pet peeves is getting an invoice or statement containing an error. When this happens, I want to call the company immediately to correct it. But, if the company has failed to print its phone number on the invoice, I must waste time looking up the number, and so waste more time fixing the company's mistake.

Carelessness and poor service are not designed into a business, but, rather like a virus, grow and spread, ultimately consuming it. By contrast, businesses which offer outstanding service do so because they have made a commitment to delivering it to their customers. That commitment is translated through an ongoing program of education and training for employees. In fact, for many of these businesses, training budgets have become part of their success, closely guarded from the competition. Even after training, this needs to be monitored regularly to ensure it is effective. Statistically speaking, only a small number of your customers will actually tell you if they are dissatisfied. The majority will simply go elsewhere. Making it even more difficult is the fact that no two people perceive service in exactly the same way. What might be good to one person may be less than exemplary for someone else. For you to maximize your efforts in this area, you must be willing to actively seek out your customers' responses to the service you provide, and be prepared to deal with whatever you turn up.

Dealing with these problems can be one of your most cost-effective avenues to building a long-term, distinctive and profitable relationship with your customers. When you can rightfully claim you have reached this level of distinctive service, you are also **managing for profit**. I have talked rather extensively about the significance of budgets and pricing your work so that you ensure your efforts will produce a profit. While all of that is true, it is also no more important than this critical issue of customer service, and, if this isn't handled properly, you won't have to worry about any of the others. Your customers are your business.

You are in a service business, selling yourself and the skills and talents of the people who work with and for you. Your customers can be a rich resource of contacts and referrals, if you will provide them with customer service.

EXCEPTIONAL CUSTOMER SERVICES

One of my former students relayed a story that illustrates this point. This student had a commercial building he wanted to have renovated. Instead of awarding a single contract to complete the work, he divided it up into four separate projects, each of which would be awarded to a different contractor. His intent was really to see who to hire on a much larger project he had in mind for the future. He was looking for a professional individual who was intent on distinguishing himself or herself by offering quality work. Each contractor completed the work, unaware that he or she was being tested. All seemed equally competent, but one individual paid more attention to detail. The work area was clean, employees were timely and they completed the work with a determination that was somehow lacking in the others. He finally settled on this contractor several weeks after the work was completed, when he received a phone call from him.

"Mr. Perry, this is Joe, the contractor who did some work for you about a month ago. The reason I am calling you is to find out if you are still as pleased with your job as you were a month ago when we finished the work. Is there anything we can do for you to correct any problems that may have developed since we were finished?" As Mr. Perry said, "This just about bowled me over, for I am accustomed to having contractors worry only about the next job, not one they did some time ago." Talk about maximizing profits!

Think about how much more mileage this contractor is getting on his investment, with just an additional phone call! This made such an impression on Mr. Perry that he is still relating this story some 15 years after the fact. How many times over these years did he have the opportunity to tell that story? How many referrals and recommendations do you suppose this contractor got because he took the time to make a call to show he cared about his customers?

Do you know how many professional sales people call their customers after the sale? Relatively few. Most of them are afraid they will hear bad news. How about you and your staff? Think about what a perfect opportunity you are passing up to help your customers resolve their problems and solidify their perception of you as a true **customer** *service provider*. Think of how you are distinguishing yourself from the competition, doing what you actually say you do! What better time to ask for referrals?

CONTRACTS PROVIDE A PROFESSIONAL PERCEPTION

I find that many service businesses don't use a written contract because they are afraid they may upset their customers. Somehow, they think it may reflect poorly on them, illustrating a lack of trust. They may be using this as an excuse, or this may be symptomatic of their inability to appreciate what a contract can do for them. The fact is, a written contract can reinforce your image as a true professional in your field. Several years ago, I overheard a conversation in a restaurant between a young couple and a man who represented himself as a full-service kitchen dealer.

The couple wanted to have this dealer build an addition for their kitchen, as well as supply the kitchen design and the products which would go into it. This dealer proceeded to write down all the details and complete his final calculations on a cocktail napkin! In about 5 minutes, he was able to come up with an exact price of only $25,000. He was either a fraud or a fool, because there was no way he could do that work for that amount of money. In all likelihood, he'd gotten himself into trouble on another job, and needed some immediate cash so he could finish it. Unfortunately, there are far too many people out there these days doing the same thing.

Think what a real professional might have done under similar circumstances. Hopefully, that person would have arranged to meet the client at the job site to see what physical limitations might exist. He or she would have brought along a portfolio, including photos of work done for other satisfied customers, and maybe a letter of recommendation. They could have all sat down and discussed the project, using feedback to uncover potential problems or ways to improve upon the owner's original idea. A real professional would have reassured the clients of what they could expect, educating the customers to help them understand the process.

After completing some preliminary drawings and calculations, our professional would then arrange to return with a written proposal, an estimate of the time required to complete the project, the cost to complete the work and the method of payment required. At that time, the professional would encourage and answer any questions the clients might have, reviewing the written contract which explained each party's rights and responsibilities under the terms of the contract. The contract would then be used as a means of closing the deal. Following this whole procedure would make the professional worth more. It doesn't take a lot to distinguish your business, but it does require some forethought and planning. You certainly won't be the cheapest around, but at least you will know that every job you are doing will make you a profit.

(You may want to review NKBA's contracts and business management forms to help you establish a professional perception.)

Customers buy from us because we are able to satisfy their needs and wants. Which of the two, needs or wants, do you think exerts the most influence on their buying decision? The answer quite simply is the one with the greatest emotional attachment. Just ask yourself whenever you have made a purchase, which has influenced you more? When there is little or no emotional attachment, we are more likely to buy the most utilitarian product, but, when there is an attachment, we are very likely to stretch our budget in order to really get what we want.

All one has to do is look in a mail-order catalog, or visit a nearby department store. They don't sell one style or model of anything. In fact, many of these merchandisers are counting on their wide variety and selections to draw you to them so that you will make your final buying decision there.

It's quite easy to forget that your potential client, that prospect sitting across from you, desires nothing less than to have his or her wants met, as well as needs.

VALUE

Throughout this book I have been saying, "Make yourself worth more, sell value." By the term "value," I do not simply mean a high-end line of cabinets. I mean to exceed your customer's expectations throughout the entire experience. You can only do that well, if you are listening, not so much to what they are saying, but rather by what they are telling you. They are not very likely to tell you much at all, unless they trust you. When was the last time you and your staff really sat down and did some brainstorming on how your company presents value to your customers?

CHAPTER 7

Reference Information—Terms

CHAPTER 7 SUMMARY OF TERMS	
TERM	**DESCRIPTION**
discounters	A term applied primarily to large retail chains or mass merchandisers who discount their products deeply.
market niche	That segment of the market which you target specifically, such as a certain neighborhood, or region of the city, which you have delineated by age and income.
price sensitive	A perception formed mentally, often only by the salesperson, as to what is driving the customer's purchasing decision. For instance, a sale made to a customer in which the parties have concluded the only real value being exchanged was price.
written contract	A written obligation to provide a service or product in exchange for some form of compensation of equal value, in most cases—money.

Chapter 8

IT'S WHAT YOU DON'T KNOW
THAT CAN HURT YOU!

In the world there is nothing more submissive and weak than water. Yet for attacking that which is hard and strong nothing can surpass it. - Lao-Tzu

There simply isn't any room to make assumptions in business. Your job is to ferret out the truth, and that isn't always an easy task. The reality is that even when you or an employee make an honest mistake, it can very well cost your business dearly. Missing a deadline for the submission of a report or the payment of taxes, as we pointed out earlier, can result in excess fines and penalties. There are thousands of other examples, as well, but I would like to focus on a few that could have a profound impact on your business.

CONTRACT ISSUES

Due to the nature of your work as designers and remodelers, you will no doubt have an opportunity to bid on work as part of a larger remodeling or new construction project. Construction contract law, which differs somewhat from the usual variety of commercial contract law, provides that the contractor, or the subcontractor, has an obligation to perform all the work specified in the contract documents. This applies even when an item of work appears in the specifications and not the drawings. You can see how critical your performance at this stage of the process can be. Imagine the consequences of overlooking something and learning after the fact that you were nevertheless responsible for it.

A standard approach to preparing estimates will surely help to limit mistakes either in the form of errors or omissions. As you and your staff become better acquainted with the process through repeated use, you should be able to realize dramatic improvement. Mistakes in the estimating process are probably the leading cause of why proposals are improperly prepared and submitted, resulting in a loss, when they are discovered too late. A uniform and consistent approach should be in place and used routinely in order to allow everyone involved in the preparation of the quote to question when an item has been overlooked.

EMPLOYEE VS. CONTRACT LABOR

There is a popular misconception among business owners and managers with respect to the issue of employees and contract labor. There is and has been an "underground economy," and it places a significant burden on those businesses which try to play by the rules. The U.S. Government estimates that more than $20 billion are lost each year in unreported taxes.

At a time that when the cost of government operations is reeling under the weight of enormous debt, it is responding by cracking down in an effort to recoup some of these lost earnings. One area they have been particularly vigilant about is the issue of independent business status and whether or not it is being used as a tax dodge. When employers illegally use this ploy, they realize several immediate benefits which give them a competitive advantage over those businesses that pay their fair share. Retirement and healthcare taxes go unpaid as do unemployment taxes. Unknowingly, the employer and independent contractor are at substantial risk, and, have no doubt placed others at risk because they have no worker's compensation insurance coverage. Employees, who are not legitimate independent contractors, may not realize that they also stand to lose substantial business deductions they may have taken in past years, and may have to invalidate contributions made to retirement programs. Beyond all this lies the prospect that if the employer is found guilty of using this as a tax dodge, the fines and penalties that can be imposed can be overwhelming for the small-business person.

What is the likelihood of getting caught? The IRS now claims that reviewing a company's 1099 reports is considered to be a part of what they refer to as a "package audit," and is an area they are continuing to emphasize. There is strong evidence they are doing just that.

A kitchen dealer told me of his company's recent experience with this very issue. It seems their business had established a relationship with an individual some 3 years prior, and had encouraged this individual to set up his own business and to incorporate it, which he did. Over the next 3 years this individual did virtually all their installation work. The IRS recently informed the dealer that they were ruling that this individual was an employee of theirs, and not a true independent contractor as they had claimed. Of course, the dealer protested on the basis that this individual had incorporated his business, and obtained the necessary business licenses. The IRS responded that since they had no proof they had ever obtained any competitive bids on their work and that the majority of the individual's income was derived exclusively from them, they were in fact his employers during the period in question. The IRS is also now requesting a further audit of some prior years' activity.

This dealer does not honestly know whether or not they can survive this crisis. Whether they close their doors or not makes little difference to the IRS. They will collect, one way or the other.

TEST YOUR BUSINESS

While U.S. laws can be a bit confusing and ambiguous concerning subcontractors, the penalties are quite clear. If the IRS determines that employees are being misclassified as subcontractors, they can force you to pay, not only back payroll taxes, social security taxes, unemployment taxes, and federal income tax withholding, but also any penalties and interest that may have accrued.

Canadian enforcement of laws pertaining to subcontractors is not nearly so stringent. However, Revenue Canada has established that if installers or other subcontractors perform work for one contractor more than 66 percent of the time, the work will be considered personal services rather than corporate services and the subcontractor will be classified as an employee. The contractor is then liable for paying taxes on the employee. Revenue Canada audits trades randomly to enforce this regulation.

The U.S. IRS, in its Training Manuals 8463 and 3142-01, lists 20 factors used to determine whether an individual is an independent contractor or an employee. If you, as an employer, have any doubts, you would be wise to check with your certified public accountant. The IRS also publishes a very thorough explanation of those 20 questions along with some excellent examples which may provide you with an idea of how they determine whether an individual is, in fact, an independent contractor or an employee. Publication 15-A, "Employer's Supplemental Tax Guide," is available through your local IRS office.

20 QUESTIONS

1. Is the individual providing services required to comply with instruction on when, where and how the work is done?
2. Is the individual provided with training to enable him or her to perform the job in a particular manner?
3. Are the services performed by the individual a part of the contractor's business operations?
4. Must services be rendered personally?
5. Does the contractor hire, supervise, or pay assistants to help the individual performing under the contract?
6. Is the relationship between the parties a continuing one?
7. Who sets the hours of work?
8. Is the individual required to devote full time to the party for whom the services are performed?
9. Does the individual perform work on another's business premises?
10. Who directs the sequence in which the work must be done?
11. Are regular oral or written reports required?
12. What is the method of payment—hourly, weekly, commission, or by the job?

13. Are business or traveling expenses reimbursed?
14. Who furnishes the tools and materials necessary for the provision of services?
15. Does the individual have significant investment in the tools or facilities used to perform his or her services?
16. Can the individual providing services realize profit or loss?
17. Can the individual providing services work for a number of firms at the same time?
18. Does the individual make his or her services available to the general public?
19. Can the individual be dismissed for reasons other than non-performance of contract specifications?
20. Can the individual providing services terminate his or her relationship at any time without incurring a liability for failure to complete a job?

OWNER'S INSURANCE

Worker's compensation insurance for owners, in many states or provinces, may be an option rather than a requirement, however, that also leads to some other little known problems for these same owners. Check with your insurance agent on your personal hospitalization or major medical policy, and ascertain whether or not you may fall under any type of clause which automatically excludes any work-related injuries or illness. Some policies will automatically exclude the owner if such coverage was available through an industrial policy and was rejected by the owner. In such a case, the coverage would not be afforded the owner and the owner would then be liable for his or her own medical bills. That may really be a problem for many people who are not aware of such a clause.

HOME OFFICES

The U.S. Supreme Court has ruled that business owners must, in effect, prove that they use their home office as the *principal place* for conducting their business, before they may legitimately claim it as a business deduction. Unfortunately, they remain rather vague on this issue as to what truly constitutes a principal place. In a ruling likely to have implications for you, the IRS issued an information release (IR 93-12), concerning this very issue. The results of this court ruling and the IRS release make it incumbent upon you to prove that you are in compliance. Even in the event that you spend the majority of the time in your office, it is where you actually conduct your business with your clients that may be the determining factor. Should that not be in your home office, you may not qualify for the home-office deduction. Check with your accountant.

OCCUPATIONAL SAFETY AND HEALTH TRAINING

There have been significant changes in the application of Occupational Safety and Health Administration (OSHA) regulations. The regulations now require you as the employer to use extraordinary care and responsibility for your employees and the various chemicals and products they may be exposed to on the job site. Training and reporting requirements have all increased significantly. Nobody wishes to see anybody hurt or maimed at work. Unfortunately, many government agencies responsible for enforcement of federal legislation are self-funded and are mandated by law to levy fines and penalties, where appropriate.

These policies make your compliance all the more critical as they can have a devastating impact on your bottom line.

Training plays a significant role in all of this and, in fact, is no longer a choice but a mandate. Record keeping is also a critical requirement and, in most cases, ignorance of the law is no excuse. To their credit, OSHA is making a new service available to the employer which allows you to request assistance and a cursory review to make sure all your policies comply with these regulations. Call your local OSHA administrator for details. For more information, refer to the Code of Federal Regulations, Part 1926.

AMERICANS WITH DISABILITIES ACT

This is another piece of legislation you may already be familiar with. Accessible restroom facilities in all public buildings and facilities have long been a requirement. Through this piece of legislation, however, small businesses are also required to comply. While you may only perform residential work, your showroom qualifies as a public commercial space and is therefore subject to the Americans with Disabilities Act (ADA) regulations. Now you also need to look into your own responsibilities as an employer under the terms of this act. Failure to comply can expose you to substantial risk.

KEEP EMPLOYEES INFORMED

If all of this information is important to employers, why shouldn't it also be important for employees? I have had some people attend my seminars with their employees, and they came away convinced it was the smartest thing they could have done. Once employees realize the scope and necessity of this information, and the corresponding responsibilities associated with running a business, they will generally have a better appreciation of the task at hand. And they can better assist you, because they do understand.

Share information with managers and supervisors. You will be creating a different environment, but one which will be more open and healthier, in terms of encouraging commitment, accountability and responsibility.

The problem with all these unknown situations is that they have serious implications. Because you are unaware of them, you don't allow for them as you develop an overall operating strategy and budget. When this happens you are forced to accommodate the additional burden they pose with your profits.

CHAPTER 8

Reference Information—Terms

CHAPTER 8
SUMMARY OF TERMS

TERM	DESCRIPTION
Americans with Disabilities Act (ADA)	Federal legislation that mandates compliance with access and egress requirements for people with physical and mental disabilities. This is also applicable to the workplace.
assumptions	Based upon available information, it is a person's best estimate of how to handle a situation. Usually, however, there is much room for improvement, such as more research to uncover previously unknown facts. An example is a financial assumption, a "guesstimate" instead of an estimate.
business deductions	Costs of sales and operational expenses, such as materials, rent and insurance, deducted from the revenues of a business in order to determine taxable income
contract laborer	An individual compensated to perform work and responsible for the results rather than the methods. Must also perform according to the guidelines in IRS Publication 15-A. An example would be an independent contractor, such as a plumbing contractor, painting contractor or electrical contractor.
employee	An individual compensated to work where, when and how he or she is directed to by a supervisor, owner or manager according to the guidelines in IRS Publication 15-A.
estimate	Frequently confused with a quote, an estimate is a price for your customer, generally based upon available information with respect to how much you intend to complete on a project and how long you calculate it will take.
mistakes	The leading cause for loss of profits on kitchen and bathroom remodeling jobs, and yet simple checklists could do much to correct these problems. Mistakes include errors, omissions, inattention to detail, poor take offs, etc.
quote	Also known as a proposal or bid, this is a written document which lays out the scope of the work, the specifications and related documentation such as drawings. An example is a firm estimate and commitment to your customer to complete the described work within a reasonable time for the agreed upon charges.
1099 reports	The IRS form on which a business reports payments it has made during the course of the previous year, to independent contractors.

Chapter 9

FINANCIAL RATIOS—
HOW OTHERS WILL JUDGE YOU

The pond sends up its lyrics from its dark in lilies, and the sun says, they are good. - Rabindranath Tagore

The gathering of vital information for the purpose of establishing your financial position requires consistency and accuracy. So, too, will the task of analyzing this information to use for comparative purposes. Unless you use some reliable measures, such as your own historical performance or the parameters for industry standards, it will be difficult for those evaluating your financial information to make an honest assessment of where you really are. You can improve the value of your financial reports if they are prepared in accordance with recognized procedures.

Accepted accounting standards might well provide you with some insight to where you should be headed, but remember there are variables unique to your business and the kitchen and bathroom industry. It would seem to make sense to use the services of your accountant to help you with the correct interpretation of the ratios you will compute after reading this chapter.

(The information used to determine the following financial ratios is taken from both the **SECOND YEAR BALANCE SHEET** and the **INCOME AND EXPENSE STATEMENT** introduced previously for our fictional business.)

BALANCE SHEET - SECOND YEAR
Projected December 31, 1996

ASSETS

Current Assets:
Cash	$26,531
Accounts Receivable	4,715
Inventory	130,642
Prepaid Expenses	8,307
Other Current Assets	0
Total Current Assets	$170,195

Net Fixed or Plant Assets:
Buildings	71,300	
Equipment & Machinery	25,637	
Vehicles	14,950	
Other Fixed Assets	22,957	
	$134,844	
Accumulated Depreciation	(9,833)	
Total Net Fixed Assets		125,011
Other Assets		0
Total Assets		$295,206

LIABILITIES & OWNER'S EQUITY

Current Liabilities:
Accounts Payable	37,080
Accrued Expenses	2,551
Income Taxes Payable	1,047
Short Term Notes Payable	0
Total Current Liabilities	$40,678

Long-Term Liabilities:
Installment Debt Payable	$98,968
Mortgage Payable	0
Other Long-Term Liabilities	0
Total Long-Term Liabilities	$98,968
Total Liabilities	$139,646

Owner's Equity
Paid-In Capital	$89,133
Retained Earnings	66,427
Total Owner's Equity	$155,560
Total Liab & Owner's Equity	$295,206

INCOME AND EXPENSE STATEMENT
Period Ending December 31, 1996

	1995 (Actual)	1996 (Projected)	(Y-T-D)
Revenues From Sales	$529,500	$635,400	
Cost of Sales			
Direct Costs			
Labor	76,672	92,362	
Equipment Rental	2,125	3,500	
Materials	189,751	201,000	
Sub-Contracts	51,787	40,500	
Indirect Costs			
License Fees	5,500	8,300	
Training Fees	1,500	2,500	
Sales Commissions		12,963	
Contingency Fees	7,943	9,531	
Total Cost of Sales	$335,278	$370,656	
Gross Margin	$194,223	$264,744	
Operating Expenses			
Administrative Salaries	$18,225	$31,350	
Payroll Taxes	6,891	8,562	
Rent	37,065	36,000	
Telephone & Utilities	4,050	4,200	
Insurance	11,040	12,000	
Advertising	23,061	20,000	
Maintenance & Repairs	1,544	2,200	
Gas & Oil	3,716	3,900	
Depreciation	9,833	9,833	
Travel & Entertainment	2,979	1,750	
Non-Income Taxes	367	450	
Owner's Compensation	39,202	40,000	
Other Operating Expenses	1,328	1,200	
Total Operating Expenses	$159,301	$171,445	
Net Operating Income	$34,921	$93,299	
Interest Expense	10,371	10,468	
Other Income	0	0	
Net Income Before Taxes	$24,550	$82,831	
Income Tax Expense	3,311	16,404	
Net Income	$21,239	$66,427	

COMPARATIVE RATIO ANALYSIS
Fictional Business
(Compares First Year Financial Reports Introduced in Chapter 3)

		1995	1996
Current Ratio	=	1.7563	4.1840
Acid Test Ratio (Quick Ratio)	=	0.8779	0.9723
Total Asset Turnover (ATO)	=	2.0026	2.1524
Average Collection Period (ACP)	=	35.0973	2.7207
Inventory Turn Over (ITO)	=	3.7365	2.8372
Daily Sales In Inventory (DSI)	=	97.6850	129.2206
Debt To Assets (D/A)	=	0.5919	0.3353
Debt To Equity (D/E)	=	1.4505	0.6362
Equity Modifier (EM)	=	2.4500	1.8977
Profit Margin (PM)	=	0.0354	0.1045
Times Interest Earned (TIE)	=	6.6672	8.9128
Return On Assets (ROA)	=	0.0710	0.2250
Return On Equity (ROE)	=	0.1793	0.4270

Ratio Analysis has its limitations. Most of this analysis is meaningful only when it can be compared to actual historical performance within your own business or to industry standards. None of these measures represent "correct" values. Ask your accountant to go over these ratios with you the first few times, so you don't misinterpret their significance. Remember as interested as you may be in the benefits of any financial decisions, you must also be able to recognize the costs associated with them as well.

RATIOS

Ratios are sets of numbers, financial calculations, which show the relationship between similar things. We can identify the major categories of financial ratios as follows: *Liquidity, Leverage, Turnover* and *Profitability*.

LIQUIDITY RATIOS

Also known as Solvency Ratios, these ratios are used to alert management to a shift in the company's financial position due to a change in the relationship between the firm's current assets and its current liabilities. *Liquidity Ratios* look at the firm's ability to access its current assets in a timely fashion in order to pay its creditors for their current claims. These consist of two separate ratios, the Current Ratio and the Quick Ratio.

Target Audience: Lenders, investors and management. You can be sure that anyone you approach to borrow or invest in your business will want to know how able you are to meet your short-term or current obligations. Additionally, you and your manager should be aware, so you can make financial decisions which will not have a negative impact on what may already be a delicate position.

Current Ratio

The *Current Ratio*, the most familiar measure of solvency, is the basic test for the ability to pay short-term debt. It is determined by dividing the company's current assets by its current liabilities. The result gives you the first part of the relationship to a dollar (?:1). If your ratio is 2:1, it means the business has $2 in current assets for every $1 in current liabilities. The higher the current ratio, the greater the cushion between the company's current portion of its debt, and its ability to satisfy that debt. A strong ratio is an indication that the current assets are significantly more than the firm's current liabilities, but the composition and character of these assets should be of paramount importance in evaluating the company's solvency.

$$\text{Current Ratio} = \frac{\text{current assets}}{\text{current liabilities}}$$

Quick Ratio

The *Quick Ratio*, also known as the *acid test*, uses essentially the same information required in determining the Current Ratio, but is a better measure of the ability of the business to pay current liabilities. This ratio employs only those current assets that can be quickly converted to cash, divided by current liabilities. If you are below the 1.0 - 2.0 range (have $1 - $2 in cash and receivables for every $1 in current liabilities), you have too little invested in your business; if it is above, you probably have too much invested.

$$\text{Quick Ratio} = \frac{\text{cash + receivables}}{\text{current liabilities}}$$

THE LIQUIDITY RATIOS

The Liquidity Ratios

> The function of these ratios is to alert management as to when the company's position is more precarious because its current or liquid assets in relation to its current liabilities is in the process of slipping. With the acid test, management gets a more realistic picture since, as a rule, inventory is generally not considered a very liquid asset. The inventory may be damaged, obsolete and either miscounted or even non-existent. These ratios can be used effectively to indentify trends in their early stages and take corrective action.

$$\text{The Current Ratio} = \frac{\text{current assets}}{\text{current liabilities}} \qquad 4.18 = \frac{170{,}195}{40{,}678}$$

Recommended 2.00

$$\text{Acid Test (also known as the quick ratio)} = \frac{\text{current assets - inventory}}{\text{current liabilities}} \qquad 0.97 = \frac{39{,}553}{40{,}678}$$

Recommended 1.00

LEVERAGE RATIOS

These ratios are used to measure the firm's indebtedness. That indebtedness may help your current position, but very likely at the expense of your future earnings. *Leverage Ratios* are used to identify the relationship of the firm's debt to the equity of the owner's in the business. Are you relying too much on debt? Maybe this debt is easing your current financial position, but you must also learn to think of it as pledging away your future earnings!

Target Audience: Lenders, investors and owners. Your friendly banker and commercial lender are going to be interested in these numbers, because they want to be sure there is some equity present that has value as collateral. Investors and owners want assurance that the debt position won't be so suffocating that there won't be future earnings.

Times Interest Earned

Times Interest Earned (TIE) is one ratio that should become an important barometer for you to watch whenever you are considering assuming deeper financial obligations. It measures earnings before the payment of interest and taxes. Why is that important? You must use those earnings in order to meet those very same obligations.

$$\text{Times Interest Earned} = \frac{\text{net operating income}}{\text{interest expense}}$$

Debt To Asset Ratio

The *Debt to Asset Ratio* (D/A) indicates which portion of the firm's assets are being financed. A sudden downturn in the economy or in the local market, reducing the effectiveness of the asset to that business, will not have a corresponding reduction on the finance charges that are due.

$$\text{Debt To Asset (D/A)} = \frac{\text{total liabilities}}{\text{total assets}}$$

Debt/Equity Ratio

The *Debit/Equity Ratio* (D/E) is an indication of the capital invested in the business by the owners (the equity portion), and how much of the business belongs to the claims of its creditors (the debt portion); in other words, it measures your business' debt load. A smaller number is better. A high ratio of debt to equity would indicate a potentially higher risk to the creditors. A lower ratio would generally be interpreted as an indication of financial safety and probably greater ease in borrowing later on.

$$\text{Debt/Equity Ratio (D/E)} = \frac{\text{total liabilities}}{\text{owner's equity}}$$

Equity Multiplier

The Equity Multiplier (EM), or total assets divided by equity, is a measure of the dollars in assets being used for each dollar of equity. A high ratio might indicate the owner's investment is being managed profitably with efficient use of those assets. A low number might indicate a more liquid position. However, it might also indicate inefficient or obsolete equipment or unsellable inventory.

Equity Multiplier Ratio $= \dfrac{\text{total assets}}{\text{owner's equity}}$

THE LEVERAGE RATIOS

The Leverage Ratios

> Are you relying too much on debt? It may be affecting your current performance, but you must also learn to think of it as pledging away your future earnings! The TIE should be one very important barometer you watch. It measures earnings before the payment of interest and taxes, because you must use those earnings in order to meet those very same obligations. The D/A indicates which portion of the company's assets are being financed. The D/E then reflects the relationship of long-term financing to its debt. The EM is the dollar amount of the assets it uses for each dollar of equity.

$$\text{Times Interest Earned} = \frac{\text{net operating income}}{\text{interest expense}} \qquad 8.91 = \frac{93,299}{10,468}$$

$$\text{Debt To Asset (D/A)} = \frac{\text{total liabilities}}{\text{total assets}} \qquad 0.34 = \frac{98,968}{295,206}$$

$$\text{Debt To Equity (D/E)} = \frac{\text{total liabilities}}{\text{owner's equity}} \qquad 0.64 = \frac{98,968}{155,560}$$

$$\text{Equity Multiplier (EM)} = \frac{\text{total assets}}{\text{owner's equity}} \qquad 1.90 = \frac{295,206}{155,560}$$

THE TURNOVER RATIOS

How efficiently is management utilizing the assets of the firm in the course of its daily operations? That question can be answered by using the *Turnover Ratios*. Turnover Ratios, also referred to as Efficiency or Asset Management Ratios, are tools used to measure how effectively the overall operation of the business is being managed.

Target Audience: Investors, owners and managers. Investors are looking for confidence that management knows how to produce optimal returns on their investments. Owners and managers will look to these ratios to provide them with a gauge to measure their progress at controlling costs and properly utilizing the resources at hand.

The Turnover Ratios consist of the following:

Average Collection Period

The *Average Collection Period* (ACP) is arrived at by taking the *accounts receivable* figure, dividing by *net sales* for the period, and multiplying that number by the number of days in the accounting period. The answer represents the average number of days to collect your money.

$$\text{Average Collection Period (ACP)} = \frac{\text{accounts receivable}}{\text{daily sales}}$$

Inventory Turnover

The *Inventory Turnover* (ITO) reflects how frequently the inventory is turned over in the course of the accounting period.

$$\text{Inventory Turnover (ITO)} = \frac{\text{cost of goods sold}}{\text{inventory}}$$

Days of Sales in Inventory

The *Days of Sales in Inventory*, (DSI), reflects how well your inventory is being managed. Too much on hand ties up funds that could be put to better use. Insufficient inventory results in lost opportunities for sales.

$$\text{Days of Sales In Inventory (DSI)} = \frac{\text{inventory}}{\text{daily cost of goods sold}}$$

Asset Turnover

The *Asset Turnover* (ATO) reflects how many dollars in sales are generated by the wise management of the firm's assets.

$$\text{Asset Turnover (ATO)} = \frac{\text{revenues from sales}}{\text{total assets}}$$

THE TURNOVER RATIOS

The Turnover Ratios

> We need tools to see how effectively you are managing the operations of the business and that's the function of the turnover ratios. ACP is a measure of how long it is taking you to convert your customer's invoices to cash. Money costs money and someone always pays. If not your customer, then you! The ITO will show you how many times in the course of the year you turn the inventory. The DSI is the reciprocal of the ITO and will show how many days worth of inventory you have on hand. The ATO informs us how many dollars in sales are generated per dollar of assets.

$$\text{Average collection period (ACP)} = \frac{\text{accounts receivable}}{\text{daily sales}} \qquad 2.72 = \frac{4{,}715}{1{,}733}$$

$$\text{Inventory turnover (ITO)} = \frac{\text{cost of goods sold}}{\text{inventory}} \qquad 2.84 = \frac{370{,}656}{130{,}642}$$

$$\text{Days of sales in inventory (DSI)} = \frac{\text{inventory}}{\text{daily cost of goods sold}} \qquad 129.22 = \frac{130{,}642}{1{,}011}$$

$$\text{Asset turnover (ATO)} = \frac{\text{revenues from sales}}{\text{total assets}} \qquad 2.15 = \frac{635{,}400}{295{,}206}$$

PROFITABILITY RATIOS

Profitability Ratios are used to measure the firm's relative profitability from the sale of its products and services. Here we are interested in learning whether or not your management of your kitchen and bathroom business is producing a return.

Target Audience: Lenders, investors, owners and managers. These ratios tell lenders whether or not you are capable of paying back whatever capital you ask to borrow. Investors and owners want to know whether they are throwing good money after bad, or whether their commitment will pay off. Managers will see these results as a yardstick of their performance.

Profit Margin

The *Profit Margin* (PM), also called *Return-On-Sales* (%) or *Net Profit*, is expressed by dividing the *Net Income* by the *Total Sales*.

$$\text{Profit Margin} = \frac{\text{net income}}{\text{revenues from sales}}$$

Return On Assets

The *Return on Assets* (ROA) is a measure of the role your assets played in producing your firm's net income. Before making a decision to replace one asset with another, however, work closely with your accountant to determine what your real costs will be.

$$\text{Return On Assets (ROA)} = \frac{\text{net income}}{\text{total assets}}$$

Return On Equity

The *Return on Equity* (ROE) is a measure of management's ability to make a good return on the stockholder's or owner's investment. A higher percentage is better. Compare this figure to the return you could receive on your money in other investments. This will show how well your small business measures up. *Net Income*, divided by *Equity*, provides us with the ratio we are looking for here.

$$\text{Return On Equity (ROE)} = \frac{\text{net income}}{\text{owner's equity}}$$

THE PROFITABILITY RATIOS

The Profitability Ratios

> The PM is an indicator of the profits generated through the sales of its products and services. In order to interpret these ratios in a meaningful way, management should have an idea of any trends within his or her own business or the industry norm. The ROA calculates the return earned by employing those assets within the operation of the business. The ROE should be of vital concern to management, because it represents the measure of the company's performance during this period of time. Are they creating wealth for themselves and/or their investors? Enough so they will able to attract new investment capital when they require it?

$$\text{Profit Margin (PM)} = \frac{\text{net income}}{\text{revenues from sales}} \qquad 10.45\% = \frac{66{,}427}{635{,}400}$$

$$\text{Return On Assets (ROA)} = \frac{\text{net income}}{\text{total assets}} \qquad 22.50\% = \frac{66{,}427}{295{,}206}$$

$$\text{Return On Equity (ROE)} = \frac{\text{net income}}{\text{owner's equity}} \qquad 42.70\% = \frac{66{,}427}{155{,}560}$$

INTERPRETING FINANCIAL RATIOS

In interpreting financial ratios, work with your performance numbers from prior fiscal periods. Together with your accountant and management team, take note of changes. Throughout much of my discussion, I have referred to your *trade secret*. The numbers themselves are not your trade secret, rather *how* you achieved them. By understanding what these numbers represent within your business, you will come to appreciate how much influence you can have over the direction of your business. With this information, you can easily redirect your business or redefine its mission and develop new goals, but only if you can appreciate what these numbers are telling you.

One important issue with respect to these numbers is that you may be easily manipulated by them. If your only focus is to make the numbers look good, then it may have a telling effect on your management objectives. For instance, none of these ratios has a *correct* value and yet people usually assume a higher value is correct, when just the opposite might be true. If you concentrated your efforts on building your cash reserves or increasing your inventory, mainly because you believed it was important to ensure a high current ratio, you might be making poor use of your resources. Use the resources available to you to their maximum benefit, not to achieve high ratios. Let's review the ratios and note what you need to look at as you evaluate your firm's performance.

The Liquidity Ratios

The *Current Ratio* is generally a ratio of 2:1 or better is recommended for most businesses. Why? Because a higher ratio indicates that you are in a better position to meet your current obligations. A lower ratio would indicate that you might have difficulty meeting those obligations, and turning to an outside source for funding may be more difficult.

The *Quick Ratio* or Acid test is an even more severe examination of your position since it eliminates inventory from the equation. While you certainly want to maintain a position balanced more in your favor than that of your creditors, any change reflecting a rapid deterioration from a prior period should be reason to investigate more closely, as to why this has happened. By using these ratios to identify trends early, you can still take corrective action before things get out of control.

The Leverage Ratios

The *Leverage Ratios* reflect your dependence upon debt. Since debt payments are fixed, they must be made even when the revenues may be off. Too many debt payments and poor revenues will result in insufficient cash flow, which could lead to default.

The *Debt to Asset Ratio*. The assets of the organization consist, among other things, of the tools and equipment used within the business. If too much of their value is claimed by the creditors, then their use affords little or possibly no benefit to the owners. Before you decide to go into further debt, examine this D/A ratio closely. There may be no return to you as the owner, because all you are really doing is working to pay off the purchase.

The *Debt to Equity Ratio* is another indicator your investors will be interested in. If it is disproportionately weighted in favor of the creditors, there may be little opportunity for you to realize a profit that can actually be distributed to them.

The *Equity Multiplier* indicates the relationship between the equity and the assets of the firm. A higher number should be a strong indicator that the investor's and/or owner's money has been used to purchase more of the assets outright. Thus their effective use should result in a greater return to those claiming an equity position.

The Turnover Ratios

Once again these *Turnover Ratios* will be used by others to gauge the effectiveness of your management style. Get in the habit of using these yourself and you will have access to important information regarding your ability to collect your money, manage your inventory and make productive use of your assets.

The *Average Collection Period* or ACP is one you can expect both lenders and investors to look at frequently. A long ACP, certainly anything in excess of 30 days should be reason for concern. If your money is out in the form of receivables owed to you by your customers, you are not earning anything with it and it may very well be the reason you are not paying your suppliers on time. You don't have to be a banker in the kitchen and bathroom industry. There are alternative means of helping your clients finance their purchases without using your money. Investigate credit card plans and third-party financing programs.

The *Inventory Turnover* (ITO) Ratio is an indicator of how many times you turn over your inventory in the course of the year. This is one ratio that might very well be skewed for the kitchen and bathroom industry. Ordinarily you would not order inventory items such as cabinets and countertops until you needed them, since your jobs are essentially custom. Thus your ratio will be rather low compared to a manufacturer. A better use of this tool might be to gauge where and when you can pare back your inventory.

Days of Sales in Inventory. How much inventory do you actually need in any given area? This is one question that only you and your own past performance might indicate. Looking to industry norms won't help. You have to have inventory, but, when it is surplus to your needs, it's costing you money that could be better spent elsewhere.

Asset Turnover (ATO) Ratio is a measure of how profitably you are using the assets of the business to generate sales. A review of this number may not pinpoint where you should look to get a handle on which assets are not being used productively; however, it will lead you to ask some tougher questions about how each of your assets is being employed. Frequently within a business, there is a rush to go out and buy the latest technology. You feel that you must have it. Aside from the question of how to finance the purchase, you would do well to analyze how effectively you are already using your existing assets. Maybe it's time to dispose of a non-productive asset that is costing you money for maintenance, insurance and space.

The Profitability Ratios

These ratios are used to measure management's success in operating a profitable business.

The *Profit Margin* reveals how much of each dollar in sales is returned in the form of profit. As you examine the results, keep in mind that, as we have already explored in this book, profit is not merely what you get to keep. These sometimes elusive profits must be poured back into the business to help it grow, develop and compete. This ratio, as a low number, without telling you where to look, alerts you to the fact that you require at least some fine tuning and perhaps more drastic measures.

The other two profit ratios, the *Return On Assets (ROA)* and *Return On Equity (ROE)*, will be used by others to evaluate your management effectiveness. The ROA ratio is a measure of your effectiveness in managing the assets of the business. Are they being utilized as effectively as they might or is this a problem area? The ROE is certainly going to be of interest to investors and to yourself. Think of this as their confidence index. A higher number is an indication of your ability to create wealth and that is the primary purpose of being in business.

SUMMARY

In summary, as beneficial as it may appear to use these ratios, keep in mind that they can be used most effectively as they apply to your own business. Even on an industry-wide basis, the type of business activity, the capital structure, size and experience of the business will all impact these ratios. They cannot replace sound judgment and they don't provide solutions to the problem areas they focus on. Work with your accountant, your employees and suppliers to develop systems that will help you monitor and prescribe corrective measures.

RETURN ON INVESTMENT

Bottom line profits are the most important *return on investments* for stockholders and owners. It is a measure of how effective you have been in meeting two stated objectives, namely to **make a profit** and to see that the business **increases in value** over time.

You need to give yourself every conceivable advantage, and using the right tool for the right job is essential to the task at hand. This chapter has discussed the tools commonly used in business to make interpretations. Those interpretations will be used by others whether you like it or not, whether or not you understand them or even use them yourself. In all likelihood, these other people probably won't even be familiar with the kitchen and bathroom industry. They will be your bankers, your lenders, your investors, and maybe even your landlords. Each one will have the ability to impact your business. (See exhibits entitled **RETURN ON INVESTMENTS**.)

RETURN ON INVESTMENTS

Return On Investments

> ROE or bottom line profits, is the most important Return On Investment for stockholders and owners for it provides the source of funding dividends or owner profits, and increasing the wealth of their equity investment. In addition to providing an inducement for new investors, it also provides capital for expansion, outside investments etc. Another important ROI, is the before-tax ROA especially when compared with the ROE. The spread or difference between them then, is the meaning of financial leverage. It simply means using debt capital on which a business can earn a higher before-tax ROA than the annual interest rate due on the borrowed capital.

Return On Equity (ROE) =	net income / owner's equity	42.70% =	66,427 / 155,560
Before-tax Return On Assets (ROA) =	net operating income / total assets	31.60% =	93,299 / 295,206
Operating earnings before interest and income tax that is earned on the capital supplied by liabilities =	total liabilities x before-tax ROA	$44,135 =	139,646 x 31.60%
	- Interest expense	(10,468)	
	= Financial Leverage Gain For The Year	$33,667	
	or this percent of your pre-tax profits *	40.65% =	33,667 / 82,831 = Net Income Before Taxes

> * Note: In a year in which a company has a poor performance, and its before-tax ROA is less than its annual interest rate, Financial Leverage on the borrowed funds will actually work against the business.

RETURN ON INVESTMENTS

Objective -
1. Calculate your correct ROE or Return On Equity.
2. Calculate your correct ROA Before Tax Return On Assets
3. Calculate your Financial Leverage or gain in pre-tax profits for the year produced on the capital supplied by the liabilities

Given: ** Locate from the Balance Sheet the following:

Total Assets	$295,206.00
Total Liabilities	$139,646.00
Total Owner's Equity	$155,560.00

*** Locate from the Income Statement the following:

Net Operating Income	$ 92,299.00
Interest Expense	$ 10,648.00
Net Income Before Taxes (Pretax Profits)	$ 82,831.00
Net Income	$ 66,427.00

Step # 1 - To find your Return On Equity. To do this divide your Net Income by Owner's Equity. (Calculation #1)
Make the following entries into your calculator.
Entry #1   66,427
Entry #2   ÷ 155,560
Results equals your ROE or   = 42.70%

Step # 2 - Calculate your before-tax Return On Assets, by taking your Net Operating Income and dividing that by Total Assets (Calculation #2)
Make the following entries into your calculator.
Entry #1   93,299
Entry #2   ÷ 295,206
Results equals your Before-tax ROA = 31.60%

Step # 3 - Subtract your Owner's Equity from the Assets to arrive at the Liabilities. (Calculation # 3)
Make the following entries into your calculator.
Entry #1   295,206
Entry #2   - 155,560
Results equals your Liabilities = $139,646.00

Step # 4 - Calculate the *Operating Earnings before interest and taxes that is **earned on the capital supplied by liabilities**.* Multiply your total Liabilities by the Before-tax ROA percentage you arrived at in the 2nd step. (Calculation #4)
Make the following entries into your calculator.
Entry #1   295,206
Entry #2   x 31.60%
Results equals   = $ 44,135.00

Calculation #1
Entry #1: 66427
Entry #2: ÷ 155560
Entry #3: = .4270

Calculation #2
Entry #1: 93299
Entry #2: ÷ 295206
Entry #3: = .3160

Calculation #3
Entry #1: 295206
Entry #2: - 155560
Entry #3: = 139646

Calculation #4
Entry #1: 139646
Entry #2: x .3160
Entry #3: = 44135

RETURN ON INVESTMENTS

Step # 5 - Calculate your Financial Leverage or Gain For The Year by subtracting your Interest Expense from the Net Operating Income. (Calculation # 5)
Make the following entries into your calculator:
Entry #1   44,135
Entry #2   - 10,468
Results equals your Financial Leverage   = **$33,667.00**

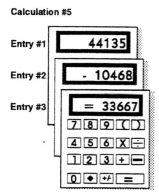

Step # 6 - Convert this Financial Leverage to a percentage of your pre-tax profits. Divide this number by your Net Income Before Taxes found on the Income Statement. (Calculation # 6)
Make the following entries into your calculator:
Entry #1   33,667
Entry #2   ÷ 82,831
Results equals your Financial Leverage as % = **40.65%**

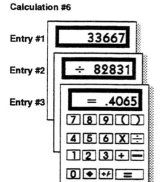

RETURN ON ASSETS

The Before-Tax *Return On Assets* (ROA) is another significant *Return On Investment* (ROI), especially when compared with the *Return On Equity* (ROE). The spread or difference between them is what is known as **financial leverage**. Whenever you borrow capital, whether it is for the purchase of equipment, expansion or inventory, you are assuming new liabilities. Stated another way, these liabilities are going to be responsible for generating new or additional sources of earnings within your business.

You realize that you are going to pay for the privilege of using someone else's money. The next question to ask is, "Will the earnings from operations attributed to the earnings of these new liabilities exceed the costs (interest expense) of the borrowed capital, and provide you with financial leverage or a gain for the year?"

Obviously, if there is an economic advantage to using other people's money after paying for the use of it, you may well be interested. Before you sign on the dotted line, however, you may want to look at the larger overall picture. How is the local economy holding up? Can you see patterns for growth sustaining your ability to pay this borrowed capital back? A word of caution—in a year in which a company performs poorly and the Before-Tax ROA is less than the annual interest charge to borrow the capital, this same financial leverage will work against you. You will still have to meet the conditions of the obligation and make timely payments, even if you haven't earned enough to cover them.

RETURN ON EQUITY

Your *Return on Equity* (ROE) is why you are still in business. Essentially, you have bet that your investment of capital coupled with the intelligence and hard work of you and your staff will result in a dividend higher than you could expect from some other investment. If you were the owners of our fictional business, and you knew you could realize a 42.70 percent return on your investment, without the frustration, risk and daily challenges of operating a business, would you still be in business? No matter how much you want to be in business, unless there is consistent and reliable delivery of some very strong numbers in your ROE, you will not remain in business. And, while we have learned that ROE is certainly critical to your success, it is by no means the only ROI that you should be familiar with.

In anticipation of the day when you ask others to make a judgment about your management capabilities, you should make it a goal to learn how, when, and where you can exercise controls to improve your own set of numbers. Using the **DU PONT EQUATION** below, and the exhibits, entitled **INCOME AND EXPENSE STATEMENT, BALANCE SHEET AND RETURN ON EQUITY**, you will note that there are, in fact, a series of relationships between all these numbers. The sooner you can appreciate the significance of these ratios and their relationships, the better prepared you will be to identify where, within your business, you need to devote more attention.

THE DUPONT EQUATION

The Du Pont Equation

As we have noted several of these ratios are related to one another. The most important relationship exist between the ROE and three of these other ratios. It provides a link or connection between a profitability ratio (PM), a leverage ratio (EM), and a turnover ratio (ATO). Thus management can better pinpoint each of the factors that may be leading to a troublesome ROE. In the overall scheme of things, producing a healthy ROE is certainly one of the primary goals of every manager and owner.

Return on equity (ROE)	=	PM	x	ATO	x	EM
42.70%	=	10.45%	x	2.15	x	1.90
		(profit)		(turnover)		(leverage)

RETURN ON EQUITY

Objective -
1. Calculate the Profit Margin (PM)
2. Calculate the Asset Turnover Ratio (ATO)
3. Calculate the Equity Multiplier (EM)
4. Calculate your correct ROE or Return On Equity. by using the relationship between your Profit Margin, a profitability ratio, your Asset Turnover Ratio, a turnover ratio, and your Equity Multiplier, a leverage ratio. Referred to as the Du Pont Equation.

Given: ** Locate from the Balance Sheet the following:

Total Assets	$295,206.00
Owner's Equity	$155,560.00

*** Locate from the Income Statement the following:

Revenues From Sales	$635,400.00
Net Income	$ 66,427.00

Step # 1 - To find your Profit Margin. Divide your Net Income by Revenues From Sales. (Calculation #1)
Make the following entries into your calculator.
Entry #1   66,427
Entry #2   ÷ 635,400
Results equals your PM or   = 10.45%

Step # 2 - Find your Asset Turnover Ratio (ATO). Divide your Revenues From Sales by Total Assets. (Calculation #2)
Make the following entries into your calculator.
Entry #1   635,300
Entry #2   ÷ 295,206
Results equals your ATO or   = 2.15

Step # 3 - Calculate the Equity Multiplier (EM). Divide Total Assets by Owner's Equity. (Calculation #3)
Make the following entries into your calculator.
Entry #1   295,206
Entry #2   ÷ 155,560
Results equals your EM or   = 1.90%

Step # 4 - Determine the Return On Equity (ROE). Multiply the PM by the ATO, and then multiply that answer by the EM. (Calculation #4)
Make the following entries into your calculator.
Entry #1   .1045
Entry #2   x .0215
Entry #3   x .0190
Results equals your ROE or   = 42.70%

Calculation #1
Entry #1: 66427
Entry #2: ÷ 635400
Entry #3: = .1045

Calculation #2
Entry #1: 635400
Entry #2: ÷ 295206
Entry #3: = .0215

Calculation #3
Entry #1: 295206
Entry #2: ÷ 155560
Entry #3: = .0190

Calculation #4
Entry #1: .1045
Entry #2: x .0215
Entry #3: x .0190
= .4270

WHERE DO YOU GO FROM HERE?

It is important that you find a competent accountant or bookkeeper who will take the time to explain and review your financial statements each month. His or her function is to record the information while helping you to make some sense out of it. If the numbers sound too good to be true, they probably are! Ask if they see any red flags, and then assist them in determining what the problems might be. Don't be lulled into a false sense of security, simply because they don't offer any comments. They probably feel that if you are interested in the interpretation of your financial reports, you will ask. Learn to ask!

It is your business, not your accountant's. You are the one who must make use of the information we have discussed here, and hopefully you will explore it in greater depth, as you begin to apply it.

CHAPTER 9

Reference Information—Ratios And Terms

SUMMARY OF RATIOS			
Term	Definition	Formula	Target Audience
LIQUIDITY RATIOS	Measures firm's ability to meet current obligations.		Lenders, investors, suppliers, owners and management
Current Ratio	Basic test to determine ability of firm to pay short-term debt	Current Assets ÷ Current Liabilities	
Quick Ratio	Same as Current Ratio, however, more stringent since it excludes inventory.	Current Assets - Inventory ÷ Current Liabilities	
LEVERAGE RATIOS	Measure of the firm's indebtedness.		Lenders, investors and owners
Times Interest Earned	Measures earnings before the payment of interest and taxes.	Net Operating Income ÷ Interest Expense	
Debit To Asset Ratio	Indication of which portion of the firm's assets are being financed	Total Liabilities ÷ Total Assets	
Debt/Equity Ratio	Indicates which portion of the assets belongs to owners and which to creditors	Total Liabilities ÷ Owner's Equity	
Equity Multiplier Ratio	Measure of the efficient use of equity as employed by the firm's assets.	Total Assets ÷ Owner's Equity	
TURNOVER RATIOS	Measures how efficiently assets are used on a regular basis.		Investors, owners and managers
Average Collection Period (ACP)	Represents the number of days required to collect your money.	Accounts Receivable ÷ Daily Sales	
Inventory Turnover Ratio (ITO)	How frequently your inventory is turned over in the course of the accounting period.	Cost of Goods Sold ÷ Inventory	
Days of Sales in Inventory (DSI)	Reflects how well your inventory is being managed.	Inventory ÷ Daily Cost of Goods Sold	
Asset Turnover Ratio (ATO)	Reveals how much in sales is being generated by wise management of firm's assets.	Revenues from Sales ÷ Total Assets	
PROFITABILITY RATIOS	Shows where the profits are being generated, and how the investor's money is being used to create wealth.		Lenders, investors, suppliers, owners, managers and employees
Profit Margin (PM)	Indicator of the profits generated through the sales of products and services.	Net Income ÷ Revenues from Sales	
Return on Assets (ROA)	Calculates the return earned by effective use of the assets within the business.	Net Income ÷ Total Assets	
Return on Investments (ROI)	Measures management's ability to earn a profit and to increase the value of the business over time.	ROE + Before-Tax ROA	
Return on Equity (ROE)	Measures the ability of management to create wealth in the form of a return on the owner's investment.	Net Income ÷ Owner's Equity	

__	SUMMARY OF RATIOS		
Term	**Definition**	**Formula**	**Target Audience**
Before-Tax ROA	Provides a look at how effectively management is earning a return from the operation of the business in the absence of any investment activity.	Net Operating Income ÷ Owner's Equity	
Financial Leverage	How effectively does management use debt capital to earn a higher before-tax ROA than the annual interest rate on the borrowed money.	(Total Liabilities ÷ Before-Tax ROA) - Interest Expense = Financial Leverage or Gain for the year.	
Dupont Equation	Offers another means of measuring your ROE and at the same time focuses your attention on where corrective measures should be invoked.	PM x ATO x EM = ROE	

CHAPTER 9
SUMMARY OF TERMS

TERM	DESCRIPTION
asset turnover ratio (ATO)	Reveals how much in sales is being generated by wise management of firm's assets.
average collection period ratio (ACP)	This number represents the number of days required to collect your money.
before-tax ROA ratio	Provides a look at how effectively management is earning a return from the operation of the business in the absence of any investment activity.
comparative ratio analysis	An internal analysis of the current financial period's performance with similar information from a prior period in order to determine areas of concern.
current ratio	A basic test to determine ability of firm to pay short-term debt.
days of sales in inventory ratio (DSI	Reflects how well your inventory is being managed.
debt to asset ratio	An indication of which portion of the firm's assets are being financed.
debt/equity ratio	An indication of which portion of the assets belongs to owner and which to creditors.
Dupont equation	Offers another means of measuring your ROE and at the same time focuses your attention on where corrective measures should be invoked.
equity multiplier ratio	A measure of the efficient use of equity as employed by the firm's assets.
financial leverage	How effectively management uses debt capital to earn a higher Before-Tax ROA than the annual interest rate on the borrowed money.
historical performance	The past performance of a business, as recorded in a variety of areas or disciplines, providing the observer with a profile of how the business performs. These consist of financial reports, job costing, customer profiles, inventory records, etc.
industry standards	Standards compiled on an industry-wide basis, usually with respect to performance in a variety of areas or disciplines, allowing management to establish its own operational standards. Examples include financial analysis of statements of businesses in the same industry, e.g., the kitchen and bathroom industry, remodelers, electrical contractors.
interpretation of ratios	An analysis of the financial ratios as determined by your bookkeeper or accountant.
Inventory turnover ratio (ITO)	How frequently your inventory is turned over in the course of the accounting period.
leverage ratios	Used to measure firm's indebtedness.
liquidity ratios	A look at firm's ability to pay its creditors in a timely fashion.
profit margin ratio (PM)	An indicator of the profits generated through the sales of products and services.
profitability ratio	Shows where the profits are being generated and where the investor's money is being used to create wealth.
quick ratio	More stringent than Current Ratio, since it excludes inventory.
return on assets ratio (ROA)	Calculates the return earned by effective use of the assets within the business.
return on equity ratio (ROE)	Measures the ability of management to create wealth in form of a return on owner's investment.
return on investment ratio (ROI)	Measures management's ability to earn a profit and to increase the value of the business over time.
times interest earned	Measures earnings before the payment of interest and taxes.
turnover ratio	Measures how efficiently assets are used on a daily basis.

Chapter 10

BY THE NUMBERS

In the midst of this chopping sea of civilized life, such are the clouds and storms and quicksands and thousand-and-one items to be allowed for, that a man has to live, if he would not founder and go to the bottom and not make his port at all, by dead reckoning, and he must be a great calculator indeed who succeeds.
— Henry David Thoreau

Why is it most of us shy away from numbers in general, and financial management in particular? Our daily routines would be very difficult to understand if we couldn't perform them by the *numbers*, i.e., time, recipes, anniversaries, birthdays, distances, our health and our children's grades. So, why is it that we, as business people who should understand the numbers of our own business, are so bewildered and mystified by them? Could it be that, for some of us, our past experiences with math have never made much sense to us?

If you have ever felt frustrated because you didn't understand the *numbers*—you are not alone. I originally researched and gathered this information because I didn't understand them either, and frankly I was tired of simply being a survivor. Do you feel that you owe it to yourself and to the people that you work with to do more than just get by?

Understanding the numbers in your business is the quickest and surest way to grasp how profitably you are operating and managing your firm. One of the distinct advantages a small business can offer its customers is its ability to meet their needs quickly. Business changes so rapidly these days, that *the numbers* are the fastest and most reliable method to determine exactly what those needs are and to position yourself accordingly. You will have a decided advantage over your competitors who don't use numbers to tell them just what is going on in their business.

Now that you have read this book for the first time, make a commitment to read it again and highlight the areas that need strengthening by you and your professional advisors. Recognize that there are some areas where you need help, and some areas where your strengths are not being utilized to your fullest capability. Use this information to begin building your *trade secret*. Involve your team in this process. There is no better time than now to offer each other your support and assistance in identifying your common mission and goals. By working together and assigning areas of responsibility, you will begin to see that profit is something you can build on. Remember, you must plan for profit, not simply hope for it at the end of the year.

HOW TO MEASURE PROFITABILITY

Is your business really making a profit or are you deceiving yourself because you have shown consistent sales growth? The growth is admirable, but only if it is accompanied by, or part of, a long-range plan to increase profits. How can you tell? By the numbers!

Why aren't you earning a profit? Are your margins too slim? Are you covering all of your expenses? Are your labor costs too high? How can you tell? By the numbers!

Could you better contain some of your expenses? Do you really understand your market and your approach to capturing a piece of it? How effective is your marketing plan? Are your advertising expenditures really targeting the right customer base? Are you blaming your competition? How can you tell? By the numbers!

Should you spend more money to train your people? Is your closing ratio improving? Are the subcontractors you work with giving you a fair shake with their pricing? Are they as productive as you might be if you were to bring some of their work in-house? How can you tell? By the numbers!

OPERATIONAL DIAGNOSIS

Develop your own simple financial diagnostic tool which, when used regularly, will show you where you are headed. (See the following exhibit, entitled **OPERATIONAL DIAGNOSIS**.) I have included this as an example, but you can develop your own. Work with your employees and your accountant to modify and adjust this one as a starting point.

MANAGING YOUR KITCHEN AND BATHROOM FIRM'S FINANCES FOR PROFIT

OPERATIONAL DIAGNOSIS

Operational Diagnosis For Period Ending: / /

Notes

Financial Information

Receipts By Department

	Sales	Returns	Adj.	Budgeted	%
Department 1 -					
Department 2 -					
Department 3 -					
Department 4 -					
Department 5 -					
Department 6 -					

Are poor sales indicative of a poor or limited selection of inventory? Have you properly identified your market niche and are you pursuing it correctly? Are excessive redos a sign of poor quality or poor workmanship or poor management? What's selling and what are your real profit centers?

Du Pont Equation

$$(ROE) = \underset{(1)}{PM} \times \underset{(2)}{ATO} \times \underset{(3)}{EM}$$

$$= \quad \times \quad \times$$

When the ROE is low look at the other ratios for these potential problems:

Profit Margin (1) $PM = \dfrac{\text{net income}}{\text{total sales}}$ *(low PM might indicate too low a mark-up or insufficient sales.)*

Asset Turnover (2) $ATO = \dfrac{\text{sales}}{\text{assets}}$ *(low sales dollars generated by non-productive use of assets.)*

Equity Multiplier (3) $EM = \dfrac{\text{total assets}}{\text{equity}}$ *(high potential for default, too much leverage of debt to be paid on a fixed basis.)*

Customer Information

By Transaction Type

	Counts	$	%	Avg.
Cash				
Charge (Commercial Only)				
Credit Cards				
3 rd Party Financing				
Totals				

Develop profile of customer base with idea of soliciting repeat business or referrals for new business. Remember "80/20 rule". Could the size of your average sale be increased by additional efforts to upsell? As an organization are you listening to your customers? What follow-up programs are in place to receive feedback from your customers?

Marketing Information

Sales Thru Advertising

	Counts	$	%
T.V.			
Radio			
Newspaper			
Flyers			
Other Publications			

Sales Thru Marketing

Referrals			
In-house Promotions			
Coupons			
Other			

Where do your customers come from? What is your most effective means of attracting new customers? Are you getting the most for your dollar with respect to advertising and promotions? How can you increase customer referrals? Are some customers being left out of the loop when it comes to marketing and/or advertising?

Productivity Information

	$
Errors & Omissions	
Labor Costs	
Staffing-hour Costs	
Training Expense	

This worksheet should be completed at the end of each financial period.
Together with your employees and your accountant you may see fit to modify or adjust it.
It is a tool which you can employ to develop your "trade secret", in this case, another aspect of your own business profile.

I suggest you consider what information is really important to your operation and why, and then include it. Ideally this report should be completed upon the close of each financial period. Just what areas might be important to you? I can't know what issues impact your business, but we would be safe in discussing the four areas I have used. These include your *financial position at the end of the period*, your *customer profiles*, your *marketing efforts* and your *productivity*.

1. What financial information do you want?

Sales, returns and adjustments by department or job name are important because such information provides you with a measurement of how effective your strategies may be working in these other areas. Compare these figures to what you had budgeted for each department during this period. Questions you might ask:

- Are poor sales indicative of a poor or limited selection of inventory?
- Have you properly identified your market niche and are you pursuing it correctly?
- What is selling and which are your real profit centers?
- Are excessive returns or complaints a sign of poor quality, poor workmanship or poor management?
- Are your sales being adequately supported by your marketing and advertising efforts?

I would also recommend that you prepare a sample *Du Pont equation* upon the close of the period, and, if there is any deterioration in your company's performance, establish why. Ask your accountant for assistance, if necessary.

2. Who buys from you and how are you reaching them?

The best customers are repeat customers. If they have already done business with you, they know who you are and how to reach you. That information alone can save you significant sums of time, money and resources. Here is the perfect opportunity to apply the *80 - 20 rule* we discussed earlier. What information might assist you in developing a customer base that provides you with repeat business and referrals? Questions you might ask:

- Are your customers essentially cash customers, credit card buyers or charge customers, and what percentage of overall sales do they represent?
- What is the value of the average sale in each of these categories?
- Are they new or repeat customers?
- How have they learned about you—radio, newspaper, referral, in-house promotion, coupons, other publications?

3. What do you want to know concerning your marketing efforts?

As you assembled the information to answer the questions in the previous two sections, you may have begun seeing a relationship that existed between them. Since you now know who your customers are, what they buy and how to reach them, you are in an excellent position to develop an effective marketing strategy. Begin by noticing that there is a difference between advertising and marketing.

ADVERTISING

Advertising provides information about your business: your hours of operation, your products and services, and your location. Its primary purpose is to inform your potential customers and make them aware that you are a player in their marketplace. Advertising is designed to get them in the front door where they can be sold by your professional sales staff. Questions you might ask:

- Are you adequately represented in the proper categories of the Yellow Pages?
- Do you use a logo and company colors? Are they strictly adhered to in all advertising?
- Do you use signage on your vehicle(s), at the front of your showroom or place of business? Are they clear and easy to read from a distance?
- Are advertising dollars available from distributors or manufacturers?

MARKETING

Marketing, on the other hand, is an educational device with far greater accuracy and purpose. It is used by the seller to first identify what the market trends are, and then to develop a strategy which will convince the buyer that a product or service offers the benefits they want. It attempts to build a relationship between the seller and the buyer through some positive interaction early in the process, ideally culminating in a sale. If your marketing efforts have been unsuccessful in producing sales, you may need to rethink your strategy and/or change your tactics. Questions you might ask:

- How well do you understand your market and the niche you have identified as the one you want to fill?
- Are you making enough of an investment in your marketing strategy, and are you getting the results you targeted?
- Are you using promotions, incentives, community projects, etc.?
- What information will you want regarding productivity?

The system needs constant refining. People require skills training. All of us could use more education. To increase productivity, constant monitoring, practice and evaluation is needed. Left to its own, productivity can deteriorate if systems and procedures are not formally set in place. Develop your questions so they provide reliable feedback on where and how the systems you employ can be improved. Questions you might ask:

- How do your labor costs look in comparison to what you have budgeted?
- Are you preparing realistic estimates regarding the time required to complete a project?
- What does the rate of errors and omissions look like?
- Have you kept track of new technologies and training?
- Should you explore new technologies and training in different areas?

As the owner or manager of a kitchen and bathroom business, you can identify numerous situations and issues that are beyond your control. However, many of these issues are accompanied by variations which you can influence. Be cautioned though, because trying to change every situation you encounter will merely waste your time, money and resources. Each issue must be identified and characterized before you decide whether or not it contributes to the mission of the business. Your *numbers* make those characterizations easier to understand and appreciate.

GET OTHERS INVOLVED

Those who are employed by kitchen and bathroom firms have as much at stake as the employer does, and, therefore, they need to be involved. Employees will actually become interested in the success of the business, when it is explained why their contribution is so important. Don't hesitate to share both the good and the bad news. Your employees cannot be very supportive, nor can they do very much about it, unless they, too, understand the economics of running a business. Let them see what the profitability of the business is. Don't be concerned that they will see how much money you make, what's really important is how you get to those numbers.

Most people have a distorted view of how much it costs to be in business. Unless you help break down the barriers, they will never be able to appreciate the challenges you face. You can't begin to make a profit, unless people understand how to operate a business by the *numbers*. Once you see for yourself how effective a tool numbers really are, you'll be convinced it is the only way to run and manage your business.

CHAPTER 10

Reference Information—Terms

CHAPTER 10
SUMMARY OF TERMS

TERM	DEFINITION
advertising	Information you make available to your customers and prospective clients to get them in your front door.
marketing	An educational opportunity to get your customer to interact with you so as to correctly identify your market's trends and then to develop a strategy to meet those demands. Some examples are polls, surveys, offers, promotions, incentives, community projects—anything that creates involvement.
numbers	Refers to financial information that management can use to build a profile of the business which then becomes an essential element in its *trade secret*.
operational diagnosis	A periodic look at the performance of the business with respect to any variations from our original projections.
variations	Alternatives to what you consider to be the norm or reasonable expectations, and yet not all variations offer valid reasons for change, such as changes in the numbers or buying habits of your customers.

Conclusion

CREATING WEALTH

*Drop a pebble in the water: in a minute you forget,
But there's little waves a-flowing, and there's ripples circling yet,
And those little waves a-flowing to a great big wave have grown;
You've disturbed a mighty river just by dropping in a stone.* - James W. Foley

Your business represents an investment in your future. In order for this investment to produce a return, it must have a track record of creating wealth. What exactly is wealth? It is the sum of one's resources, including real property and intangible assets. Ideas, concepts, associations, systems and relationships are all examples of one's resources. Your company culture and the environment in which your business functions is also an intangible asset and part of the organization's wealth. This environment, in which these resources may already flow among the players—your employees, suppliers, distributors and your customers—becomes part of the system for the creation of wealth.

YOUR FIRM'S ENVIRONMENT

Since every business takes on a life of its own, the owners have a responsibility to manage that environment, reinvesting money and resources to guarantee its continued health and prosperity. Anyone who has a role to play within your company is also creating wealth. As they become more dependent upon it and more proficient at it, they add to its quality of life. Such quality of life measures job satisfaction, which means less employee turnover. Greater dependence upon one another within the company leads to stronger and healthier relationships. This creates less stress and a more positive working environment. With such a healthy environment, your business becomes more responsive to the needs, wants and requests of your customers—an environment which results in repeat sales and greater profits.

Its inherent value lies in the flexibility it provides as an ever-changing system. You must use a multiplicity of resources in your efforts to seek solutions and alternatives to the challenges facing your business. Tomorrow's marketplace will come under the stewardship of those organizations that foster an environment of creative expression. These **customer** service providers; designers of prosperity and builders of wealth will reap the return on their investments by maintaining such an environment. How you refine and perfect the methods used to create wealth within your business then become part of your success.

I know that two and two make four—and should be glad to prove it too if I could—though I must say if by any sort of process I could convert two and two into five it would give me much greater pleasure.
- **Lord Byron**

GLOSSARY

GLOSSARY	
accounts payable	Money you owe your suppliers and other creditors for purchases you have made and charged to your account.
accounts receivable	Revenues from sales which you have agreed to accept on a delayed payment schedule.
accrual method	Recognizes income as it is earned rather than as received and expenses as they are incurred rather than when they are actually paid. These are your accounts receivables and accounts payables.
accrued expenses	Services or products you have received, yet have not been billed for, as of the close of the accounting period. An example would be your cabinets that arrived yesterday from your supplier, yet the bill may not arrive for another 2 or 3 days.
accumulated depreciation	That portion of an asset's value which has been written off to date.
acts of commission	Acts of responsibility attributed to contractor, employees, subcontractors and subcontractor's employees, such as mistakes committed and directly attributed to you as the prime contractor on a kitchen or bathroom remodeling job; a good reason to carry liability insurance.
acts of omission	Omissions attributed to contractor, employees, subcontractors and subcontractor's employees. These are omissions directly attributed to you as the prime contractor on a kitchen or bathroom remodeling job. Another good reason to carry liability insurance.
adjustments	As they apply to the budget process, these might certainly apply to seasonality factors or influences on the local economy, thus impacting your own business performance. Possibilities include regions subject to extremes in weather, tourism shifts, areas heavily dependent on manufacturing and their accompanying business cycles.
advertising	Information you make available to your customers and prospective clients to get them in your front door.
aged receivables	Generally, a reference to the older and dated accounts receivables.
Americans with Disabilities Act (ADA)	Federal legislation that mandates compliance with access and egress requirements for people with physical and mental disabilities. This is also applicable to the workplace.
asset turnover ratio (ATO)	Reveals how much in sales is being generated by wise management of firm's assets.
assets	Any type of property possessed by the business which may be of some future financial benefit. This could be tangible property (buildings, land, equipment, etc.) and non-tangible property (patents, copyrights, formulas, designs) valued on your balance sheet.
assumptions	Based upon available information, it is a person's best estimate of how to handle a situation. Usually, however, there is much room for improvement such as more research to uncover previously unknown facts. An example is a financial assumption, a "guesstimate" instead of an estimate.
average collection period ratio (ACP)	This number represents the number of days required to collect your money.
balance sheet	A financial report designed to accurately represent the ownership and debt of the business.
basic balance sheet equation	This equation is used to insure Balance Sheet is in balance. assets = liabilities + owner's equity
before-tax ROA ratio	Provides a look at how effectively management is earning a return from the operation of the business in the absence of any investment activity.

GLOSSARY	
bonds	A financial commitment that certain work will be completed if the contractor defaults. It protects third parties only; contractor remains responsible to bonding company. Examples are surety bonds such as lien bonds, payment bonds and performance bonds.
break-even point	That point at which a business can expect their efforts to contribute directly to their bottom line, usually as measured in dollars or units of production.
business deductions	Costs of sales and operational expenses, such as materials, rent and insurance deducted from the revenues of a business in order to determine taxable income
business plan	A detailed strategy designed to communicate to you, your investors, employees and others, your mission and plans to execute these strategies.
cash dividends to stockholders	A return of a portion of the net income to the stockholders of a corporation for their sharing in the risk of the operation of the business, i.e., the quarterly earnings; the annual return to investors of a corporation.
certificate of insurance	Instrument issued to subcontractors which they then supply to prime contractor as proof they have obtained worker's compensation insurance coverage for their employees. Kitchen and bathroom dealers should require these from subcontractors who work on their client's properties.
certified public accountant	An individual recognized for educational and professional achievement and licensed in the state in which he or she practices.
charge sales	Sales made to customers who choose a payment method you offer, other than immediate cash payment, such as credit card sales and third-party financed projects.
chart of accounts	A structure of the various accounts your business uses to account for all its financial transactions.
checklists	An affordable, convenient tool everyone within an organization can use to make better use of time and resources. Some examples are: materials checklist, job sequence checklist, punch lists.
Circular E	Employer's tax guide; IRS Publication 15.
collateral	Security for a loan. This would be a physical asset that has come unencumbered equity remaining.
commission basis	Compensation plan for salespeople paid as a percentage of gross sales. A salesperson's commissions.
comparative ratio analysis	An internal analysis of the current financial period's performance with similar information from a prior period in order to determine areas of concern.
contingency costs	Job-related costs outside your control, but which are, in fact, real costs of doing business, such as delays caused by customers, subcontractors and mandatory inspections.
contingency fees	Remuneration necessary to assist you in offsetting some of the contingency costs.
contract laborer	An individual compensated to perform work and responsible for the results rather than the methods. Must also perform according to the guidelines in IRS Publication 15-A. An example would be an independent contractor, such as a plumbing contractor, painting contractor or electrical contractor.
controls	A built-in system of checks and balances, such as checklists and standard operating procedures, that you can employ in your business to avoid problems.
co-op funds for advertising	Advertising monies available to dealers through their distributors for products produced by various manufacturers, requiring compliance with their guidelines.
cost of sales	Costs associated directly or indirectly with a project or sale. Labor, materials, subcontracts and equipment rental are examples.
current assets	Those assets which can typically be converted to cash within the next 12 months. They may be cash, securities, accounts receivable, inventory or checking account.
current ratio	A basic test to determine ability of firm to pay short-term debt.

	GLOSSARY
customer service	The totality of the experience you offer to distinguish yourself from the competition when it comes to fulfilling your customers' wants. Look at your bottom line, and, if it is not healthy and growing, you have room for improvement.
days of sales in inventory ratio (DSI	Reflects how well your inventory is being managed.
debt to asset ratio	An indication of which portion of the firm's assets are being financed.
debt/equity ratio	An indication of which portion of the assets belongs to owner and which to creditors.
depreciation expense	A non-cash outlay; a recognition of the loss of an asset's value due to time and wear, such as depreciation on a kitchen and bathroom dealer's showroom display unit.
direct costs	Costs attributed directly to the production of a finished project, such as a remodeling project's directly related costs of sales (cabinets or countertops).
discounters	A term applied primarily to large retail chains or mass merchandisers who discount their products deeply.
Dupont equation	Offers another means of measuring your ROE and at the same time focuses your attention on where corrective measures should be invoked.
early payment discounts	Discounts offered by your suppliers as an incentive to pay early, such as 2% 10 days net 30.
employee	An individual compensated to work where, when and how he or she is directed to by a supervisor, owner or manager according to the guidelines in IRS Publication 15-A.
equity multiplier ratio	A measure of the efficient use of equity as employed by the firm's assets.
estimate	Frequently confused with a quote, an estimate is a price for your customer, generally based upon available information with respect to how much you intend to complete on a project and how long you calculate it will take.
estimating process	Method used by dealers to arrive at the cost of their products and services, which recognizes their expenses and calculates a margin of profit for their investment.
Federal Insurance Contributions Act (FICA)	At present, this amounts to 6.2 percent on wages up to $62,700 for both the employee and the employer. These are Social Security taxes which are deducted from one's paycheck.
financial leverage	How effectively management uses debt capital to earn a higher Before-Tax ROA than the annual interest rate on the borrowed money.
financial reports	Reports prepared for and used by management and others to evaluate the company's financial performance. Most commonly these refer to the Balance Sheet, the Statement of Income and Expenses and the Statement of Cash Flow.
Financial Standards Accounting Board (FSAB)	A watchdog committee recognized by the accounting profession to establish guidelines and principles.
forecasting	Also called budgeting, attempts to predict where and how the business will perform in the future, generally by looking at past performance and analyzing it.
generally accepted accounting principles (GAAP)	Industry standards adopted by the accounting profession.
gross profit (margin)	Revenue income remaining after deducting cost of sales. Not a true profit, since overhead has not been deducted yet. Revenues - Costs of Sales = Gross Profit Margin.
hidden costs	This refers to expenses not recognized until it is too late to avoid them, such as fines and penalties.
historical performance	The past performance of a business, as recorded in a variety of areas or disciplines, providing the observer with a profile of how the business performs. These consist of financial reports, job costing, customer profiles, inventory records, etc.

GLOSSARY

income and expense statement	A financial report designed to determine whether or not the business' income exceeded its expenses or vice versa during a given period of time.
income tax payable	The amount of income taxes due to either the federal or state governments based upon the earnings of the business in the prior accounting period. This is based on the Net Profit before Taxes amount reflected on your Income And Expense Statement.
indirect costs	Those costs attributed indirectly to your producing a finished project, such as unique training, shop drawing, long-distance phone calls.
industry standards	Standards compiled on an industry-wide basis, usually with respect to performance in a variety of areas or disciplines, allowing management to establish its own operational standards. Examples include financial analysis of statements of businesses in the same industry, e.g., the kitchen and bathroom industry, remodelers, electrical contractors.
interpretation of ratios	An analysis of the financial ratios as determined by your bookkeeper or accountant.
inventory	Materials, parts and products sold by the business and maintained on hand, such as cabinets, countertops, hardware and laminates.
Inventory turnover ratio (ITO)	How frequently your inventory is turned over in the course of the accounting period.
job costing records	The process of recording costs on the basis of job-by-job detail, in order to build a profile as to how your business operates.
leverage ratios	Used to measure firm's indebtedness.
liabilities	The creditors' claims against the assets of the business, i.e., accounts payable, accrued expenses, payroll taxes payable.
line of credit	Prior arrangement for funds as needed, with a cap, through your bank or commercial lender.
liquidity ratios	A look at firm's ability to pay its creditors in a timely fashion.
long-term assets	Those assets, also known as fixed assets, which are usually expected to have a service life of some future time frame, such as the physical plant, property or equipment you own and use in your business.
long-term financing	Third-party financing available to your customers in order to accommodate large and expensive purchases such as a kitchen and bathroom remodeling project. This would be provided by credit card companies, commercial lenders and banks.
long-term notes payable	Obligations of the business with a duration in excess of the next 12 months. This appears on your balance sheet as the long-term liabilities such as Notes Payable, Mortgages.
manufacturer's suggested retail price (MSRP)	A price which manufacturers deem to be competitive based upon their own marketing research, and presumably on the product's features and benefits.
market niche	That segment of the market which you target specifically, such as a certain neighborhood or region of the city which you have delineated by age and income.
marketing	An educational opportunity to get your customer to interact with you so as to correctly identify your market's trends and then to develop a strategy to meet those demands. Some examples are polls, surveys, offers, promotions, incentives, community projects—anything that creates involvement.
marketing plan	A detailed strategy designed to identify and reach your market niche, maximizing the results of your efforts by properly utilizing the resources available to you. For instance, a kitchen and bathroom dealer's overall marketing strategy as it relates to advertising, customer service, employee training and management support.
markup	The calculation of the correct amount of charges required to produce a selling price that will cover the seller's costs, overhead and provide the seller with a margin of profit.

GLOSSARY	
Material Safety Data Sheets (MSDS)	Forms available through your suppliers for each chemical you use in your business containing its makeup and recommended first aid in the event your employees inhale, ingest or are exposed to them. They are required to be available as part of your office and job-site safety program.
Medicare	At present, this amounts to 1.45 percent on all wages for both the employee and the employer. These Medicare taxes are deducted from one's paycheck.
mistakes	The leading cause for loss of profits on kitchen and bathroom remodeling jobs, and yet simple checklists could do much to correct these problems. Mistakes include errors, omissions, inattention to detail, poor take offs, etc.
monthly budgets	Projections of the financial operations of the business during future monthly periods. This is an annual budget broken down into monthly units in order to provide management with an idea of its responsibilities in a more timely fashion.
net income	Also known as the bottom line, this figure is a measure of your ability to create wealth. It is arrived at only after you have subtracted all costs, expenses and taxes associated with the operation of your business. The is the Net Profit amount reflected on your Income and Expense Statement.
net worth of the business	Your assets minus your liabilities equals owner's equity which is another way of determining the net worth of a business.
notes payable	Payments owed against a note held by one of your creditors, reflected as the notes payable amount on your balance sheet.
numbers	Refers to financial information management can use to build a profile of the business which then becomes an essential element in its trade secret.
Occupational Safety And Health Administration (OSHA)	Agency which governs the standards for a safe workplace.
operating expenses	Those expenses necessary to operate the business on a day-to-day basis, such as salaries of office staff, rent, utilities and insurance.
operational diagnosis	A periodic look at the performance of the business with respect to any variations from our original projections.
other assets	These assets are tangible or non-tangible in nature, however, they possess some future potential value to your business. They might include patented processes or designs as well as secret formulas, copyrights or other proprietary knowledge.
other income and expense	Revenues or expenses produced other than through the sale of the business' primary product or service. This could be revenue from the sale of an asset or expense realized because of a liability.
overhead costs	Those expenses you must absorb each day just to keep your doors open, such as rent, utilities, salaries of office staff and advertising expense.
owner's equity	Also known as partner's equity or stockholder's equity, this is direct (Investments) or indirect (Retained Earnings) accounting of the owner's claims against the assets of the business. This appears on your Balance Sheet.
payroll burden	Additional costs to management, beyond hourly pay or salary for which management is responsible, i.e., worker's compensation insurance, unemployment taxes, matching Medicare and social security payments.
payroll taxes	Known also as federal or state withholding, these are income taxes assessed to the business or individual or both on the earnings for a given period.
prepaid expenses	Those expenses which the business must pay in advance, such as rent and insurance premiums.

GLOSSARY

price sensitive	A perception formed mentally, often only by the salesperson, as to what is driving the customer's purchasing decision. For instance, a sale made to a customer in which the parties have concluded the only real value being exchanged was price.
productivity	Output of goods or services, possibly listed by department or individual, and frequently based on some predetermined and standard measure. The output can also be listed by dollar volume of work, material installed or number of projects sold during a given period.
profit	Residual value or surplus from a sale or investment transaction that remains after satisfying any claims for goods and/or services rendered, relative to that transaction, and after deducting the seller's expenses. An example is Net Profit as determined on the Income and Expense Statement.
profit based on costs	A selling price arrived at by adding the percentage of profit to the costs associated with the finished project.
profit based on selling price	A selling price arrived at, after careful consideration of costs, expenses, the market and the desired return on investment. This is the price that will provide the desired profit margin after deducting all costs and expenses associated with delivering the finished project.
profit from operations	As distinguished from Gross Profit Margin or Net Profit, this profit is recognized as earned from the primary operation of the business. On the Income and Expense Statement, this is frequently referred to as Net from Operations.
profit margin ratio (PM)	An indicator of the profits generated through the sales of products and services.
profitability ratio	Shows where the profits are being generated and where the investor's money is being used to create wealth.
projections	Also known as pro-formas. A company's financial performance as anticipated in reports assembled for future periods. Some examples are: annual budgets (Income and Expense and Cash Flow Statements) and adjusted ownership at end of accounting period (Balance Sheet).
quick ratio	More stringent than Current Ratio, since it excludes inventory.
quote	Also known as a proposal or bid, this is a written document which lays out the scope of the work, the specifications and related documentation such as drawings. An example is a firm estimate and commitment to your customer to complete the described work within a reasonable time for the agreed upon charges.
ratios	Relationships between financial calculations which allow for meaningful interpretations of management's abilities, including profit ratios, leverage ratios and turnover ratios.
referrals	Leads and/or prospects known to your clients, that you must ask for. The opportunity to ask for leads can present itself on at least three occasions during the selling process—at the close, upon completion and 30 days after completion when you call to follow up.
retailer	A person or business owner who conducts business, such as a department store or a mass merchandiser, by reselling that which others manufacture or make, and profit by the sheer volume.
retained earnings	A portion of the net income used to satisfy some of the outstanding debt of the corporation, or to be invested in other capital expenditures, in either case increasing the value of the stockholder's existing investment. This is the amount reflected on your Balance Sheet under Owner's Equity.
revenue	Income derived from sales of primary products or services sold by the business, such as kitchen cabinets, countertops, bathroom vanities, or an entire remodeling job.

	GLOSSARY
return on assets ratio (ROA)	Calculates the return earned by effective use of the assets within the business.
return on equity ratio (ROE)	Measures the ability of management to create wealth in form of a return on owner's investment.
return on investment ratio (ROI)	Measures management's ability to earn a profit and to increase the value of the business over time.
sale	Transaction consummated when something of value is exchanged for something else of value, usually money. Example: A contract between you and your customer has been completed to your mutual satisfaction.
scheduling	Designation of time, personnel and resources to insure the most productive and therefore profitable means of completing a project. Scheduling informs management, subcontractors and tradespeople of available time slots and delivery dates
shortfalls	A cash shortfall refers to a cash position relative to what must be paid out, or when there's less in the bank than what you must pay out.
short-term financing	Third-party financing available to your customers in order to accommodate less-expensive purchases, such as individual components in a remodeling project. This would be provided by credit card companies, commercial lenders and banks.
short-term notes payable	Short-term obligations of the business, meaning they are due and payable within the next 12 months
spreadsheet (electronic)	A computer worksheet which allows you to work with and manipulate numbers; handy for preparing budgets.
statement of cash flow	Financial report designed to assess both short- and long-term obligations of business.
strategy	A game plan or concept of how you will conduct your business in order to achieve the mission of the business.
target market	That segment of the market you will focus your efforts to reach and sell to. These are buyers whom you will educate to the value of using your services.
target pricing	Using the Profit Based on Selling Method. Target pricing is the price to sell at, with the most competitive and profitable return. This would be the ideal price assuring customer value and business profit.
tax deposits	Federal and state income taxes that have been withheld, FICA and Medicare taxes plus employer's share of matching amounts of FICA and Medicare; also called 941 taxes.
third-party financing	Project costs provided through a source of funding other than directly by the customer or contractor, such as local banks, finance companies, mortgage companies.
times interest earned	Measures earnings before the payment of interest and taxes.
trade secret	A business advantage that is yours because you thoroughly understand how your business operates, which gives you an edge over your competition, or perhaps you possess some unique information that benefits your firm
turnover ratio	Measures how efficiently assets are used on a daily basis.
up-sell	Recommending services or products that enhance and make more valuable your customer's purchases, such as appliances you sell with a remodeling job.
variations	Alternatives to what you consider to be the norm or reasonable expectations, and yet not all variations offer valid reasons for change, such as changes in the numbers or buying habits of your customers.
written contract	A written obligation to provide a service or product in exchange for some form of compensation of equal value, in most cases—money.
80 - 20 rule	Also called the Pareto Principle, this means that 80 percent of your business will come from 20 percent of your customers.
1099 reports	The IRS form on which a business reports payments it has made during the course of the previous year to independent contractors.

BIBLIOGRAPHY

NKBA PUBLICATIONS AND RESOURCES

BRINGING TOTAL QUALITY MANAGEMENT TO YOUR KITCHEN AND BATHROOM BUSINESS, David Newton, CKD, CBD. National Kitchen & Bath Association, 1996.

KITCHEN AND BATHROOM INSTALLATION MANUAL, Volume 2, Installation Project Management, Walt Stoepplewerth and Darel Lewis. National Kitchen & Bath Association, 1996.

LEVERAGING DESIGN: Finance and the Kitchen and Bathroom Specialist, Debi Bach. National Kitchen & Bath Association, 1996.

THE GREAT CASH HUNT, Leslie L. Vlachos, M.Ed. and Stephen P. Vlachos, CKD, CBD. National Kitchen & Bath Association, To be published, 1997.

BUSINESS MANAGEMENT

CONSTRUCTION CONTRACTING, Sixth Edition, Richard H. Clough and Glenn A. Sears. John Wiley & Sons, Inc., New York, NY, 1994.

IF IT AIN'T BROKE...BREAK IT, Robert J. Kriegel and Louis Patler. Warner Books Inc., New York, NY, 1991.

THE E-MYTH, Michael Gerber. Harper Collins Publications, 1986.

THE E-MYTH REVISITED, Michael Gerber. Harper Collins Publications, 1995.

THE GREAT GAME OF BUSINESS, Jack Stack. Currency Books, New York, NY, 1992.

THINKING ABOUT QUALITY, PROGRESS, WISDOM AND THE DEMING PHILOSOPHY, Lloyd Dobbins and Clare Crawford-Mason. Times Books, a Division of Random House, Inc., New York, NY, 1994.

CUSTOMER SERVICE

IN SEARCH OF EXCELLENCE - Lessons From America's Best-Run Companies, Thomas J. Peters and Robert H. Waterman Jr. Warner Books Inc., New York, NY, 1982.

POSITIVELY OUTRAGEOUS SERVICE, New & Easy Ways To Win Customers For Life, T. Scott Gross. Mastermedia Limited, New York, NY, 1991.

THE QUEST FOR SERVICE QUALITY, Rxs for Achieving Excellence, Phillip S. Wexler, W.A. Adams, Emil Bohn. Maxcomm Associates, Sandy, UT, 1993.

THE SERVICE EDGE, 101 Companies That Profit From Customer Care, Ron Zemke with Dick Schaaf. PLUME, Penguin Books USA Inc., New York, NY, 1989.

FINANCIAL MANAGEMENT

BUSINESS PLANS THAT WIN $$$, Lessons From The MIT Enterprise ForumSM, Stanley R. Rich and David E. Gumpert. Harper & Row Publishers, New York, NY, 1987.

HOW TO READ A FINANCIAL REPORT, John A. Tracy. John Wiley & Sons Inc, New York, NY, 1989.

THE ENTREPRENEUR'S GUIDE TO CAPITAL, Jennifer Lindsey. Probus Publishing Co., Chicago, IL, 1990.

THE NEW VENTURE HANDBOOK, Ronald E. Merrill and Henry D. Sedgwick. AMACOM, a Division of American Management Association, New York, NY, 1987.

SELLING

INFLUENCE, THE PSYCHOLOGY OF PERSUASION, Robert Cialdini, Ph.D. William Morrow & Co., Inc., New York, NY, 1993.

THE SALES BIBLE, The Ultimate Sales Resource, Jefferey H. Gitomer. William Morrow & Co., Inc., New York, NY, 1994.

ZIG ZIGLAR'S SECRETS OF CLOSING THE SALE, Zig Ziglar. Berkley Books, New York, NY, 1982.

PERSONNEL ISSUES

EMPOWERMENT TAKES MORE THAN A MINUTE, Ken Blanchard, John P. Carlos and Alan Randolph. Ken Blanchard Family Partnership, John P. Carlos and W. Alan Randolph, Berrett-Koehler Publishers Inc., San Francisco, CA, 1996.

LEADERSHIP IS AN ART, Max DePree. Dell Publishing Co., New York, NY, 1989.

PERSONAL DEVELOPMENT

IN THE SPIRIT OF BUSINESS, Robert Roskind. Celestial Arts, Berkley CA, 1992.

PSYCHO-CYBERNETICS, Maxwell Maltz. Prentice-Hall, Inc., Printed by Wilshire Books, 1996.

THE 7 HABITS OF HIGHLY EFFECTIVE PEOPLE, Stephen R. Covey. Fireside, Simon & Schuster, Inc, 1989.

RECOMMENDED SOFTWARE

Spreadsheets:
Lotus 1-2-3
Microsoft's Excel
Quattro-Pro

Accounting:
Peachtree
Quick Books Pro by Quicken
One Write

Business Packages:
Lotus SmartSuite
Microsoft Office

Project Management:
Primavera Systems Inc.'s SureTrak, Project Manager For Windows
Microsoft's Project

INDEX

accounts payable, 36, 38, 54

accounts receivable, 36, 38, 52, 65, 166

accrual method, 35

accrued expenses, 36, 38

accumulated depreciation, 38

acts of commission, 10

acts of omission, 11

adjustment, 6, 58, 65, 71, 108, 130, 188

advertising, 5, 18-19, 35, 55, 58, 62, 65, 67, 117, 122, 141, 186, 188-189

aged receivables, 72

alternative approach, 97-101

Americans with Disabilities Act, 153

asset turnover, 166, 171

assets, 26, 34, 36-38, 52, 54, 72, 161, 163-164, 166, 168, 170-172, 177, 193

assumptions, 7, 25, 149

average collection period, 65, 166, 171

balance sheet, 26, 34, 36-38, 41, 51-55, 58, 75, 157-158, 177

basic balance sheet equation, 36-37, 52

before-tax ROA, 177

bonds, 3, 10-11, 24, 26, 52

borrow, 67, 117-121, 161, 163, 168, 177

bottom line, 3, 21, 36-38, 62, 73-74, 97, 153

break-even analysis, 73-75

break-even point, 19, 73-74, 130

budget, 3-4, 19, 22, 26-29, 55, 58-59, 63, 65, 68, 70, 73, 75, 89-92, 97, 115, 117, 130-131, 143, 145, 153, 188, 190

business deductions, 150

business management, 12 17, 19, 97, 145

business plan, 3-4, 19, 21

cash dividends to stockholders, 37

cash flow, 4, 26, 34, 38, 42, 51, 63-69, 71-73, 75, 117, 170

certificate of insurance, 11

certified public accountant, 33, 151

charge sales, 66

chart of accounts, 37

checklists, 11, 115, 132

collateral, 118, 163

commission, 65, 127-130, 133-134, 151

commission basis, 127

communication, 6, 18, 26, 60, 83, 132-134

comparative ratio analysis, 160

contingency costs, 24

contingency fees, 61

controls, 115, 177

co-op funds for advertising, 117

cost of sales, 23, 25, 55, 60-62, 74, 84, 89-91, 97, 102

current asset, 52, 72, 161

current ratio, 161, 170

customer service provider, 1-3, 11-12, 73, 83, 89, 131, 144, 194

days of sales in inventory, 166

debt to asset, 163, 170

debt/equity, 163

depreciation expense, 35

direct costs, 23-24, 60, 62

discount, 1-2, 19, 25, 63, 66-67, 72, 87, 89, 116-121, 129, 132, 139-141

discounters, 140

Dupont equation, 178

early payment discounts, 25, 72, 116

earnings, 5, 26, 35-36, 38, 54, 61, 102, 122, 150, 163, 177

employee, 6, 10-12, 18-19, 21, 23-24, 35, 60, 71, 73, 106, 108, 115, 122-125, 127, 130-133, 143, 149-153, 172, 186, 190, 193

employer, 10, 23, 122, 125, 150-153, 190

equity multiplier ratio, 164

estimate, 3, 21, 25, 90-92, 104, 106, 108-109, 133-134, 141, 144, 149-150, 190

estimating process, 90, 150

financial leverage, 177

financial management, 13, 17, 19, 33, 185

financial reports, 19-20, 33-34, 75, 157, 160, 180

Financial Standards Accounting Board, 38

fines, 5, 72, 115, 149-150, 152

forecasting, 73

formula, 36, 52, 81

generally accepted accounting principles, 35

gross profit, 25, 35, 60

guarantees, 12

hidden costs, 61, 63, 115

historical performance, 157

hourly charges, 104, 108

income and expense statement, 34-38, 40, 51-52, 54-57, 60, 73, 75, 157, 159, 177

income tax payable, 38

indirect costs, 23-24, 60-62

industry standards, 51, 104, 157

Internal Revenue Service, 36, 115, 116, 122, 150-152

inventory, 2, 36, 38, 52, 55, 71-72, 83, 117, 164, 166, 170-171, 177, 188

inventory turnover, 166, 171

job-costing records, 24, 106, 125

kitchen and bathroom, 1-3, 5, 12, 17, 19-20, 23-24, 33, 37, 63, 65-66, 89-90, 117, 131, 157, 168, 171-173, 190

leverage ratio, 163, 165, 170

liability, 10, 23, 36-38, 71, 152

liabilities, 26, 34, 36-38, 52, 54, 161, 163, 177

line of credit, 118

liquidity ratios, 161-162, 170

long-term assets, 52

long-term financing, 65

long-term notes payable, 38

manufacturer's suggested retail price, 84

market niche, 132, 139, 188

marketing, 2, 18, 54, 130-131, 139-141, 186, 188-189

marketing plan, 18, 54, 131, 186

markup, 83-85, 89, 91, 97, 108

material safety data sheets, 10

Medicare, 122

mistakes, 7, 10-11, 60-61, 132-134, 149-150

money, 4-5, 9, 11, 23-24, 34-36, 38-39, 65-66, 72-73, 104, 108, 115-118, 129-130, 132, 141, 144, 166, 168, 171, 177, 186, 188, 190, 193

monthly budgets, 58-59, 63, 65, 73, 91

net income, 36-38, 73, 75, 168

net worth, 54

notes payable, 36, 38, 54

numbers, 22, 25, 54, 58, 65, 71, 74-75, 83, 90-91, 97, 104, 108, 139-140, 161, 163, 170, 177, 180, 185-186, 190

Occupational Safety and Health Administration, 10, 152

operating expenses, 4, 23, 25, 35, 38, 55, 60, 73, 84, 89-91, 104

operational diagnosis, 186-187

other assets, 52

other income and expense, 26

overhead, 24-25, 74, 84, 89, 91, 97, 102, 104

overhead costs, 24

owner's equity, 36-38, 52, 54, 163-164, 168

payroll burden, 19, 23, 25, 104, 106, 122, 125

payroll taxes, 151

penalties, 5, 72, 115-116, 149-152

prepaid expenses, 36

price sensitive, 139

productivity, 12, 17-18, 106, 122, 125, 132, 188-189

professional advisor, 20, 186

profit, 1-6, 13, 17-19, 21-22, 24-26, 34-36, 51, 54-55, 58, 60-63, 66, 68, 71-75, 83-89, 91-92, 102-104, 106, 108, 115, 125, 127, 129-130, 132-134, 139-143, 145, 152-153, 161, 163-164, 168-169, 171-173, 186, 188, 190, 193

profit based on costs, 102

profit based on selling price, 102

profit from operations, 26

profit margin, 35, 63, 84, 87, 89, 102, 127, 168, 172

profitability ratio, 168-169, 172

projections, 52, 65, 71, 73

quick ratio, 161, 170

quote, 90, 116, 150

ratios, 35, 54-55, 157, 161, 162-163, 165-172, 177

referrals, 2, 12, 18, 33, 131, 140, 143-144, 188

retailer, 1, 2, 3, 73, 83, 132, 140

retained earnings, 37-38, 54

return on asset, 168, 172, 177

return on equity, 168, 172, 177, 179

return on investment, 129, 173-177

revenue, 22, 25, 35-37, 55, 58, 60, 62, 65, 67, 72-74, 90, 102, 129, 166, 168, 170

Revenue Canada, 151

safety, 10-11, 19, 61, 152, 163

sale, 2-3, 7, 9, 12, 17, 19, 22-26, 35, 55, 57-58, 60-63, 65-68, 71, 73-74, 84, 87, 89, 90-91, 97, 102, 117, 125, 127-129, 134, 141, 144, 166, 168, 171-172, 186, 188-189, 193

scheduling, 19, 108

shortfalls, 63

short-term financing, 66

short-term notes payable, 38

spreadsheet, 22

statement of cash flow, 26, 38, 51, 63-65, 67-69, 71, 73, 75

steps for pricing, 84, 91, 93-96, 98-101

stockholder, 37, 54, 168, 173

strategy, 4, 21, 55, 63, 65-67, 71, 83, 139-140, 153, 189

subcontractor, 6, 10-11, 13, 18, 23, 60, 91, 97, 142, 149, 151, 186

target market, 18

target pricing, 129

tax, 20, 24-26, 34-36, 38, 54-55, 60, 62-63, 68, 73-75, 84, 102, 115-116, 122, 133-134, 149-151, 163, 177

tax deposits, 116

third-party financing, 9, 65, 171

times interest earned, 163

trade secret, 73, 170, 186

turnover ratio, 166-167, 171

United States, 10, 20, 102, 106, 122, 125, 142, 150-152

up-sell, 131-132

variations, 190

worker's compensation, 11, 25, 106, 122, 150, 152

written contract, 9, 12, 144

80 - 20 rule, 131, 141-142, 188

1099 reports, 150